Performing Piety

The publisher gratefully acknowledges the generous support of William and Sheila Nolan as members of the Literati Circle of the University of California Press Foundation.

Performing Piety

Making Space Sacred with
the Virgin of Guadalupe

Elaine A. Peña

UNIVERSITY OF CALIFORNIA PRESS
Berkeley · Los Angeles · London

University of California Press, one of the most distinguished university presses in the United States, enriches lives around the world by advancing scholarship in the humanities, social sciences, and natural sciences. Its activities are supported by the UC Press Foundation and by philanthropic contributions from individuals and institutions. For more information, visit www.ucpress.edu.

University of California Press
Berkeley and Los Angeles, California

University of California Press, Ltd.
London, England

Library of Congress Cataloging-in-Publication Data

Peña, Elaine A., 1979–
    Performing piety : making space sacred with the Virgin of Guadalupe / Elaine A. Peña.
        p.   cm.
    Includes bibliographical references and index.
    ISBN 978-0-520-26833-3 (cloth : alk. paper)
    ISBN 978-0-520-26834-0 (pbk. : alk. paper)
        1. Guadalupe, Our Lady of—Cult.   2. Anthropology of religion—Mexico.   3. Sacred space—Mexico.
    4. Guadalupe Hidalgo (Mexico)—Religious life and customs.   I. Title.
    BT660.G8.P45   2011
    232.91'7097253—dc22

                                                2010032664

Manufactured in the United States of America

20 19 18 17 16 15 14 13 12 11
10 9 8 7 6 5 4 3 2 1

This book is printed on Cascades Enviro 100, a 100% post consumer waste, recycled, de-inked fiber. FSC recycled certified and processed chlorine free. It is acid free, Ecologo certified, and manufactured by BioGas energy.

Para Sandra Ojeda Martínez (1953–2007) y Dwight Conquergood (1949–2004), guías extraordinarios

Contents

Illustrations

MAPS

Acknowledgments

Several institutions and colleagues supported this project. My adviser at Northwestern University, Dwight Conquergood, reassured me throughout my journey; he listened to all my field reports, nitpicked at my presentations and papers, shared APTP shows and multiple-course meals, prepared me for qualifying exams in spite of the excruciating pain that signaled his impending death, talked me through "messy" fieldwork moments in Mexico, and inspirited the completion of this book.

There were other key players who challenged me to make this study rigorous and interdisciplinary. The historian Josef Barton helped me tie together what seemed to be disparate locations on a map and inspired me with descriptive accounts of Sunday morning walks—prose that I could only dream of aspiring to. The performance theorist Margaret Thompson Drewal's courses pushed me to think about the links between performance and ritual that exist beyond the immediately perceptible. The anthropologists Mary Weismantel and Micaela di Leonardo helped me become a better writer, each in her own way. Robert Launay's courses and critical eye prompted me to make connections outside of Guadalupan studies. E. Patrick Johnson, my favorite performance practitioner and scholar, never lets me forget that it can be done. Alan Shefsky, resident poet and department assistant, saw me at my best and worse. As did my workmates: Tatiana Andronova, Pedro Díaz del Río, Michelle Campbell, Bishupal Limbu, Frantom Hutchins, and Jacob Juntunen. At Northwestern, this project was generously supported by a Dissertation Year Fellowship, an Alice B. Kaplan Center for the Humanities Mellon research grant, the Center for International Comparative Studies, and Latin American Caribbean Studies, as well as what is now officially, thanks to Mónica Russel y Rodríguez, the Latino Studies Program. Last but not least, I would like to thank David Roman for listening to me and genuinely caring about my work at the earliest and most precarious stage of my graduate studies.

There were many scholars outside of Northwestern that critically engaged this research. Diana Taylor read many drafts of the chapters early on, as did Robert Orsi, William Taylor, Timothy Matovina, Davíd Carrasco, and Horacio Sentíes Rodriguez. As will become evident, their personal comments and scholarship helped me advance the scope and breadth of this study. I must also thank the many scholars who asked questions and offered enthusiastic comments throughout my travel and especially during conversations at the University of Michigan, El Colegio de Michoacán, El Centro de Investigaciones y Estudios Superiores en Antropología Social (CIESAS), the University of Notre Dame, New York University, Yale University, the University of Oxford, Georgetown University, and Princeton University. My affiliation with the 2010–12 Young Scholars of American Religion (YSAR) cohort and our mentors, Anne Braude and Mark Valeri, has also strengthened this work. In addition, certain generous souls—Alicia Bazarte Martínez, Guillermo de la Peña, Gail Mummert, Antonio Prieto Stambaugh, Guillermo Gómez-Peña, Eduardo Flores Castillo, Laura Velasquez, Veronica Gonzalez, Theresa Delgadillo, Sergio Suarez, Alvaro Pombo, Lesley Cordova, Denise Khor, José Luis Ledesma, Suleiman Osman, Tom Guglielmo, and Kathryne Beebe—offered support and critical insights at key moments.

During my time as a postdoctoral associate in Latina/Latino Studies at the University of Illinois Urbana-Champaign (2006–7), Ricky Rodriguez, Alejandro Lugo, and Alicia Rodriguez offered encouragement. Victoria Gonzalez helped me find my way. Stephen Pitti's unfailing support when I was a postdoctoral associate and lecturer at Yale's MacMillan Center for International and Area Studies (2007–8) helped me grow professionally and personally. Alicia Schmidt Camacho, Gil Joseph, Patricia Pessar, and Joe Roach provided valuable feedback. The indomitable Nancy A. Phillips oriented me. At Yale, this project also benefited from intellectual and financial support provided by the Ethnicity, Race, and Migration Program; the Women, Religion, and Globalization Faculty Colloquium; and the Council on Latin American Iberian Studies. I would also like to thank my colleagues in the American Studies department at the George Washington University and at the Smithsonian Institution's Latino Center for their support during the final stages of this project. This book would not have come to fruition without the always positive and equally helpful interventions of Reed Malcom and his colleagues at the University of California Press.

Family members made my institutionalization and the pursuance of this project bearable. They are, and will always be, my touchstone—pockets of joy and comfort on the darkest days. My mother, Sandra Ojeda Martínez (1953–2007); my sister, Sandy P. Rodríguez and her son, Osiel; as well as my brothers, Fernando Peña Jr. and Gustavo Peña, remind me that life is hard and that coping is an art. My extended family members Ric and Pam Slocum, Marisela Chavez, Amada Chavez, Andi Garcia-Linn, jesse moreno, Veronica Solis, Denise Solis, Michael Avila, Miriam Diaz, Chela and Tony Gonzalez, Alvaro Muñoz, Maria Teresa Martín-Bourgon, and my better half, José Maria Muñoz, show me how to enjoy life.

This project's most important contributors do not have academic jobs. They are too smart to go through the trouble. The Guadalupanos with whom I worked in Chicago, Des Plaines, Mexico City, Zitácuaro, and Querétaro accepted me into their homes and their communities and shared the most intimate details of their lives. More important, they let me practice alongside them. Without their help this study would provide nothing more than empty ideas.

Washington, D.C., 2010

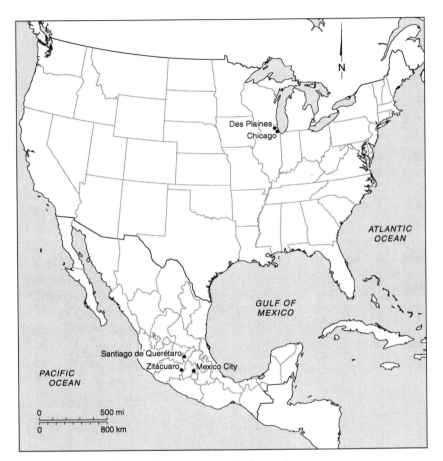

MAP I. Sites of Guadalupan devotion across North America.

Introduction

Locating Transnational Devotion

I first met la Virgen de Guadalupe in Laredo, Texas. As I was born and raised less than a mile from Nuevo Laredo, Tamaulipas, it was inconceivable for me not to recognize her image—petite hands, palms together, solemn brown face gazing downward, her thick and forgiving eyelashes—impossible not to appreciate the way her celestial blue robe and gold aura made her beautiful and magical. Although quintessentially Mexican, she belonged to all Americans just the same. Later I would learn that she inspires communities beyond the Americas—from the inner sanctum of Nôtre Dame in Paris, France, to the Church of Guadalupe in Cebu City, Philippines.

My elders taught me early on that piety is not something you talk about; it is something you do. Moreover, faith helps us survive hardship and allows us to look forward; it assures us that tomorrow can bring good news and better circumstances. My day-to-day realities did not exactly substantiate the idea that piousness resolves all, but they certainly made it an attractive possibility. Learning and growing in an environment where binational trade, intricate political networks, and ubiquitous power circuits thrive alongside drug cartels, horrific violence, and severe economic disparity unequivocally taught me that devotion—venerating la Virgen de Guadalupe, la Virgen de San Juan de los Lagos, la Santa Muerte, San Judas, San Miguel Arcángel, and el Sagrado Corazón—and self-preservation often go hand in hand.

Although she was always near, la Virgen de Guadalupe's presence became pivotal when I moved to Chicago to attend graduate school. In a field methodology course at the end of my first year, my mentor, Dwight Conquergood, aware of my interest in the links among religion, economy, and political change, told me about a recent apparition of la Virgen de Guadalupe on a tree in Rogers Park—a multiethnic neighborhood on Chicago's Far North Side. Divided by Clark Street into East and West Rogers Park, each block along that main axis reflects the changing shifts of immigration to this modern port of entry: from quick-to-close West African and Peruvian eateries, to Jamaican jerk joints, to Mexican *taquerias,* the neighborhood showcases its high diversity index for commercial purposes. On the East Side, the vicinity exhibits leafy trees, generally well-kept single-family homes, apartment buildings, Loyola University, and easy access to Chicago's coveted lakefront property. The West Side, where I conducted my fieldwork, has a different feel. There are parks and big trees, but the houses are noticeably worn. Families inhabit multiunit buildings, some sharing two-room apartments. Along the edges of these buildings are pathways indicated by actual carpeting, which some residents use as either a shortcut to their houses or to stay off the main streets. There are also waves of gentrification evidenced by apartment buildings turned condo. From Howard Street, which separates Chicago from Evanston, to its southern border, Devon Street—considered a principal marker of the neighborhood known as little India—the contrast between East and West Rogers Park is tangible.

Dwight astutely suggested that I consider the occurrence in West Rogers Park as a possible case study for the practicum component of the course. I did. And inadvertently began to shape what would become a multiyear, multisited, transnational research project. Learning about the theoretical underpinnings of critical performance ethnography in the seminar room that spring quarter while realizing the practical and political implications of Dwight's favorite aphorism—"Opening and interpreting lives is radically different than opening and closing books"— in Rogers Park inspired the conceptual and methodological foundations of this study. Speaking from decades of experience as a performance ethnographer, he advised (1) the art of fieldwork is performance; (2) people are not fools; and (3) imagine culture as a matrix of boundaries, borders, intersections, turning points, and thresholds. He also cautioned, "If anything can go wrong in the field, it will." Many things did go wrong. On occasion I misspoke. I sometimes stumbled. I include some of those moments, not to draw attention to the researcher, but to relate the pitfalls and possibilities of *co-performative witnessing*—an approach that privileges embodied action as both an object and a method of study.[1] This mode of research is a deeply politicized way of seeing and being in the field. Its point of departure is twofold. First, the ethnographer and the "subject" are always, and have always been, despite the insistence of more traditional ethnographic methods, engaged as interlocutors. Second, co-performative witnessing does not rely solely on texts housed in archives, oral histories, maps, or statistics but also foregrounds sensual communication—the rich subtext and often deeply coded moments of bodied exchange—that produce knowledge, ideas, opinions, mores, and traditions.

This intimate method guided me as I conducted my fieldwork and took courses. Most days I would attend seminars, lectures, and other requisite meetings in Evanston and then walk from Northwestern University's landscaped campus to the prayer/community meetings held every evening on a street corner in West Rogers Park. I also took part in Guadalupan assemblies at the Second Tepeyac of North America in Des Plaines, Illinois—an institutionally sanctioned replica of the sacred hill of Tepeyac in Mexico City. The Second Tepeyac is situated in the borderland between urban and suburban space. Enclosed in a ninety-six-acre campus, it is further isolated by a panorama of trees on three sides and by a cemetery. This Guadalupan pilgrimage site, which maintains close ties (mimetically and officially) with its counterpart in central Mexico, has green areas, parking spaces, and *peregrinos* (pilgrims) to spare.

Many times, I traveled to Des Plaines with Rogers Park Guadalupanos, the majority of whom are "unauthorized migrants" originally from traditional sending states such as Michoacán and Guanajuato but who also hail from Veracruz and Nuevo León.[2] This migratory tie is important because it illuminates the long-standing transnational networks that bind Guadalupan sacred spaces together. Early-twentieth-century and post–World War II migration circuits connecting western and central Mexico—Michoacán and Guanajuato, for example—with the Midwest, especially South Chicago and the Pilsen and Little Village neighborhoods, help us trace the Virgin of Guadalupe's historical and contemporary influence in both countries. The case studies presented here are implicitly and deeply connected not only by shared interest in and devotion to the Virgin but also by underlying political economic ties. They offer examples of the living, breathing expressions of past devotees. Many of the Guadalupanos with whom I worked in the Chicago area are "new-comers" (or post-1965) migrants, but some are second- and third-generation residents. It is more important to acknowlege that the Virgin of Guadalupe was already traveling with train-track-laying and meat-packing migrant laborers well before that watershed moment in the master narrative of U.S. migration.[3] Moreover, devotees in several places, along the pilgrimage route from Zitácuaro, Michoacán, to Mexico City or at the Second Tepeyac, revealed that they share family and social networks that connect these spaces every day (e.g., Mexico City to Des Plaines, Zitácuaro to Chicago).

Newly arrived or long since established, the majority of adherents that congregated in Des Plaines did not find themselves aligned with fellow devotees at the Second Tepeyac on the basis of nationality. What connected them were their allegiance to la Virgen de Guadalupe and their determination to rise above the xenophobic realities of life in "el Norte." Those weekend pilgrimages to the Second Tepeyac provoked a set of key questions that ultimately determined the shape and scope of this study: (1) When is space sacred? Who determines its boundaries? How is it sustained and legitimized? (2) How do conceptions of sacred space in the United States and Mexico differ from place to place, from community to community vis-à-vis urban, suburban, and rural settings? (3) How are different forms of knowing, socioeconomic and political coping tactics, conceptions of history, and faith-based traditions circulated within and between these sacred spaces?

Framing the project in this way requires a site-specific analysis, one that simultaneously privileges the production of space and the production of the sacred. Putting these two goals side by side presumes that space is not absolute,[4] that the process of sacred space production embraces both religious and secular elements, often in unison. In the context of exploring Guadalupan shrine development in central Mexico and the Chicago area, it is imperative that we view the migration networks and the approaches to local integration as a process—as layers of culture, history, and traditions imbued in specific locations at specific times.[5] Moreover, looking at the ways in which devotees have claimed (and will continue to) claim space gives us a chance to look critically not only at the categories of ethnicity, race, gender, class, and citizenship but also at the alliances and antagonisms that follow any immigrant group. This study seeks to reinforce the idea of connectivity among sacred spaces in disparate locations based on comparable embodied practices, oral traditions, and aesthetic/architectural choices, but it does so without defaulting to compartmentalizing or paraphrasing heterogeneous populations and deeply complicated intracommunity relationships that frequently transcend understandings of local context.[6]

After conceptualizing the project using a space production framework and co-performatively witnessing the construction of Guadalupan shrines in Rogers Park and Des Plaines over two and a half years (i.e. listening; witnessing devotees fight among themselves about money and power; seeing how devotees maintained sacred space with their labor, their expressions, and their material goods; fund-raising at dances and block parties; praying the rosary; laughing; remembering; singing; having heated discussions with police officers; negotiating with xenophobic neighbors; working alongside immigration lawyers; translating naturalization documents; tidying the shrine; cleaning up the mess left by vandals; weathering Chicago's extreme seasons; preparing and selling a wide assortment of Mexican dishes; celebrating the Virgin far from home with and alongside Guadalupanos who were far from home as well), it only made sense to try to grasp the fuller complexity of what Eric Wolf calls a "master symbol" by considering the Virgin's presence in central and western Mexico—a region where many Midwest-based devotees were born.[7] That year I spent my time conducting archival research, learning about the backstage logistics of sacred space maintenance, co-performatively witnessing all-female walking pilgrimages, interviewing church officials, working with staff members in the Basilica's public relations office, speaking with peregrinos at Tepeyac and in their homes, and witnessing diverse modes of sacred space production. It became clear at the end of this fieldwork period that the project was, at its base, about the various processes—material, spatial, ideological, aesthetic, rhetorical, cultural, embodied—underwriting the production of Guadalupan shrines across the U.S.-Mexico border.

EXCAVATING SACRED SPACE: THE MEMORY OF A COLONIAL CULT

One of the Virgin's geographic and temporal starting points is the hill of Tepeyac in the former metropolis of Tenochtitlán, capital of the Aztec empire (and present-day Mexico City).[8] When Hernán Cortés and Spanish forces arrived in 1519 in Tenochtitlán they encountered a meticulously constructed island metropolis sustained by a well-oiled, tributary and warfare-based political-economic system.[9] The Franciscan missionary fray Bernardino de Sahagún, among others, noted the verdant beauty and architectural perfection of the city's canal transportation system.[10] In *La Villa de Guadalupe: Historias, Estampas, y Leyendas*, the historian Horacio Sentíes Rodríguez describes the sixteenth-century Tenochtitlán landscapes as possessing protective mountain ranges—the Sierra de Guadalupe and Sierra de Pachuca to the north, the Sierra de las Cruces to the west, the Sierra Nevada to the east, and the Sierra del Ajusco to the south—as well as bountiful lakes—Texcoco, Zampango, Ecatepec, Xaltocan, Chalco, and Xochimilco—that supported an intricate transportation system that guided goods and people across the city.[11] Three *calzadas* (causeways)—Tlacopan, Iztapalapa, and Tepeyac—constructed in the pre-Tenochtitlán era by the Tlatelolcans, enhanced intracity communication and business networks.

The hill of Tepeyac's geographic position guaranteed its political and economic importance through the pre-Hispanic and colonial epochs. Located at a northern point of the Calzada de Tepeyac, the *"nariz del cerro"* (lit., "nose of the hill"), operated as an important entryway into the city, not only for trade, but also for high-ranking ecclesiastical and civil figures arriving from the Iberian Peninsula.[12] They announced and celebrated their arrival in the New World at Tepeyac before entering the city proper. It is important to note, however, that while Tepeyac was indeed an important religious stop, its appeal came primarily from its physical location.

Accounts of this early colonization period also suggest that Spanish *conquistadores* (conquerors), in addition to bringing warfare, disease, and their dreams of accumulating wealth, transposed their cultural practices and their religious beliefs to the New World. Cortés, Francisco Pizarro, Vasco Nuñez de Balboa, Hernando de Soto, Sebastián de Balalcázar, Pedro de Alvarado, and other important figures from Extremadura, a region in central/western Spain, worshipped the Virgin Guadalupe of Extremadura in different locales across New Spain.[13] Cortés, for example, is said to have worshiped the Extremaduran Virgin on the hill of Tepeyac after his arrival in 1521.[14] His devotion transpired ten years before the Virgen de Guadalupe appeared to Juan Diego.

Cortés's devotion, however, came after the well-established adoration of the Aztec goddess Tonantzin—a prototype, like Guadalupe (of Extremadura), of the young Virgin who appeared atop the hill of Tepeyac in December 1531.[15] Tracing a sixteenth-century lineage through the mythology of powerful indigenous goddesses, the cultural theorist Gloria Anzaldúa firmly positions the Virgin of Guadalupe (of Mexico) as a symbol imbued with Aztec, Totonac, and Spanish histories:

La Virgen de Guadalupe's Indian name is *Coatlalopeuh.* She is the central deity connecting us to our Indian ancestry. *Coatlalopeuh* is descended from, or is an aspect of, earlier Mesoamerican fertility and Earth goddesses. The earliest is *Coatlicue,* or "Serpent Skirt." She had a human skull or serpent for a head, a necklace of human hearts, a skirt of twisted serpents and taloned feet. . . . The male-dominated Azteca-Mexica culture drove the powerful female deities underground by giving them monstrous attributes and by substituting male deities in their place, thus splitting the female Self and the female deities.[16]

By citing la Virgen de Guadalupe's pre-Cortesian history, Anzaldúa debunks the dichotomization of women's roles and the insistence that they are mere receptacles—benignly passive and perhaps ignobly so. Her analysis also challenges the reproduction of a virgin/whore dichotomy, promulgated not only in private and public spheres but also (as I witnessed) among devotees within sacred spaces.[17] Although many would argue, myself included, that the cult of la Virgen de Guadalupe can empower women (in particular), dimensions of the base of Guadalupan devotion—the apparition story—do indeed propagate a binary perspective.[18] But let us judge for ourselves.

According to the *Nican mopohua* ("Here is recounted")—the narrative of Guadalupe's apparitions to Juan Diego written in Náhuatl[19]—between December 9 and December 12, 1531, la Virgen de Guadalupe appeared four times in New Spain.[20] During the early morning hours of December 9, a Christianized indigenous man, Juan Diego Cuauhtlatoatzin, was walking toward the calzada of Tepeyac when he heard a lovely singing voice beckoning him to climb the hill. There he encountered a Náhuatl-speaking young woman, neither entirely indigenous nor Spanish, with long, black, straight hair parted in the middle. She wore a sash tied around her natural waist, which was customary for a woman with child. This young virgin asked him to circulate a message: build a temple in my honor. Juan Diego, awed and overwhelmed, proceeded directly to the quarters of fray Juan de Zumárraga, the first archbishop of Mexico City. After unsuccessfully attempting to communicate her request, he returned to Tepeyac where the celestial figure appeared a second time. He begged her to find another emissary, but she insisted that he persevere. Courage renewed, Juan Diego paid a second visit to the skeptical clergy, only to be denied again. He returned to Tepeyac a third time, and the Virgin promised to give him a sign on the following day. But Juan Diego did not return as promised because his uncle, Juan Bernardino, fell ill. The omniscient figure, aware and sympathetic to his hardships, forgave his absence and later cured Juan Bernardino. The fourth and most famous apparition occurred around six o'clock in the morning on December 12. On this propitious day, she filled Juan Diego's *tilma*—a garment made of maguey fiber worn across the torso—with scores of roses, which were uncommon in that region and especially during the winter months. Juan Diego, humbled but empowered, returned to Zumárraga with the evidence. He revealed the Virgin's image miraculously imprinted underneath the roses. His tilma, also known as the *"ayate de Juan Diego,"* is protected today in the Modern Basilica by bulletproof glass and state-of-the-art heat sensors. Further, inscribed on the walls of that sanctuary are portions of the following message: "No estoy yo aquí que soy tu Madre? No estás bajo mi sombra y resguardo? No soy la fuente de tu alegría? No estás en el hueco de mi manto, en el cruce de mis brazos?" (Am I, your mother, not here? Are you not under my shadow and shelter? Am I not the source of your happiness? Are you not inside my cloak, in my embrace?).

Many have construed the Virgin's acquiescence to Juan Diego as a representation of a woman's capacity to be instinctually compassionate—a trait that many women must fulfill or risk social and familial consequences. Scholars have addressed this implicit gender bias,[21] but the poet Sandra Cisneros does so humorously when she questions the illogical precept that the Virgin is indeed a realistic role model. She writes, "I was angry for so many years every time I saw the Virgin of Guadalupe, my culture's role model for brown women like me. She was damn dangerous, an ideal so lofty and unrealistic it was laughable. Did boys have to aspire to be Jesus? . . . As far as I could see, *La Lupe* was nothing but a goody-two-shoe meant to doom me to a life of unhappiness."[22] The Guadalupanas with whom I worked, both in central Mexico and in the Midwest, never explicitly mentioned this aspect of Guadalupan devotion. It is true that many devotees admitted to emulating the Virgin, but they took their goal with a grain of salt. Most saw it as a process, an ideal they moved closer to through everyday and exceptional devotional performances.

Using gender as a lens is not the only way we can analyze the Virgin's appearances in New Spain. Like any great story, the dominant symbols, images, and characters, the conflict, and the resolution of the narrative give rise to manifold interpretations and usages. Canonized by Pope John Paul II in 2002, Saint Juan Diego Cuauhtlatoatzin, for example, represents the destitute, doubt-ridden, and affronted devotees who through faith and humility acquire redemption and guidance from their mother—

la Virgen Maria de Guadalupe. Juan Diego is, in many respects, the protagonist of the legend. Guadalupanas/os appropriate and reinterpret his classic hero's journey as the first *peregrinación* (pilgrimage), using it as a model to overcome their own hardships and circumstances. Celebrants and devotees alike propose, "La vida es una peregrinación y todos somos peregrinos" (Life is a pilgrimage, and we are all on the journey). On an institutional level, fray Juan de Zumárraga, the Spanish missionary who legitimized the apparition, despite his initial hesitations now epitomizes the benevolence and understanding inherent in the upper echelons of the Catholic Church. But there is also an aspect of eager appropriation. Guadalupan clergy in Mexico City continue to use the apparition story to sustain religious, political, and cultural power and authority in Mexico, to foster Guadalupismo throughout the Republic,[23] and to recuperate preconquest indigenous history as they see fit.

Further, la Virgen de Guadalupe's image, the principal product of the narrative, is both a Roman Catholic icon and a malleable symbol of strength for devotees across the Americas. Guadalupanas/os from Miguel Hidalgo to César Chávez, from Emiliano Zapata to Alma López have used her iconic image to spark upheaval, foster civil rights and gender equality, strengthen political campaigns, create art, preserve identity, and build communities. These material and symbolic realizations indicate some of the ways devotees entangle belief in the cult of the Virgin of Guadalupe with cultural and sociopolitical aspirations. As the Guadalupan scholar Antonio Pompa y Pompa sardonically proposes, "Se ha dicho que si durante la Guerra con los norteamericanos en 1847, las tropas mexicanas hubieran tenido por bandera la Virgen de Guadalupe, habríamos ganado la guerra" (It has been said that Mexican soldiers would have claimed victory during the war against the United States in 1847 if they would have used the Virgin of Guadalupe's image on their battle flag).[24] Certainly, as a wide range of scholarship has shown, the cult of la Virgen de Guadalupe operates as a fundamental building block in conceiving and circulating Mexico's national identity. This study acknowledges that emphasis but focuses on the ascendancy and scope of the cult, in particular, how Guadalupan devotion circumvents affiliation and/or allegiance to one nation, especially when it befits the practitioner.

THE REGENERATIVE EFFECTS OF THE INEFFABLE

La Virgen de Guadalupe's sixteenth-century apparition and the sanctuaries that followed functioned as a catalyst for the Christianization and colonization of Mexico. Not only did this colonial figure—the embodiment of Iberian and indigenous spirituality—receive a shrine atop the hill of Tepeyac, but outposts also sprang up across the United States and as far away as the Philippines, Kenya, and Korea.[25] Simply put, "the accumulation of capital has always been a profoundly geographical affair."[26] This project concerns itself with that history. It privileges, however, the regenerative geosocial effects of that colonial moment—how adherents continue to develop Guadalupan sacred spaces across North America; how their stories and experiences cut across what the map has cut up.[27]

Using the three aforementioned Guadalupan shrines—Tepeyac in Mexico City (est. 1531); its replica, the Second Tepeyac of North America, in Des Plaines, Illinois (est. 2001); and a sidewalk shrine constructed by Mexican nationals on Chicago's Far North Side (est. 2001)—this project considers the institutional and noninstitutional production of sacred spaces among ethnoreligious communities between the Midwest and central/western Mexico on three levels: (1) spatial practices and rhetorical strategies, (2) the perspectives of those who conceptualize space production, and (3) ideas and tactics that are coded, or communicated, through symbols. I focus less on how these communities are transnational, an extensively studied idea,[28] and more on the transnational spaces they produce with the continual transposition and circulation of idioms and practices.[29]

Considering those transnational exchanges alongside the sociopolitical and economic dimensions of built environments, this study argues that by offering the Virgin their *devotional labor* (e.g., pilgrimage, prayer, song, dance, and shrine maintenance) adherents develop, preserve, sanctify, and connect not only spaces but also histories and traditions across several boundaries: geopolitical, social, and institutional. Genuflection, for example, is labor. It may be a simple gesture, but it takes on a more complex valence when you take into account the history of the action—walking for hours across icy Chicago roads in early December or for days across central Mexico. Genuflection also involves social labor, which entails organizing job, family, and day-to-day responsibilities. These practices engender *devotional capital,* which is not "capital" in the standard sense of the term. Capital, according to a classic economist like David Ricardo, is a production factor that is neither human labor nor land property.[30] Although Karl Marx distinguished among different kinds of capital, for him the epitome of capital was financial capital, that is, money that produced, and immediately, more money.[31]

Devotional capital reinforces our understanding of the regenerative links between religious practice and socioeconomic forces; it proposes that religious practice is capital. The devotees with whom I worked create a type of "symbolic" capital that, in Pierre Bourdieu's words, "is one for which economism has no name" and one that does not generate direct or instantaneous monetary benefits.[32] Bourdieu speaks to the narrowness of defining exchanges as profitable based solely on monetary gain. His point is that one may acquire advantages or attain profit as easily or as effectively through symbolic exchange as through traditional business or monetary negotiation.

Within and between Guadalupan sacred spaces, adherents determine, create, and circulate devotional capital according to a site-specific faith-based value system. Moreover, devotional capital may also be thought of as a vehicle; adherents communicate ways of remembering, knowing, interpreting, and coping (which may or may not be written down in a church bulletin or the latest migration/remittance report) that affect not only the quality of life for these religious communities but also the legacies they leave behind. Devotional capital thus attends to how Guadalupanas/os' religious work, however ephemeral, informs their day-to-day experiences and how the specificity of their interactions—the ways in which they themselves sort what Geertz calls "winks from twitches," or differentiate between backstage and front stage piety—yield regenerative social, economic, cultural, and political benefits.[33]

Numerous texts interpret, celebrate, and/or criticize the Virgin of Guadalupe's presence in the Americas. Certain scholarly and exegetical texts form the base of what I have come to call critical Guadalupan studies.[34] Although wide-ranging, the canon does not include an analysis of the long-standing transnational dimensions of Guadalupan devotion—the dynamic symbolic, architectural, material, ideological, rhetorical, and cultural exchanges and transpositions occurring among devotees in different locations. Offering a multisited examination of the production of sacred space is the principal way in which this project contributes to the expansive corpus of Guadalupan literature. In addition, this project continues discussions in the study of primarily Spanish-speaking ethnoreligious communities residing in North America.[35] Although there are terrific explorations of Latino religious cultures and idioms,[36] I hesitate to use the blanket term because this study does not only focus on "Latinos", but it also attends to the ways in which individuals and groups from a range of subject positions engage, confront, and/or counter the cult of the Virgin of Guadalupe. Moreover, many of the people with whom I worked identified themselves not as Latino but with a precise response about their regional and cultural bearings. This precision sheds light on the complex questions informing this study. Understanding how conceptions of sacred space production differ among urban, suburban, and rural areas, for example, begins with how and where devotee-residents have developed their identities. This study complements ethnographic, sociological, and historical analyses that consider the transmigration and settling processes of ethnoreligious communities.[37]

Many studies about diasporic religion, Guadalupan and otherwise, elide a discussion of the secular regenerative effects of spiritual practices, specifically, the ways in which religious rituals engender socioeconomic benefits.[38] I attend to these aspects of religious practice with the terms *devotional labor* and *devotional capital,* examples of which are interwoven throughout the text. For many devotees, many of whom are struggling working-class and/or undocumented, day-to-day coping tactics are contingent on the *recitation* of prayer, *attending* church, *giving* tithe, *sustaining* sacred space, and *demonstrating* belief in public. What follows is a contextualized examination of those processes. It is an inspired study equally informed by theory and practice; a true labor of love, as Dwight would say, earnestly trying to address the complexity of three disparate but undeniably interconnected spaces that have risen (and continue to rise) across North America.

NOTE ON ORGANIZATION

The conceptual order of a book can take many forms. This project began in Chicago and crossed not only the U.S.-Mexico border but also the Atlantic Ocean several times. Writing the manuscript did as well. The research process is in many ways a system of checks and balances. Even so, it is difficult to avoid Geertz's all-too-true assertion that "culture exists in the trading post, the hill fort, or the sheep run, anthropology exists in the book, the article, the lecture, the museum display, or, sometimes, nowadays, the film."[39]

I was urged during the copy editing stage of the book to change the chapter sequence: to begin the anthropological analysis in central Mexico, which would undoubtedly highlight the compelling stories and socioeconomic analysis of women making space sacred. After giving it serious thought, I decided to keep the initial conceptualization. I do not want to suggest that central Mexico is a logical starting point. Nor do I want to perpetuate origin myths or notions of religiocultural authenticity. We do not have to default to the geopolitical boundaries that establish the Mexican nation-state and by association Mexican symbols to truly understand the Virgin of Guadalupe. As we will see, Guadalupan devotion exists in a realm of simultaneity. Therefore, we begin the journey with our feet firmly planted in two places—in Mexico City and Des Plaines—our eyes on multiple communities, their diverse histories in our pockets, and, most important, sensuous attentiveness.

NOTE ON LANGUAGE

Because this is a multisited ethnography of primarily Spanish-speaking devotees in central Mexico and the Chicago area, I interweave Spanish words and phrases throughout. I have translated all quotes from Spanish to English. This includes formal and informal interviews, scholarly texts, and periodicals. I have left proper names and places in their original tongue.

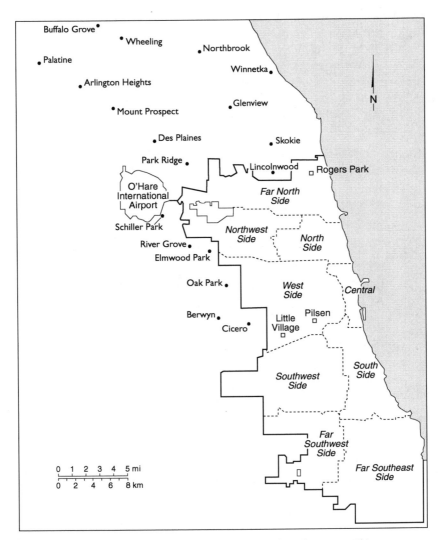

MAP 2. Location of Des Plaines, Illinois, and Rogers Park in the greater Chicago area.

PART ONE

Building

CHAPTER I

Virgen de los Migrantes

Transposing Sacred Space in a Chicago Suburb

One crisp fall day in a northwest suburb of Chicago, Mexican, Salvadoran, Guatemalan, and Honduran Guadalupanas/os gathered in the gymnasium-cum-sanctuary at the Second Tepeyac of North America—a sanctioned replica of the hill of Tepeyac in Mexico City. The Second Tepeyac is not visible from the street. Not far from the Des Plaines River, it is surrounded by acres of landscaped trees and foliage; occasional clusters of buildings that constitute Maryville Academy divert attention from the open-air shrine. Keeper of a thousand souls, the All Saints Cemetery, located across the street from Maryville, lends silence and tranquillity to the edges of the metropolis. On that afternoon, a passerby would be drawn by hues—steel gray streets that continue as far as the eye can see, dense green trees, and a slate blue sky blended with cirrus clouds—not by the presence of a congregation flourishing in response to a Guadalupan outpost.

Hundreds of devotees celebrated Juan Diego, the unsung hero of the apparition story, that day at the Second Tepeyac. The cover of a special issue of *El Católico*, the Chicago archdiocese's official Spanish-language periodical, featured an illustration of Pope John Paul II holding Juan Diego's hand and la Virgen de Guadalupe's luminous figure in the background. The accompanying headline read, "Canonización de Juan Diego Cuauhtlatoatzin: ¡Nuestra Señora de Guadalupe ha cumplido lo que ha prometido!" (The canonization of Juan Diego Cuauhtlatoatzin: Our Lady of Guadalupe has accomplished what she promised!).[1]

Fulsome reports of the cult's historical and contemporary influence in Mexico and beyond filled the pages of the glossy magazine. Positioned between each article were job notices—"Cooks: Applebee's Zion, Illinois. Flexible Schedules, Excellent Pay, Health Insurance"—as well as advertisements for schools, shops, services, and congratulatory notes from various social clubs operating in the Chicago area. Second Tepeyac committee members and the officiating priest had also designated that Sunday to formally welcome Guadalupanas/os from El Salvador. After the prayer service the priest asked Salvadorans in the audience to raise their hands. A handful in a room of five hundred responded. A couple of those devotees let out a prideful holler. Giggles and applause rolled in soft waves across the crowded gym. Next he called out for families of Guadalupanos from Honduras to respond and then motioned toward a small group of adherents from Guatemala. Each party responded in turn, equally proud if underrepresented. The priest then asked the *mexicanos* to declare their presence. More than 90 percent of the attendees offered an assortment of *gritos*, cheers, whistles, and outstretched arms. Nervous giggles and reserved approval were now roars and toothy smiles. Finally, he called for *americanos* to make their presence known. A wave of silence fell over the crowd. Standing against the back wall of the gymnasium, I timidly began to raise my hand with the three other "Americans" I saw positioned in the crowd like the cardinal directions of a compass. Being marked as an American, I thought, didn't really capture the fact that I was raised on the U.S.-Mexico border, traversed both Tamaulipas and Texas with ease, and am a U.S. citizen because I was born, literally, less than a mile north of the Rio Grande. José, my compadre from Rogers Park with dual citizenship, sensing my apprehension, grabbed my thinking hand and raised it far over my head.

I attended prayer assemblies at the Second Tepeyac of North America over a two-year period (2002–4). These experiences were familiar but always a bit strange. No longer surrounded exclusively by border-Mexican and Tejano-American devotees in South Texas but by Guadalupanas/os from across North and Central America, my understanding of piety, devotion, and the sacred became infused with diverse cultural perspectives, distinct idioms, and different life experiences. I spent the majority of my time working alongside immigration lawyers and shrine coordinators whose primary objective was to mitigate the pressures of undocumented life in the United States. Often I traveled to Des Plaines with Mexican nationals living on Chicago's Far North Side. What connects adherents at the Second Tepeyac, however, is shared allegiance to la Virgen de Guadalupe, not necessarily national or even regional affiliation.

Although scholars have attended to the intersections between the cult of Guadalupe, geographic resettlement, and national affiliation, those efforts position Guadalupan devotion, and justly so, as an evocation of Mexican spirituality, culture, and history. Of particular importance to the following discussion is scholarship that focuses on Guadalupan devotees' identity formation outside of Mexico, specifically, the nationalistic elements underwriting the development of ethnoreligious spaces.[2] Renderings of Mexican exiles in the 1930s escaping religious persecution, for example, and their conceptualization of a México de Afuera, "unyielding dedication to nationalism, Mexican national symbols, the Spanish language, Mexican citizenship, and the Catholic faith rooted in devotion to Mexico's national patroness, *Nuestra Señora de Guadalupe*," set a precedent for contemporary analyses.[3]

Although Mexican Guadalupanas/os in Des Plaines display analogous convictions, the intercultural and multinational dynamics sustaining the Second Tepeyac demand that we refocus our optic. That Guadalupe is an inherent part of Mexico's identity is undeniable. Her presence, however, does not offer solely a "Mexican" perspective; the Second Tepeyac provides an atmosphere in which communities are encouraged to celebrate their distinct heritages and homelands. Devotees, many of whom learn about and circulate religious practices along migration circuits, acknowledge each other's nationalist affiliations, but their religious principles often exceed secular identifications, even when national symbols such as flags formed part of their devotional spaces. Further, they appeal explicitly to the sacred when expressing collective pro-immigrant subjectivities. Manuel A. Vásquez and Marie F. Marquardt suggest:

> Released from the disciplinary power of the modern secular nation-state, religion is free to enter the globalizing, regionalizing, and localizing dynamics described here to generate new identities and territories. . . . Cities [and suburbs] become places where those displaced by globalization—be it Latino immigrants in the United States or peasants migrating to growing metropolises in Latin America—try to make sense of their baffling world by mapping and remapping sacred landscapes through religious practices like making pilgrimages, holding festivals, and constructing altars, shrines, and temples.[4]

Inter-American sacred space development and ethnoreligious community formation, even at its early stages, encourages polyvalent expressions of the divine that enable devotees to overcome the debilitating material and societal effects of anti-immigration narratives. Here I offer a comparative examination of those expressions—the architectural, rhetorical, and embodied practices that not only produce Guadalupan sacred space in Des Plaines but also create an open line of communication with Tepeyac in Mexico City.

THEORETICAL AND HISTORICAL CONSIDERATIONS

Understanding the links among the transposition of ritual performances, socioeconomic practices, and the development of sacred space across national borders necessarily builds on theories and methodologies that consider the material, ideological, social, and temporal components at work within the production of space. Henri Lefebvre, for example, conceptualizes the production of space as a dialectical relationship between what is perceived (or what he refers to as "spatial practices"), what is conceived ("representations of space"), and what is lived ("representational spaces").[5] His categories are grounded by certain requisites, but the boundaries separating them are porous. Each informs the other's development. I use the triad as an optic through which to analyze distinct but related locations. My emphasis throughout this study lies in the production of sacred space, primarily within the realm of spatial practices, which Lefebvre defines as that "which embraces production and reproduction and the particular locations and spatial sets characteristic of each social formation. Spatial practice ensures continuity and some degree of cohesion. In terms of social space, and of each member of a given society's relationship to that space, this cohesion implies a guaranteed level of *competence* and a specific level of *performance*."[6]

Guadalupanos' devotional practices in Mexico City and Des Plaines—their pilgrimages, dances, songs, prayers, and shrine maintenance—ensure not only the success of sacred space construction and the circulation of Catholic doctrine but also the transmission of knowledge, coping strategies, cultural practices, and histories across different sites throughout North America. Embodied acts, however, are but one dimension of production. In order to understand the full extent of their contribution, I want to pay equal attention to those individuals and agencies that determine "representations of space"—in other words, the "scientists, planners, urbanists, technocratic subdividers and social engineers" that manipulate "frontal" relations and impose "order" on sacred space.[7] This is not to suggest that devotees cannot conceptualize sacred space. In fact, as I suggest in Part II, a *peregrina*'s (female pilgrim's) decision to put one foot in front of the other during pilgrimages, for instance, also imposes "order," albeit not quite institutionally. The places peregrinas traverse become imbued with their faith-based actions, thereby creating sacred space that parallels and complements Tepeyac, as well as its outposts.

The last category of the triad—what is lived—allows us to attend to the deeply complex and often-coded regenerative effects that are born of sacred space production. Lefebvre cites the "sun, sea, festival, waste, expense" as that which resides and develops, for example, within neo-capitalism's "representational spaces."[8] In this study notions of Guada-lupan sanctity, as experienced by devotees, dominate this realm. Living through images and nonverbal symbols associated with consecrated en-vironments, adherents may assimilate their experiences and negotiate their spatial realities.

Indeed, Guadalupan devotion in the suburb of Des Plaines continues a long history of ethnoreligious community migration and Guadalupan sacred space production across North America—developments inspired by faith in and consumption of the Virgin of Guadalupe's image. Mi-grant laborers traveled between western Mexico and the Midwest in the early twentieth century, for example, replacing the war-bound white ethnic workers who supported the city's unprecedented industrial ex-pansion.[9] Newly arrived, they introduced their specific cultural and re-ligious ideals onto the urban landscape. External factors also helped guide the settlement process. The Illinois Steel Company and the arch-bishop of Chicago, Cardinal Mundelein, organized the construction of Our Lady of Guadalupe Parish in 1923. Illinois Steel donated $12,000 to finance the construction project, while the archdiocese, which had previously denied the merit of establishing a parish, "blessed" the proj-ect.[10] Founding institutional spaces in migrant neighborhoods such as the Back of the Yards and the Near West Side continued the legacy of the church's strategy to cater to diverse communities. In 1846 the arch-diocese offered St. Peter's and St. Joseph's Churches to German settlers and St. Patrick's Church to the Irish population. In 1880 the Italian com-munity received Assumption BVM, and in 1889 John Augustine Tolton, the first African American ordained in the United States, helped build St. Monica's for the black community.[11]

Pierette Hondagneu-Sotelo and her colleagues term these processes "religio-ethnic cultural expansion," or "the ways in which a distinc-tively ethnic and religious form is adopted, transformed, and expanded to new inclusiveness in the United States."[12] Karen Mary Davalos's

Chicago-based study of the Via Crucis (Stations of the Cross) in the Pilsen neighborhood, which demonstrates how generations of residents continue to use this port of entry to perform rituals, offers a terrific exemplar.[13] Since 1977 that Easter Holy Week ritual, in which devotees reenact Jesus Christ's agonizing walk toward crucifixion, has attracted thousands of "Mexicanos and other Latinos" from the Chicago area and the Midwest. "The crowd itself," Davalos suggests,

> has become a symbol of the event and the people comment on its size, strength, and security for 'the undocumented who normally remain hidden.' . . . Pilsen residents and other Mexicanos forge a relationship as a community, speak in a nearly unified voice against forms of oppression, and transcend space and time from Mexico to Jerusalem, Mexico to the United States, Chicago to Calvary.[14]

Similar to Guadalupan devotional rituals enacted at the Second Tepeyac, the Via Crucis offers disenfranchised communities an opportunity to mobilize. They not only celebrate their respective cultures and homelands but also articulate a collective political subjectivity that appeals to the sacred.

There are productive differences, however, that relate to the site-specific components of each case study. Davalos argues, "Material barriers, physical dangers, and social inequalities [in Pilsen] constitute the architecture of domination."[15] With the term *architecture of domination,* she critically pinpoints Chicago's problematic race/urban space politics, specifically, how the city selectively provides basic services and infrastructure maintenance according to neighborhood demographics shaped by industrialization processes.[16] In contrast, and pivotal to this comparative study, are the ways in which Chicago's deindustrialization has transformed not only urban space but also suburban cities like Des Plaines.

Des Plaines, like Chicago and its outskirts, was introduced to a period of economic restructuring after World War II. Lower land costs and unionization rates, a growing labor pool, an expanded highway system, and the shifting consumer market repositioned the base of industrial operation outside of the city. Race, especially the "explosive political militancy of the civil rights struggles of the late 1960s," equally influenced Chicago's deindustrialization.[17] By 1981 Chicago had lost 25 percent of its factories and 27 percent of its manufacturing jobs to the wider metropolitan area. Many laborers followed work to the suburbs; others entered the tertiary labor market: retail, restaurants, and hotels. The development of the city's transit system and O'Hare International Airport, which is adjacent to Des Plaines, attracted raw material and product distribution centers, corporate headquarters, and the laborers, who may or may not be documented, that sustain these industries and the accompanying service sector.[18]

Statistically a predominantly white suburb,[19] Des Plaines seems a peculiar choice for a sanctioned replica of Mexico's most important colonial-era sacred space.[20] At one time, Des Plaines, like other suburbs across the nation, theoretically catered to a certain type of resident and performed a particular social function. "The invention of the suburb," Joseph Roach notes, "[is a] bourgeois simulacrum of heaven where decency allots to every proper person an inviolable place, detached or semidetached, and where ownership is individually privatized for eternity along its silent, leafy avenues."[21] Likelihood aside, Maryville Academy, the isolated ninety-seven-acre property that hosts the Second Tepeyac, offers a secure venue where Guadalupanos may worship and mobilize (simultaneously if they wish).

Initially opened to help orphaned children displaced after the Great Chicago Fire in 1871, Maryville Academy, which is currently managed jointly by the archdiocese of Chicago and the state's Department of Children and Family Services, is one of Illinois's largest facilities for treating battered and neglected children.[22] The verdant campus surrounding *"el cerrito"* (little hill; Tepeyac) draws thousands of devotees on foot, on bicycles, on buses, and even on planes. This is not to suggest that this institutional space is ideal. The Catholic Church, with its modes of production and expansion, is a power industry laden with hierarchies and stratification. Although coordinators and volunteers are committed to social justice issues and to advancing cultural, economic, and educational development within the congregation, the situation is far from perfect. Community members, for example, do not talk openly about gay rights. Moreover, I do not wish to imply that Chicago's suburbs are immune to "urban" problems: xenophobia, poverty, gang violence, and so on. Instead, I seek to acknowledge the varying trajectories of intracity and transnational migration circuits and to draw a distinction among urban, suburban, and rural spaces, specifically, Mexican/urban- and U.S./suburban-based developments of sacred space. To do justice to this narrative, however, we must first travel to New Spain to consider how Tepeyac's specific historical and geographic progression advanced the production of transnational sacred space.

DIVINE INTERVENTION AND CONQUEST:
TEPEYAC, 1531–1800

According to the *Informaciones de 1666*, Spanish ecclesiastical and civil authorities inaugurated the first Guadalupan shrine known as the Church of Zumárraga on December 26, 1531, approximately two weeks after the Virgin's appearances. Today Basilica officials conserve a portion of the shrine within the Parroquia Vieja de los Indios (Old Parish of the Indians). In 1556, the second archbishop of Mexico, fray Alonso de Montúfar, constructed the eponymous church of Montúfar.[23] Anti-apparitionists maintain that Guadalupan officials placed a copied image of la Virgen de Guadalupe (modeled after a European representation) in this second church to lend legitimacy to the sanctuary. Coincidentally, the Franciscan fray Francisco de Bustamante gave the first documented anti-Guadalupan sermon on September 8, 1556, in this space.[24] The third church in this early sequence is the Iglesia Artesonada (Coffered Church). Laborers completed the building "adorned with silver and precious materials" in 1622.[25] Constructed more than a century after Cortés set foot in Tenochtitlán, the building evinced the Catholic Church's growing control and appropriation of New World resources.

Indeed, the development and promotion of these holy places advanced the spiritual conquest and produced innumerable local and regional socioeconomic and political networks. One example is *cofradías*—fraternities of devotees who simultaneously supported religious and social growth in the community. According to the historians Alicia Bazarte Martínez and Clara García Ayluardo, the clergy actively organized cofradías in New Spain with the objective of "evangelization, race integration, as well as developing solidarity within the Christian community and native communities disenfranchised by the aggressive effects of colonization."[26] A key example of this work is the aforementioned church of Montúfar. A cofradía of four hundred silver workers in collaboration with the church's first chaplain, don Antonio Freire, and two civil administrators, don Alonso de Villaseca and Domingo de Orona, oversaw and financed the project. They expanded the church of Zumárraga, constructed a small hospital, and adorned the renovated temple with a "beautiful cross engraved with scenes from the passion."[27] Indigenous subjects of the crown who resided in Tepeaquilla and the surrounding areas of San Lorenzo and San Bartolomé de las Salinas supplied the manpower to build these edifices.[28] The main work of these laborers was harvesting salt on ranches and haciendas, or plantations, in the area, but they also worked in the fishing and agriculture industries. The physical division of these slave-labor communities was widespread in this early period and continued well into the eighteenth century. In 1736, for example, don Luis Díez Navarro planned three residential areas surrounding Tepeyac, which he divided along race and class lines. Ecclesiastical officials resided to the east of Tepeyac, the Spanish population to the west, and the indigenous populations near the salt-producing zones alongside the Guadalupe riverbank.[29] Acts of segregation such as this one, in conjunction with the development of cofradías, illustrate New Spain's categories of class, as well as prejudices based on phenotypic characteristics. The skin privilege and kinship-based hierarchies that shaped those secular/religious brotherhoods powerfully affected the evangelization project and the growth of the colony.[30]

Tepeyac's physical transformation enhanced its reputation as a power player within the colonial state. In 1748, for example, five years after the completion of an aqueduct that connected the shrine with the center of the city,[31] Tepeyac officially became la Villa de Guadalupe and operated with an independent government.[32] Aqueduct maintenance and repairs to the causeway of Guadalupe in 1786, still a major entrance road for religious and civil actors, strengthened la Villa's relationships with city officials as well as area merchants and laborers. To complete the repairs to the Calzada de Guadalupe, Viceroy Conde de Gávez ordered that all *pulque* (a pre-Hispanic alcoholic beverage made from the fermented juice of the maguey plant) deliveries to and from Mexico City also transport building materials to repair the road.[33] With the completion of these public projects, la Villa de Guadalupe developed a sophisticated infrastructure, including the addition of internal posts such as "protector of the sanctuary, superintendent of the aqueduct, and superintendent of development and public relations."[34] Moreover, these sixteenth- and seventeenth-century renovation projects advanced the development and legitimacy of the cult of Guadalupe by creating physical access routes to the sacred space.

La Villa de Guadalupe entered a new realm of national and theological importance during the eighteenth century.[35] In 1754 Pope Benedict XIV declared la Virgen de Guadalupe *"patrona de Nueva España"* (patroness of New Spain) and designated December 12 as her feast day. His famous proclamation, taken from Psalm 147—"Non fecit taliter omni natione" (It was not done thus to all nations)—differentiated Mexico from other colonized/Christianized territories and positioned the Virgin as a Catholic icon for subjects of the crown throughout New Spain, which then spanned from (present-day) Northern California to El Salvador.[36] Two centuries later, Pope Pius XI, following his predecessor's declaration, reconfirmed la Virgen de Guadalupe's position as empress of Latin America and the Philippines.[37]

The construction of three new buildings also increased the symbolic currency of the burgeoning religious tourism center—the Basílica Antigua (1695–1709), El Pocito (1777–91), and el Convento de Capuchinas (1782–87).[38] The Basílica Antigua, finished in 1709 at a total cost of 800,000 pesos, provided ecclesiastical officials with an emblematic structure for the celebration of religious ceremonies and a sanctified place to safeguard the *"ayate de Juan Diego."* Pedro de Arrieta, the principal architect, designed the building to reinforce the authenticity and theological importance of the apparition accounts. In addition to placing images of the Virgin and Juan Diego alongside images of prophets and apostles, he designed the four towers of the structure to mimic the Temple of Solomon in Jerusalem. The concept behind these aesthetic choices was to demonstrate that "New Spain was also a sacred territory chosen by the Mother of God."[39]

The Spanish Constitution of Cádiz in 1812 compromised the Catholic Church's religio-political capital and set off what analysts have called the birth of the modern state in Mexico.[40] This document followed the fight for independence in New Spain led by Fr. Miguel Hidalgo y Costilla, who waved a banner imprinted with an image of the Virgin of Guadalupe to forge solidarity among would-be soldiers. Through the Mexican Constitution of 1857 and the nationalization law in 1859, liberal politicians contended that in order for the country to disengage completely from oppressive colonial power structures, the Catholic Church—a primary beneficiary of colonial rule—must be disentangled from government processes. Specifically, civil officials must strip the Catholic Church of its vast property holdings and deny use of state structures to finance any accumulation or growth. In 1848 ecclesiastical corporations in Mexico City represented only 4.34 percent of the city's proprietors, yet they maintained 38.52 percent of the city's property value. By 1864 their numbers had dropped significantly, to less than one percent in both instances.[41] The state secularized religious spaces across the nation, including the Convento de Capuchinas in 1867, but not without cost to both traditionalist and reformist camps. In addition to property expropriation, the state denied the Catholic Church use of public space, thus making it illegal for clergy or devotees to perform religious acts—

ceremonies and processions—outside of designated spaces. Postinde-pendence national and international political shifts such as periods of imperial rule—Maximilian von Hapsburg (1864–67)—the invasion of U.S. soldiers in the 1840s, the start of the Mexican Revolution (1910), and the Cristero War (1926–29), however, made the country too vul-nerable to sustain its postcolonial expectations of disempowering the Catholic Church. [42]

Every political transition, however, has a blind spot. The Basílica Antigua, for example, which protected the "ayate de Juan Diego" and hosted important international and national events such as the signing of the Treaty of Guadalupe Hidalgo in 1848 and the inauguration of Mexico's rail service in 1857, was often an aberration.[43] The first train, which joined the port of Veracruz with Acapulco, carried the name "Guadalupe" on the conductor's car. As Antonio Pompa y Pompa notes, "In 1861, when Church property was being nationalized in Mexico City, the shrine of la Virgen de Guadalupe was always the exception. In the event that valuable objects were confiscated from the property, they were always returned the next day by way of a superior order."[44]

Reform conflict and government corruption waged into the twenti-eth century incited the Mexican Revolution, the 1917 Constitution, and the 1926 reforms of the penal code—all of which continued to chal-lenge the church's presence in state processes.[45] One way the church compromised reform laws without legal consequences was by unoffi-cially advising armed forces such as the Liga Nacional Defensora de la Libertad Religiosa (National Defense League of Religious Liberty) and Acción Católica (Catholic Action), both of which defended Christ and Catholicism against secularization and played a key role in the Cristero War. [46] Several scholars suggest that liberals and conservatives alike were apprehensive during the Cristero War and through Lazaro Cardenas's presidency. Both parties, however, always practiced a form of accom-modation. As Roberto Blancarte suggests, "It was during the 1930s that the church and state defined their future behavioral patterns in regards to social strategies and mutual relations."[47] Understanding this tumultu-ous period as one of maneuvering and compromise by both factions explains, in part, how la Villa de Guadalupe was able to achieve unpre-cedented local spatial renovation and expansion across North America in the twentieth century.

RELIGIOUS TOURISM AND EXPANSION IN THE TWENTIETH CENTURY

The state and the church attended strategically to the legitimacy of the Basilica as a national space and as a tourist attraction after the Cristero War. Theoretically, the period between 1940 and 1980 was an era of tolerance, which gave ecclesiastical officials license to realize extensive physical renovations. Cooperative action taken by the state during this period set the stage for the physical expansion of la Villa de Guadalupe and the continued growth of Guadalupismo as an integral part of the nation's identity and a center of religious tourism.[48] A pivotal performance occurred at a 1940 press conference when newly inaugurated President Manuel Avila Camacho (1940–46) stated, "Yo soy creyente, soy católico" (I am a believer, I am Catholic).[49] This statement, articulated by the highest-ranking civil official in the Mexican republic, directly compromised the credibility of the 1917 Constitution. Soon after, in 1943, la Villa de Gustavo A. Madero officially regained its pre-Reforma title: la Villa de Guadalupe Hidalgo with a Senate vote of seventy-nine (for) to three (against).[50] In tandem, ecclesiastical officials initiated a new era of religious tourism and commercial expansion with the construction of the Guadalupan museum. On October 12, 1941, Monsignor Feliciano Cortés y Mora, the twentieth abbot of the Basilica, inaugurated el Museo Guadalupano—a museum that features the institutional history of the cult of Guadalupe through paintings and sculptures. Much like the Basílica Antigua's architectural representation of history and tradition, the museum's permanent exhibit visually reinforces Guadalupan doctrine to the millions who spend time at the space each year. Visits to the shrine by national politicians and international figures (President John F. Kennedy and the First Lady visited in 1962) reinforced these local changes on several levels.[51] The shrine has also been important for presidential hopefuls. In summer 2008, presumptive Republican presidential candidate John McCain (R-Ariz.) presented the Virgin of Guadalupe with white roses at the Modern Basilica during the last stop of his Latin American tour.[52]

Another significant transgression occurred in November 1952 when President Miguel Alemán (1946–52) visited the Basilica to inaugurate the Plaza de las Américas. It was the first time in a century that a president of the republic set foot on the sacred space (or that such an act was documented or publicized). He justified the visit with the following declaration:

Habíamos sido invitados a inaugurar las obras de la Plaza de la Basílica, y así lo hicimos, puesto que se trata de un lugar que es visitado por el pueblo de México, que es creyente y católico, y nosotros tenemos la obligación de atender a las necesidades y deseos del pueblo.[53]

[We were invited to inaugurate the Basilica's Plaza [de las Américas] and we did so because it is a place that is visited by the people of Mexico, people who have faith and who are Catholic. We have the obligation to attend to the needs and wishes of the country.]

Building on Alemán's authority, architects, planners, and clergy emphasized the shrine's inherent "Mexican" qualities during the conceptualization, construction, and promotion of the Plaza de las Américas (1952) the Modern Basilica (1976), and el Jardín de la Ofrenda (the Offering Garden)—which later served as the model for the Second Tepeyac.

The Plaza de las Américas—a 35,000-square-meter atrium with the capacity to hold approximately 30,000 persons—was the most important development after the construction of the museum. The architect, Manuel Ortiz Monasterio, designed the space with "Mexican-made materials" to express an architectural style that was "very ours, traditionalist, with the flavor of eighteenth-century colonial Mexico."[54] La Villa's public relations machine successfully defused this problematic colonial reference by placing it within an international framework. Planning officials displayed twenty-one flags, one from each American nation, and one flag representing Hispanic America, thereby creating an attractive multinational tourist space.[55] They promoted the local benefits of the project, claiming the Plaza was important "not only from a religious point of view but also in terms of economics and the beautification of the city. La Virgen de Guadalupe's shrine is a center of universal tourism and it deserves all of the attention and enthusiasm of prestigious persons it has received."[56] The Committee of Guadalupan Pilgrimages used similar rhetoric, advertising Tepeyac as a global tourist attraction and promising foreigners moral and visual gratification. The following is an excerpt from a 1949 advertisement found in the *Voz Guadalupana* (Guadalupan Voice), Tepeyac's monthly magazine.

Our cordial invitation to visit the Basílica de Guadalupe is justified. In the Basílica de Guadalupe, known worldwide as "the Shrine of America," you will bear witness to the ties that unite us as brothers and as Catholics; our colonial monuments, archeological jewels, our customs and traditional places, our beautiful panoramas and ideal climate all year round. . . . We are sure that when you leave Mexico, you will take with you an imperishable souvenir of our country, rich in Catholicism and history as well as traditions and legends. Mexico and Tepeyac await you!

To ensure a successful niche in the tourist economy, Plaza producers actively solicited city funding and cooperation, specifically, the elimination of "dirty" businesses, with promises of "urban development" throughout the area.[57] Municipal officials cooperated and even subsidized the construction of a market—the Mercado Villa Zona—adjacent to Tepeyac.[58] The construction of the Plaza and the two markets—Mercado Peregrino and the Mercado Villa Zona—required the demolition of three hundred houses and businesses in the vicinity.[59] Officials countered critics by suggesting the alterations would give the Basilica the same brilliance as Mexico City's then newly renovated areas such as Cuauhtémoc, México-Tacuba, and Miguel Angel de Quevedo.[60] In addition to seeking city-level support, producers asked for nationwide financial assistance. The entire project cost approximately 25 million pesos, which planners divided among three patrons: the federal government, the *delegación* Gustavo A. Madero, and parishes/devotees across the republic. Archbishop Dr. Luis María Martínez publicly called for the people, "regardless of social class or status," to contribute to the project.[61] The executive committee in the capital organized central offices in Monterrey, Guadalajara, Mérida, San Luis Potosí, León, Aguascalientes, Puebla, Saltillo, and Querétaro to collect donations.

If the production of the Plaza de las Américas placed la Villa de Guadalupe as a symbolic tourist space on local, national, and international stages, then the construction of the Modern Basilica intensified the bid. Architects and ecclesiastical officials conceptualized the project in the 1940s as a way to remedy the structural problems of the Basílica Antigua.[62] It took more than thirty years, however, to gain sufficient political and financial support. Why raise millions of pesos for an enormous church when we lack schools, hospitals, and other basic services? critics asked. The nationally acclaimed architect Pedro Ramírez Vázquez countered, "Like the city arena or the Azteca stadium, the Basílica de Guadalupe is paid for by the people who want to use the services. Ticket sales pay for the construction of a boxing arena. Why not build a temple if devotees will pay for the costs."[63] But devotees did not subsidize the entire project. On December 10, 1974, President Luis Echeverría Alvarez authorized the project and offered federal funds to cover construction costs. The plan received additional capital when Pope Paul VI proclaimed the shrine a "Basílica menor" days before its inauguration in October 1976.[64]

Monsignor Schulenburg Prado and Ramírez Vázquez oversaw the design and construction of the Modern Basilica and were clear about project priorities. Ramírez Vázquez and his design team gave precedence to devotees' embodied and spectatorial practices, and with good reason. La Villa/Tepeyac receives countless visitors annually, approximately 9 million to 12 million peregrinas/os during the month of December alone. It is the second most visited Catholic shrine in the world after the Vatican. Adherents arrive on foot, on bicycle, by car, or by bus. Also, numerous international tourists/pilgrims use air transportation. In August 2003, for example, I interviewed a travel agent/Guadalupano who organizes an annual expedition from Paris to Mexico City. He carried a custom-made French flag adorned with an image of la Virgen de Guadalupe on the center stripe. The juxtaposition of a Mexican symbol on the French banner delighted everyone around him, including newspaper and television journalists from Telemundo and Univisión who were anxious to hear his story. In addition to these high-profile tour groups, there are thousands of individual and family visits.

Considering these factors, architects designed the building to impress many millions of visitors annually, from individuals to large groups, such as the annual 35,000-devotee pilgrimage from Toluca, Mexico.[65] They justified the modern design of the edifice, which critics deprecated for being too similar to a stadium or a big top, by arguing that it was functional and met the organization's demands. Ramírez Vázquez agreed that the design of the space was stadium-like but a stadium designed for prayer and pilgrimage.[66]

Ramírez Vázquez fought against suggestions that he construct the Basilica atop the hill of Tepeyac: "Will [exhausted] devotees be expected to climb hundreds of stairs or should we install an elevator? Won't the tradition of performing a 'manda' [an exchange between the deity and the devotee in which the latter party gives thanks for a miracle or special guidance] be altered if devotees are expected to walk on their knees part of the way and then take an elevator?"[67] His focus on devotees' embodied practices prompted officials and planners to reenvision the possibilities and limitations of religious tourism. The act of pilgrimage also influenced Monsignor Schulenburg and his colleagues who took the theoretical and practical components of the devotional performance into account by asking, "What does a pilgrimage to the Basilica consist of? What is a peregrino looking for? What are their demands? What may they receive or obtain from the experience?"[68] These questions, which have cross-cultural and international implications, inspired and disciplined this particular incarnation of sacred space production. These uncertainties, which often defy resolution, continue to influence Tepeyac's local and transnational development during an ongoing era of reconciliation. This period of legal conciliation was launched by President Carlos Salinas de Gortari (1988–94) and Monseñor Schulenberg, "the last abbot of the Basilica" (1963–96),[69] when they publicly negotiated the amendment of anticlerical laws imposed in the 1917 Constitution.[70]

TOWARD "EL NORTE" (AGAIN): TRANSNATIONAL SACRED SPACE PRODUCTION IN THE MIDWEST

In October 2001 the Institute for Historical and Theological Worship for the Virgin of Guadalupe in Mexico City, under the guidance of Cardinal Norberto Rivera Carrera, proclaimed the Church of Maryville in Des Plaines, Illinois, the "Second Tepeyac of North America."[71] The reproduction of sacred space, however, does not commence with proclamations alone. This process began in 1987. Joaquín Martínez, then a lay volunteer at a church in the Chicago suburb of Northbrook solicited a statue of la Virgen de Guadalupe from relatives in San Luis Potosí. Inspired by a call for a Marian year by Pope John Paul II, Martínez organized a Chicago-area tour, which took the statuette to schools, parishes, seminaries, convents, hospitals, and retirement homes, as well as to Daley Plaza, Mayor Richard Daley's home, and eventually, after much uncertainty, Maryville Academy.[72]

In 1991 Martínez, using the apparition scenario as a primary point of reference, conceptualized the construction of a "second Tepeyac."[73] He enlisted Chicago-area architects to study Tepeyac/la Villa's physical layout, a formidable challenge considering the range of architectural styles and design options offered by the colonial-era sacred space. This collaborative effort created one of the first tangible lines of communication between Tepeyac and the Second Tepeyac. Deliberating among multiple possibilities, a shrine committee, organized and led by Martínez, decided that reproducing Tepeyac's outdoor sanctuary—el Jardín de la Ofrenda—would best fit Maryville's resources and devotee's needs. First and foremost, planners could easily modify the size of the garden to fit the suburban landscape; and second, the original structure prominently displays the key players in the Virgin's apparition scenario—Juan Diego and fray Juan de Zumárraga. Transposing the narrative and the milieu in a single swoop is a transnational strategy. It not only instantaneously bestowed legitimacy on the design plans but also solidified institutional ties between Mexico City and Des Plaines. The presence of multiple representations of the apparition scenario in both locations creates dialogue among devotees, clergy, architects, and patrons who may be separated by national borders.

After securing authorization, donations, and fund-raising support, the burgeoning Guadalupan community began to oversee the ten-year construction period of the outdoor structure known as el Cerrito. Although Joaquín Martínez envisioned, conceptualized, and organized the construction of el Cerrito, Rev. John P. Smyth, who served as executive director of Maryville for thirty-five years, officially holds the title "Fundador de Maryville Cerrito del Tepeyac de Chicago" (Founder of the Maryville Hill of Tepeyac in Chicago) because he authorized the project and presided over its inauguration in 2001.[74] Under Smyth's guidance, the Church of Maryville supports the burgeoning Guadalupan community as well as various Christian groups in the area, including an established Assyrian population, by offering space for worship services and organizational meetings.

The replica maintains a strong transnational connection with its counterpart in Mexico City. One Sunday morning in spring 2006, for example, the presiding priest offered to personally deliver notes, prayers, and other personal items during his official visit to Tepeyac the following week. A year earlier, he and a group of Chicago-based Guadalupanos had journeyed to Tepeyac as ambassadors. They shared their photos, relics, and memories of the trip with the rest of the congregation that spring morning, which only added to the allure of the priest's call. In 2006 top clergy from the Basilica in Mexico City, including Monsignor Diego Monroy, returned the favor. A group of top officials journeyed for the first time to the Chicago area, and the Second Tepeyac in particular, to bless the replica, thereby strengthening devotees' faith in the Catholic Church and the cult of Guadalupe. At the Second Tepeyac, Monsignor Monroy offered the following words:

> Sigan siendo maternales, Muestran su bondad, su ternura, y sus valores, que han testificado en las marchas por sus derechos y dignidad de migrantes. . . . Estoy seguro de que muchos han cambiado su concepto de ustedes con esta actitud de paz en las marchas donde no solo se han ondeado las banderas de México, sino de otros países . . . y la de Santa María de Guadalupe, en sus estandartes, y en su corazón, porque asi se expresaba en su actitud constructiva. . . . Nos animan los valores y la fe en esta lucha que es por la justicia y la paz. Que Dios los bendiga a todos.[75]

Here Monroy accomplishes many things. He urges spectators to fight for justice and peace using their shared faith in the Virgin of Guadalupe, while also acknowledging that the struggle is not just about securing immigration rights for Mexican migrants but that the endeavor involves devotees from other countries as well. He says, "I am sure that many have changed their perception of you while watching peaceful marches where not only the Mexican flag waves but also flags from other countries, as well as images of the Virgin of Guadalupe on your banners, and in your heart, because in this way is expressed your constructive attitude." For Monroy, the common denominator in Chicago is faith.

In addition to upholding the Virgin of Guadalupe as a symbol for migrants' rights, this official visit opened a public and institutional line of communication between the two sacred spaces. The regenerative effects of this outreach strategy toward the replica not only create a deeper sense of ownership and veritability among adherents but also initiated physical changes to the built environment in Des Plaines.

As is, the open-air replica displays an eight-by-six-foot portrait of the ayate de Juan Diego. Strategically placing her image front and center also legitimizes the replication process. It presents the evidence of the Virgin's fourth apparition—the moment when she filled Juan Diego's ayate with roses and miraculously imprinted her likeness, thereby materializing the ineffable. The representation's aged appearance, the contrast between the deep warm tones of her aura and the tranquil blue of her robe, and the multihued haze of pale sky that seems to maintain her form in perpetual levitation encapsulate the historic moment in which Christianity secured its place in the New World. This depiction and not, for instance, an interpretation featuring an altered color scheme, roses, a Mexican flag, or a close-up of the Virgin cuddling Pope John Paul II, is the only representation that has the historical and symbolic currency to legitimize the replica. Thus, Maryville officials insist that it remain prominently showcased behind bullet-proof glass on the simulated landscape.

Directly to the right of the image stand two bronze statues enacting the Virgin's fourth apparition to Juan Diego. Maryville-contracted architects drew the likeness of these statues directly from the seventeen bronze statues mounted in Tepeyac's Offering Garden. The original configuration in Mexico City, designed by Aurelio G. D. Mendoza and sculpted by Alberto Pérez Soria and Gerardo Quiróz, symbolizes and celebrates the conquered peoples' rapid acceptance of the cult of Guadalupe and the birth of a new mestizo population—the sons of Indians and Spaniards. Among those immortalized are fray Juan de Zumárraga and generic in-

FIGURE 1. El Jardín de la Ofrenda, Tepeyac, Mexico City. All photos courtesy of the author.

digenous devotees offering Guadalupe *maíz* (corn), flowers, and incense. Maryville designers imitated the aesthetic of the statues precisely, but the message is different from the one offered in Mexico City. The configuration of the statues adorning el Cerrito signifies something different not because the replica has two instead of fifteen bronze statues but because la Virgencita's gaze rests on Juan Diego and not on Zumárraga. By focusing on the upright Spanish church official and not on the kneeling indigenous man, el Jardín de la Ofrenda reinforces the superiority and authority of the church over the conquered. In Des Plaines the statue's focused gaze on Juan Diego emphasizes the Virgin's position as mother and protector of the conquered. Promoting the latter idea is the most effective approach for unifying an ethnically and culturally diverse congregation. The most recent addition to the shrine, two large stones engraved with the words "In Memory of Blessed Mother, St. Juan Diego, Indians & Emigrantes," memorializes the Virgin's benevolent role—her deep connection and commitment to those experiencing hardship. By placing "emigrantes" alongside Juan Diego and "Indians," committee members combine the foundations of the colonial cult and the diverse requirements of a U.S. congregation to produce a transnational sacred space that is distinct from the prototype but that transfers the ideological foundation of the sect. (See figures 1 and 2.)

FIGURE 2. Simulated landscape, Second Tepeyac, Des Plaines.

Many Guadalupanas/os with whom I have worked explain that they are drawn to the serenity and sanctity of the landscaped gardens. Some who have worshiped at the shrine in Mexico City readily admit that the replica is not as awe-inspiring as Tepeyac's gardens. But no one denies that the Second Tepeyac is a sacred space, despite the fact that there is no tradition of a Marian apparition. As two women from Michoacán (via Pilsen) explained to me while we were selling tamales and cups of *champurrado* (a warm drink made of corn flour that is sometimes flavored with chocolate or vanilla) to peregrinos on a bitterly cold December 12 morning, "Ella, sí está" (She is [here]). It only takes *"un grano de arena"* (one grain of sand), they agreed emphatically. This saying literally suggests that any measure of sacred space, no matter the size, when transposed, will make its new surroundings sacred, like making tap water instantaneously holy by mixing it with water blessed in a church.[76] The Second Tepeyac's legitimacy, in formal and popular senses, rests on this adage. This expression, however, also suggests a localized form of time-space compression. Building on David Harvey's concept that describes the acceleration and wide-reaching potential of business and communication networks, we can imagine how notions of the sacred, like global capital, can transcend the nation-state.[77] Maryville's built environment inspires these women to exceed time and space on their own terms, to link the original with its counterpart in a way that surpasses a state-based framework.

But there are additional ways that the Virgin appears in different locations, through performance—praying, dancing, building, and singing. Consider these lyrics from "Las Apariciones Guadalupanas" (The Guadalupan Apparitions):[78]

> *DEs-del ci-e-lo U-na Ermosa ma-Nia-na*
> One beautiful morning from heaven
>
> *DEs-del ci-e-lo u-na Ermosa ma-Nia-naaa*
> One beautiful morning from heaven
>
> *La Gua-da-lu-pa-na, la Gua-da-lu-pa-na, La Gua-da-lu-pa-na bajO*
>   *alTe-pe-yaac*
> the Virgin of Guadalupe,
> the Virgin of Guadalupe,
> the Virgin of Guadalupe
> descended to Tepeyac
>
> *Su-pli-cante juntaba las manos*
> She clasped her hands together pleadingly (repeat)
>
> *Y eran mexicanos, y eran mexicanos, y eran mexicanos su porte y su faz*
> Her bearing and her face were Mexican, and they were Mexican, and
>   they were Mexican

This song, which aurally relates the Virgin's apparition scenario, has local and transnational significance.[79] Devotees, clergy, and lay leaders alike voice this mythic story to celebrate the cult of Guadalupe across national borders and for international communities. Paradoxically, the text pinpoints the nationalist components inherent in the cult. In practice, however, adherents do not necessarily subscribe to the composition's implicit secular distinction but to the Virgin's power to protect them. As we shall see, performances shift shapes; practitioners modify meaning to accommodate their immediate and long-term needs.

THE VIRGIN'S APPARITION MADE FLESH

One way in which we may understand the persistence of "Las Apariciones Guadalupanas" and its transnational circulation is to think about the Virgin's apparition story as a scenario.

> The scenario [the often-rehearsed Christian/Moor conflict, for example] includes features well theorized in literary analysis, such as narrative and plot,

but demands that we also pay attention to milieu and corporeal behaviors such as gestures, attitudes, and tones not reducible to language. . . . All scenarios have localized meaning, though many attempt to pass as universally valid. Actions and behaviors arising from the setup might be predictable, a seemingly natural consequence of the assumptions, values, goals, power relations, presumed audience, and epistemic grids established by the setup itself. But they are, ultimately, flexible and open to change.[80]

The performance theorist Diana Taylor proposes further that the cult of la Virgen de Guadalupe is an excellent example of the way non-text-based modes of communication can also transmit knowledge.[81] Each enactment and each devotional song share a historical link in the apparition story, but as Taylor suggests, the enactments that ensue are malleable. Devotee-actors script and choreograph their performances to build and maintain a sacred space that fits their specific needs. This is true both in Mexico City and in the Chicago area. At Tepeyac in Mexico City, tourists/devotees/employees have multiple opportunities to witness the Virgin's apparition story. Every hour, the clock tower, el Carillón, located at the easternmost point of the Plaza de las Américas becomes a stage on which Guadalupe's story is reenacted by mechanical bodies. Originally constructed as part of the Modern Basilica project, architect Ramírez Vásquez intended to continue the colonial custom of placing a cross at the far end of the atrium to remind visitors that the space in-between was an extension of the temple. Life-sized figures of the Virgin, Juan Diego, Juan Bernardino, and fray Juan de Zumárraga housed in the center of the cross present the four-part apparition story to spectators standing in the atrium. The space in the middle of the tower opens up to show Juan Diego, a soft-spoken, humbly dressed, brown man. In other presentations, such as posters, postcards, prayer booklets, and church statues, this iconic Indian is sometimes whitened—his skin tone lightened and his facial features Europeanized. But in this performance, his colored body is a key element of this daily reenactment. He remains native for the natives who sustain the shrine. These figures move seamlessly from left to right, guided along a circular track custom-designed in Holland. There are no special light or sound effects. Their gestures are simple; their facial expressions singular. But the dioramas the robotic dolls create are effective. This hourly performance, combined with the presence of the ayate de Juan Diego in the new Basilica, allows each visitor the opportunity to consume the myth and the evidence in one location.

By contrast, when Guadalupanas/os in Des Plaines embody the apparition story, they make it flesh. It has become customary in the early morning hours of December 12, between three and four o'clock, for select devotees to present a theatrical version of the apparition story in the gymnasium-cum-chapel (it is too cold to hold the event by the outdoor structure). Festival organizers choose the actors from the congregation based on their participation in Cerrito activities and their institutional connection with Maryville Academy. The young pregnant woman who embodied the Virgin during the 2005 celebration, for example, worked as a secretary in the Maryville office. The participants use all the gym space to present the story and often inadvertently involve spectators in the telling. The elevated altar, which priests, bishops, and other official figures of the Catholic Church use for the duration of the twelve-day celebration, doubles as the sixteenth-century quarters of fray Juan de Zumárraga. Devotees use the area during the most pivotal moment of the apparition story—which is Juan Diego's presentation of the Virgin's image to Zumárraga—and to honor congregation members who have made exceptional contributions to the shrine. In December 2005, for instance, two devotees presented the Virgin with a ten-by-eight-foot crown cut from thick sheets of metal. At the indoor makeshift altar, the devotees publicly presented their labor to the congregation and, in turn, Father Miguel gave them a special blessing. Later, those devotees placed the crown behind her image on the outdoor sanctuary.

During the theatrical interpretation of the apparition scenario, devotee-actors use a freestanding mural of Tepeyac and an archway/portal to frame Guadalupe each time she converses with Juan Diego. The scenery is especially effective because it gives only an impression of the surrounding landscape—the hill of Tepeyac and the sky from which Guadalupe descended—thereby foregrounding the living actors who tell the narrative. This scenic arrangement gives a curious valence to the story. Depending on one's perspective, the spectator may juxtapose the apparition scenes with an image of a national flag—Brazil, Spain, the United States, or Japan, for instance (see figure 3). This detail gives another frame of reference to the spectator and reinforces Tepeyac/Maryville's appeal as an international sacred space. Further, the production and consumption of the myth by members of the community from different nations underlines Guadalupe's presence among them.

Following a tradition practiced in Mexico City, the congregation in Des Plaines stages a *docenario* (a twelve-day prayer cycle) to build toward the theatrical reenactment. At la Villa/Tepeyac, officiating priests dedicate each day to a particular faction of society—employees and volunteers, the faithful, able and disabled persons, the sick, the young,

FIGURE 3. Apparition made flesh, Second Tepeyac, Des Plaines.

families, colleges and universities, seminarians and novices, San Juan Diego Cuauhtlatoatzin, and the Republic of Mexico. At the Second Tepeyac, organizers use this technique to reinforce the shrine's dual role as a sacred space and an inclusive international political haven. In addition to dedicating the prayer service to an extensive list of laborers (construction workers, gardeners, waiters, cooks, secretaries, bakers, athletes, carpenters, journalists), the congregation recognizes countries from across the Americas and families, individuals, or businesses that have performed as the *padrinos* (benefactors) of the day's events. On the tenth day of the 2005 celebration, for instance, the Guadalupan community dedicated religious ceremonies to artists and musicians from Guanajuato, Sinaloa, Zacatecas, and Surinam, and they credited Angel Córtez and his family, as well as the communications corporation Telemundo, as padrinos. The strategies by which both shrines cultivate devotion, who is given a voice and where these voices may come from, are significantly different. By naming a wide range of occupations and geographic locations while keeping the traditional framework, the Second Tepeyac is identifying itself as a U.S.-based sacred space that caters to an ethnically, geographically, and culturally diverse congregation.

In that respect, it is quite clear that Guadalupan coordinators are intent on creating a culture of inclusion. According to Martínez, one of the main objectives in founding the Second Tepeyac was to celebrate la Virgencita's presence with others, regardless of race, citizenship, or class status. He and his colleagues aspire to cultivate a meeting place for Catholics from the five continents who reside in the Chicago area and to work toward that goal by officially naming the annual December gathering La Fiesta Guadalupana de los 5 Continentes del Mundo (The Guadalupan Festival of the Five Continents of the World). Celebrating the shrine's place in a global context by means of "blessing the five continents of the world," employing an international-themed aesthetic strategy, and publicly recognizing that the Guadalupan community as a mix of various nationalities and histories are only some of the ways in which the shrine is not solely a Mexican or Latino phenomenon. Much like the Basilica's Plaza de las Américas, which displays flags from each American nation and one flag representing Hispanic America, Maryville officials have created an attractive global space by adorning the shrine with an array of flags from around the world, including Switzerland, Mali, Austria, Jamaica, Brazil, China, Great Britain, and Greece. Juxtaposing these banners with prayer services, devotional performances, and political speeches produces interesting, and at times confusing, results. Placing Sweden's flag behind la Virgen de Guadalupe's representation because the banner's yellow and blue color scheme complements her image, for example, effectively illustrates how intentionality and arbitrariness overlap, especially at the beginning stages of space development.

"[SACRED] SPACE IS A PRACTICED PLACE"

The number of Guadalupanas/os who worship and network at the Second Tepeyac has grown exponentially since the inaugural ceremony in 2001. In December 2002 approximately 20,000 devotees journeyed to Des Plaines. There were three walking pilgrimages from the Chicago suburbs of Cicero, Rolling Meadows, and Northbrook, as well as pilgrimages from Michigan, Wisconsin, and California. The next year, between 50,000 and 60,000 adherents visited the shrine. In 2005 Maryville officials estimated that 130,000 Guadalupanas/os participated on different days of the docenario, with the highest attendance on the twelfth.

Institutional involvement and media coverage have also intensified in response to the sacred space's growing and diverse congregation. In 2005 Auxiliary Bishop Gustavo García-Siller, John R. Manz, an administrator of the Migration and Refugee Services Church in Latin America (based in Chicago), Father Claudio Díaz from the Office for Hispanic Catholics, Bishop José Trinidad González from the Archdiocese of Guadalajara, Jalisco (Mexico), and local clerics Fr. John Smyth and Fr. Miguel Martínez celebrated mass during the docenario. Univisión Chicago now covers the annual celebration with a special program called "Desde el Cerrito del Tepeyac" (From the Little Hill of Tepeyac) and popular Spanish-language radio stations, including La Ley 107.9 FM, broadcast the arrival of walking, bicycling, caravanning pilgrims from across the Chicago area and beyond.

At 10:00 P.M. on December 11, 2003, for instance, approximately two hundred Guadalupan devotees left their respective parishes on Chicago's Lower West Side/Pilsen neighborhood and walked more than seven hours in single-digit weather toward the Second Tepeyac. On arriving at 5:30 A.M. they first paid homage to the Virgin at el Cerrito, serenading her with song and prayer, before entering the gymnasium. The moment this walking pilgrimage of young and old devotees entered the space of celebration was unforgettable. An older volunteer opened the industrial-sized doors, letting in blasts of below zero wind, and announced the peregrinos would soon be arriving. Mariachi band members rose to attention, lifting their instruments in anticipation, and the congregation rustled in their seats. Coordinators instructed us to clear the first four rows of the seating space for the tired and cold Guadalupanas/os "who walked the entire night to get here," they emphasized. There was a moment of hesitation before they entered the space. We could hear the faint sound of their voices getting stronger as they approached the building. It could not have been more than two minutes, but this pause, during which bodies were moving from one space to another, was tangible within this improvised religious space. If I were to construct a spatial ethnopoetic transcription marking this pause, it would not be a blank space on the page. Rather, it would be like a moment in performance when an ultra dim light slowly becomes brighter to expose an important object or a person, redirecting and focusing the spectator's gaze.

The arrival of the travelers was overwhelming. They walked down the center aisle of the gymnasium to loud applause and the synchronized sound of trumpets. Once the crowd settled, Martínez invited members of the pilgrimage to speak. Dolores de los Angeles, a woman perhaps in her late forties, was the most articulate. She commented the walk was cold and long, and she was tired, but her love for la Virgencita was greater than her discomfort. De los Angeles also spoke of the need to keep and teach *"nuestra cultura, nuestra lenguaje"* (our culture, our language) to our children. "We cannot lose where we come from." At this point, the space performed on multiple levels. The celebration was no longer solely about religious devotion; de los Angeles had involved the cultural politics that complement devotion to la Virgen de Guadalupe. Her statements made layers of time and history, tradition and migration, spirituality and affiliation explicit.

Michel de Certeau's claim that "space is a practiced place" provides an optic through which to examine the idea that the specters of past performances, in particular, the embodied acts that have previously imbued space with the sacred, are always active. Space, as de Certeau suggests, is always in the process of transformation.[82] The Second Tepeyac's development is contingent on the multiple layers of institutional and popular history, shifting political and economic climates, and the living, breathing bodies that give meaning and make sense of the space. The act of reproducing a place—the replication of physical/aesthetic elements from Mexico City to Des Plaines—is only the first step. Left at this initial stage, the shrine would remain a superficial structure invoking but never realizing the vibrancy and legitimacy of its counterpart. The replica becomes a sacred space only when devotees' embodied performances—their voices raised in ecstasy, their praying and dancing bodies in motion, the labor and care they offer to maintain the shrine—inscribe their histories, beliefs, and aspirations on the environment. Their acts contribute additional layers of meaning and relevancy to the apparition scenario being displayed at the Second Tepeyac.

Past performances include annual bicycle pilgrimages. In 2005 devotees from Chicago's South Lawndale, Uptown, Lower West Side, and Northwest Side neighborhoods braved bitterly cold weather to pay homage to the Virgin. Peregrinos on bicycles travel through the city unaccompanied until they reach the Des Plaines city limits. At that point Des Plaines police officers escort them to the shrine. The officers sometimes stopped by the gymnasium and often frequented a taco stand for some complimentary food provided by Monica's Mexican Restaurant and Pizzeria, which operates out of Prospect Heights. Most peregrinas/os wore nondescript puffy jackets, gloves, and jeans, but one young man, originally from Jalisco, Guanajuato, used the journey to demonstrate his faith and his national pride. In addition to draping a Mexican flag around his shoulders like a cape, he had adorned his bicycle with two Mexican flags, one on each handle, and had placed his *distintivo* (pilgrimage badge), which featured an image of la Virgencita, above the front wheel. The act of adorning body and vehicle is one example of the transposition of the sacred space and patriotic sensibilities that occurs at the Second Tepeyac. It bears mentioning that while this incorporation of the Mexican flag evokes a particular expression of patriotism, it is a diasporic form of Mexican cultural identity that is not reducible to state nationalism. Similarly, in 2004, while conducting fieldwork at Tepeyac in Mexico City, I met a young peregrino from Tlaxcala who had placed an image of Guadalupe on his bicycle and wore a T-shirt with an image of la Virgencita framed by the word *Mexico* in white boldface (see figure 4).

These two devotees arrived at their destinations exhausted, with their bodies battered and stomachs empty. Both were actively contributing to the sanctification of space, but their devotional labor also imbued their bodies and keepsakes with a form of the sacred.[83] Many peregrinas/os with whom I have worked in the Midwest and central Mexico explain that their pilgrimage relics become important elements on their home altars or deeply personal gifts for loved ones who could not journey. The powerful presence of calluses, scabs, and scrapes, however ephemeral, also evince the journey. Further, the transformative experience made unique and public by physical marks inspires letters, phone calls, emails, anecdotes, and gossip—narratives communicated locally and transnationally among kinship networks.[84]

FIGURE 4. *Peregrino* and his bicycle at Tepeyac, Mexico City.

Chicago-area Guadalupan *danzantes* (dancers) also legitimize sacred space and perform cultural subjectivities by combining their suffering/devotion with artistic expression. *Matechine* dancers bless the space through ritual movement. Even though their costumes, dance steps, instruments, and headdresses may not replicate exactly those found beyond the United States, their presence is evocative. Not all

FIGURE 5. Devotee struggling to keep the gymnasium floor clean, Second Tepeyac, Des Plaines.

Guadalupanas/os, of course, worship in such a public way, and the regenerative effects of embodied devotion are not always obvious. But each act counts. Volunteer workers, the people who keep the sacred space tidy, for example, are backstage players who are indispensable at both shrines (figure 5). These individual acts combined with collective efforts such as singing and praying make space sacred. They also forge ties among devotees, create networks that persist long after the devotional act is completed.

THE REGENERATIVE LEGAL EFFECTS OF SACRED SPACE PRODUCTION

On a chilly November morning in fall 2003 I did not join the congregation gathered for Sunday service but walked toward a back area of the gymnasium-cum-sanctuary, which a mock wall hid from plain sight. Entering a cold, concrete space, I faced a line of waiting Guadalupanas/os, several people seated at long brown tables, a photographer, and a woman binding documents near a copy machine in the far corner of the room. Congregation members, shrine officials, volunteers, and local immigration lawyers, I soon found, had transformed the back room of the gymnasium into an assembly line for U.S. naturalization. The organization of the room allowed lawyers and bilingual volunteers to walk devotees through every step of the N-400: Application for Naturalization process. At the end of the assembly line, a volunteer handed each participant a ready-to-mail package addressed to the Department of Homeland Security that included (1) form N-400, (2) a copy of the applicant's Resident Alien card, (3) a photograph of the applicant, and (4) a money order for $310 for the filing fee (which increased to $675 in June 2007). That morning, like many others thereafter, I translated N-400 forms for Spanish-speaking Guadalupan devotees seeking free legal assistance.

In addition to offering free consultation and supervision, lawyers sold a $25 "citizenship" box, complete with bilingual flash cards featuring questions such as "¿Cúantas estrellas aparecen en la bandera de los Estados Unidos?" (How many stars appear on the American flag?) Answer: *cincuenta estrellas* (fifty stars). This kit also included a bilingual answer booklet and a compact disc intended to prepare Spanish speakers for their citizenship interview in English. As the head lawyer explained between consultations, "You do not have to learn this material. You have to memorize it. This kit gives you all the tools to learn the questions in Spanish but answer confidently in English. At the interview it is all about confidence."

This *taller de ciudadanía* (citizenship workshop) was undetectable to anyone who was not aware of the developing connection between el Cerrito as a sacred space and as a platform for immigration reform and legal services. Shrine organizers did not offer this opportunity as part of the front-stage activities of the Sunday church service; only active and embedded members of the Guadalupan community were privy to this knowledge. In tandem with the recent wave of immigrant rights rallies and public discourse on comprehensive immigration reform, this type of activity at the Second Tepeyac solidified its dual role as religious sanctuary and political safe haven. It demonstrates one of the many ways in which devotees use the sacred to address secular issues, or put another way, challenge a sacred/secular binary. By frequently hosting naturalization workshops with the National Immigrant Justice Center, for example, Maryville has become part of a city- and statewide circuit of centers, academies, and high schools that perform as improvised legal centers for both newly arrived and established immigrants. In addition, el Cerrito is now considered not only a destination point for peregrinas/os but also starting location for caravans of volunteers and devotees traveling to rallies in downtown Chicago and the state capitol in Springfield or participating in nationwide events such as the Immigrant Workers Freedom Ride across America.[85]

Most devotees at the Second Tepeyac, documented or undocumented, have one thing in common: they have a direct link, whether lived or witnessed, to a relocation experience. Even those few whose families have resided in the Chicago area for three generations hear tales, listen to songs, and recite prayers inspired by migration. Throughout the year, for example, devotees recite the prayer "Virgen de los Migrantes" (Virgin of the Migrants) on the grounds of the Second Tepeyac.

> *¡Ay, Virgencita Morena! Guadalupe, mi esperanza, del Cielo tu amor alcanza para aliviar toda pena; cuídame con tu alma Buena y dame en esta ocasion tu sagrada bendición pues con cariño constante, para venir de migrante, te traje mi corazón.*

> [Oh, young, dark-skinned virgin! Guadalupe, my hope, your love reaches down from the heavens and alleviates my worries; take care of me with your good soul and give me your sacred blessing, your constant affection, I came as an immigrant, I brought you my heart.]

Joaquín Martínez often alludes to this prayer when speaking with migrants who have been deported (sometimes several times) from the United States to Mexico or from Mexico to Guatemala (sometimes regardless of whether migrants were Guatemalan or not). This was a trigger for him, he explained. Hearing stories of hardship that occurred mostly in cramped and dark areas such as train cars, the interior of a car or truck, or under a cold desert sky inspired him to push the political utility of the sacred space. The stories were so disconcerting, the hardships so unimaginable, that they compelled him to act. Those conversations were constant reminders of the on-the-ground realities of migration. He also found it necessary to treat each story on its own terms. Discourses about migration to the United States in many ways revolve around Mexicans, but Martínez saw the need to single out or focus on the Central American experience—specifically, refugees who traveled to el Norte to escape their war-torn countries or those seeking a better life in established urban outposts in the United States such as New Orleans and Los Angeles.[86] He proposed several times, "They need their stories to be heard. The Virgin listens."

With this strain of political activism in mind, Martínez promotes the sacred space as a place where devotees can learn about pending legislation. The Second Tepeyac does not quite adhere to the Sanctuary Movement model, but it would not resist it either.[87] It promotes education and provides resources regardless of the legal consequences. On October 12, 2003, for example, two attorneys from the American Immigration Lawyers Association (AILA) gave compelling speeches at the foot of el Cerrito. Rosalba Piña and Royal Burge used the shrine on el Día de la Raza as a platform from which to encourage Guadalupan devotees to support the amendment of the Immigration and Nationality Act to Promote Family Unity 240A(b). On this day of solidarity with citizen-children, the lawyers, priests, and Guadalupan officials staging the gathering asked parents to dress their children in white shirts and blue pants or skirts. Differentiating them from other participants would make for a powerful press photo. Coordinators aimed at gathering one thousand children at the shrine to send a message to Congress, which was about to discuss the amendment. As written, the act recommends that citizen-children under the age of eighteen should relocate to their parents' nation of origin in the event of the parents' deportation. A judge would allow undocumented parents to stay in the United States if they had resided in the country for more than ten years, had demonstrated good moral conduct, did not have convictions or a police record, and could prove that the family would face "exceptional, extreme, or unusual suffering" in the home country. Piña argued that "extreme or unusual suffering" would begin at "the moment of deportation." The act of one judge, one human being, she suggested, would deny the child's rights as a citizen—specifically, their right to life, liberty, and the pursuit of happiness. Because these children are minors, Piña reasoned, they do not have a voice, and their parents, who are undocumented, cannot speak for them. "Therefore, we must send a message to Congress," she said. "We must give our children a voice. We must promote our right to family unification."[88]

As these lawyers spoke passionately in English and Spanish, I listened from a small table collecting signatures. Auxiliary Bishop John R. Manz, a key representative for the diocese regarding immigration issues, sat among the children on the raised platform in front of the hill.[89] Approximately two hundred Guadalupan devotees listened patiently to the statements, but only those devotees with citizenship, about 10 percent, were able to sign the petition. Regardless of the success of this gathering, shrine coordinators, the archdiocese, and these immigration lawyers collaborated to inform devotees who otherwise would have remained unaware of specific laws directly affecting their day-to-day existence.

REPRESENTATION AND EXCEPTION

As several historical and contemporary studies have shown, the transposition of sacred space and/or religious practices often forces representatives from different ethnic and socio-political groups to interact.[90] Spanish speakers intent on practicing Catholicism in the nineteenth century, for example, produced intracultural and cross-ethnic encounters throughout the United States. Mexican, as well as Central and South American, immigrants, "in the face of oppositional forces such as military conquest and occupation, indiscriminate violence and lawlessness, political and economic displacement, [and] rapid demographic change, [practiced] Spanish-speaking Catholic feasts and devotions [that] provided ongoing means of communal expression."[91] One of the earliest documented mobilization efforts occurred in 1871, when an alliance of Spanish-speaking Catholics in San Francisco successfully lobbied for the establishment of a national parish. Consuls of Chile, Perú, Nicaragua, Colombia, Bolivia, Costa Rica, and Spain, as well as various other Hispanic residents, formed this coalition to accommodate Spanish-speaking communities.[92] As Timothy Matovina and Gerald E. Poyo's fine study of nineteenth- and twentieth-century mobilization efforts makes clear, the development, maintenance, and legitimization of worship sites depends on many actors. Moreover, those church-related developments may have advanced sociocultural identity formation based on shared language.

Similar to those antecedents in the United States, the Second Tepeyac has evolved primarily among Spanish-speaking adherents and faces the obstacles posed by ethnic, class, generational, and citizenship differences.

It is tempting at this juncture to propose that shared language and shared admiration for the Virgin of Guadalupe are not the only factors at play in Des Plaines. It would be easy to suggest the presence of a pan-identity, to propose that perhaps mobilization at Maryville Academy occurs around the idea of a communal Latino identity. But that would be disingenuous. Polite and ambitious terminology such as pan-Latino or generalized social scientific processes of becoming—assimilation, ethnic resilience, or acculturation—although conceptually useful, do not attend to the complex intracultural and cross-cultural processes that engender such community formation.[93] Beyond those complications, there are internal conflicts and hierarchies—the ways in which one group may have more power, numbers, or influence than another—that complicate any rosy vision of pan-Latinoism.

Shrine organizers are well aware of the fact that Mexican Guadalupanos physically and symbolically claim the space with their sheer numbers, yet they avoid conflating adherents' histories or the specificities that make up their national identities. There is always an explicit effort on the part of coordinators to produce an atmosphere of inclusiveness among the congregation—a space in which devotees may retain their individual affiliations or preferences and work toward securing workers' rights, health care, legal documentation, and increased human rights through religious practice. In that respect, the Second Tepeyac may be an exceptional case. As we shall see in the following chapters, the cult of Guadalupe, particularly in central Mexico, can also promulgate an agenda that classifies and categorizes adherents along lines of class, gender, skin privilege, geographic location, and lack of institutional affiliation.

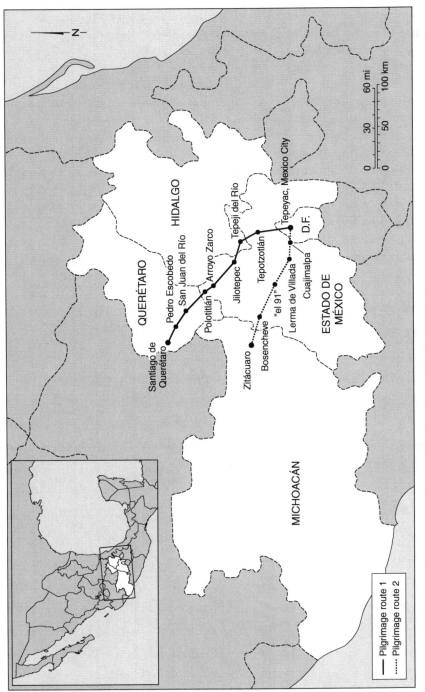

MAP 3. Pilgrimage routes from Santiago de Querétaro, Querétaro, to Tepeyac in Mexico City and from Zitácuaro, Michoacán, to Tepeyac.

PART TWO

Walking

CHAPTER 2

"¡Qué risa me da!"
(Oh, how it makes me laugh!)

HA, HA, HA!	**HA, HA, HA!**	HA, HA, HA!
he, he, he!	**he, he, he!**	he, he, he!
HAA, HAA, HAA!	**HAA, HAA, HAA!**	HAA, HAA, HAA!
hee, hee, hee!	**hee, hee, hee!**	hee, hee, hee!
Qué risa me da!	**Qué ri-sa me da!**	Oh, how it makes me laugh!
ES-ta jorrrnadita!	**ES-ta jorrrnadita!**	This itty-bitty walk,
Y otras veinte mas!	*Y OOtras veinte mas!*	and another twenty more![1]

—Chant performed by Guadalupanas on foot to Tepeyac, July 2005

The uphill march from Tepejí del Río to Tepotzotlán was almost unbearable. Listening to the rhythm of marching feet and the hypnotic murmur of praying women, I walked with my head down and my hands behind my back. I would often fall into a state of meditation where I felt light and aware. Other times I would respond reflexively to the call and response of the rosary: "Santa María Madre de Dios, ruegue Señora por nosotros los pecadores, ahora y en la hora de nuestra muerte, Amén" (Holy Mary Mother of God, pray for us sinners, now and in the hour of our death, Amen). We walked for kilometers on end between dry, bush-strewn fields and streams of speeding cars and trailer trucks. We would take our *descansos* (rest stops) on the side of the highway, laying down our red, yellow, lavender, and baby blue *útiles*—blanket-sized squares of plastic that offered some protection from the sweltering pavement. Some women would climb through barbed wire, two-by-two, to find a semi-private spot to relieve themselves. Others made conversation to alleviate the tired silence. Most of us sat quietly with our heads bowed, hiding from the relentless sun under our floppy hats adorned with ribbons and flowers.

After hours of following the paved highway, we turned onto an isolated dirt road toward Tepotzotlán. Everyone looked exhausted. Peregrinas who had previously lifted morale with their song and prayer were now silent. Our once-organized two-mile-long *columna* (marching procession) was in shambles. Women ahead of me kicked up clouds of dirt with their dragging feet. Layers of dust and sweat covered our bodies. I was thankful when the *jefas* (bosses) snapped at us to get back into formation. This was the first signal that we were approaching our destination. The second was the resurgence of chanting and singing.

Groups of locals waited for us on the side of the road as we entered the outskirts of town. We began to chant, "Ha, ha, ha! He, he, he!" The families on the side of the road applauded; they smiled, pointed, threw confetti along our path. Some offered us clear plastic bags filled with tamarind- or melon-flavored water. "Qué ri-sa me da," we continued. We were now their guests and their customers. Clusters of teenage boys checked us out. Mothers held their children close and explained who we were. Little boys ran about and shouted, "¡Qué Viva México!" Their admiration revived us. We sang louder and *con más ganas* (with more enthusiasm), "ES-ta jorrrnadita! Y OOtras veinte mas!" (This little journey! And another twenty more!).

Traveling on foot from Santiago de Querétaro to Tepeyac—the Virgin of Guadalupe's shrine in Mexico City—is no small endeavor (see cover photo). It requires physical, mental, emotional, and, above all, spiritual investment. The opening vignette grasps at that oblation, but it intimates something more. It highlights the modes of performance and spectatorship that are key to understanding this phenomenon. It also suggests that the practice of pilgrimage exceeds its canonical definition. According to institutional guidelines, a Christian pilgrim is a person who "leaves his home or residence to journey to a church or a sacred space, the tomb of a saint (St. Peter at the Vatican, Santiago de Compostela), or a distinguished relic or a miraculous image (Our Lady of Guadalupe or one of her multiple incarnations) to venerate and ask for favors, to give thanks and offerings, or to realize other acts of popular piety."[2] The objective of a Guadalupan pilgrimage is to encounter Christ by venerating his mother, Our Lady of Guadalupe. In the specific case of female devotees, the church asks that practitioners make the experience more powerful by emulating the Virgin in everyday life, beyond the extraordinary time and space of the annual ritual.[3]

Co-performatively witnessing the nine-day journey—walking, chanting, eating, sleeping, bathing, and shopping with and alongside the women, conversing with them about their pilgrimage histories, and considering the backstage economic logistics that support the ritual—has shown that their devotional practices, although contained by the ritual and guided by doctrine, exceed those realms.[4] Backstage and front stage ideological, symbolic, and material motives shape dimensions of the tradition; both "formal" motives, which are "structured around the clergy, the sacraments, and the individual's relationship with God," and "popular" religious motives, which devotees hide from official surveillance, also inform the sacred performance.[5] Inspiration to act, however, is not simply a matter of faith. Guadalupan doctrine forms the base and vehicle for the journey; love and respect for la Virgencita outweigh all other motives. But pride, money, family ties, the quest for freedom, curiosity, devotional capital, and the need for guidance, protection, and forgiveness also mold the experience. Each peregrina's motivation for walking is distinct. Pursuing a performance studies approach, one that takes seriously the gestures, movements, the moments of interaction between self and environment—the time and space that exists alongside written and spoken exchanges—will help us locate the details that make each act unique. To understand the diversity and complexity of this annual tradition as well as how practitioners not only legitimize the cult of the Virgin of Guadalupe with every step but also develop and maintain their private sacred spaces, we must position their devotional labor at the forefront of our analysis. Again, de Certeau inspires: "Their story begins on ground level, with footsteps. They are myriad, but do not compose a series. They cannot be counted because each unit has a qualitative character: a style of tactile apprehension and kinesthetic appropriation. Their swarming mass is an innumerable collection of singularities. Their intertwined paths give their shape to spaces. They weave places together."[6]

I was able to enter this culture of pilgrimage devotion by introducing myself to Basílica officials as a graduate student from the United States conducting research in the fields of performance studies and cultural anthropology. I submitted a *solicitud* (request letter), specifying my aim to investigate the links between gender and faith vis-à-vis embodied devotional practices. I promised to respect the cult, the devotees, and the sacred space, as well as to submit a copy of my findings to the Lorenzo Boturini Library located on the fifth floor of the Modern Basilica. In exchange, Tepeyac personnel offered me library privileges and admittance to high-profile events and put me in touch with key organizers of all-female pilgrimages across central Mexico. This institutional access worked both as an opportunity and as an encumbrance. The most important benefit was meeting with coordinators and securing permission to walk alongside the women. Regrettably, my presence during the ritual, or more precisely the idea of a representative from the Basílica, altered the behavior of some peregrinas. At one point, word spread among the women that the Basílica had sent a "spy." This created paranoia among devotees and in particular the women in charge of organizing and collecting money. Literally, from one day to the next, leaders who were previously unaware of my institutional affiliation took it upon themselves to welcome and protect me. I mention this part of my journey with the intention of relating, as clearly as possible, my privileged position as a scholar as well as a reluctant representative of the Catholic Church. Moreover, I cannot claim unimpeachable solidarity with the women; many differences divide us—class, cultural values, and national affiliation, among others.

Even so, this performance-based approach proved effectual. It showed that pilgrimage is more than a demonstration of religious belief. It may also be a patriotic act, a declaration of independence, a powerful mode of communication, and an overt commercial venture. Reflect, for example, on the formal and informal economic impact of 16,000 devotees praying, purchasing, and networking for nine days across central Mexico. Consider that 20,000 of their male compatriots, their husbands, sons, fathers, brothers, and friends, follow their trail on a Guadalupan pilgrimage that has its roots in the late nineteenth century.[7] It was often commented during the journey that males walk the day after so that they can scoop up any woman left behind en route to Tepeyac. Combined, these two events involve 2.5 percent of Querétaro Arteaga's population.[8] The pilgrims' common ground, aside from their allegiance to the Virgin of Guadalupe, is their regional affiliation. Querétaro is unlike any other state in the republic. It profits from direct access to the Pan-American Highway—a major throughway for the transnational movement of freight, capital, and laborers—and has the highest proportion of foreign manufacturing investment in the country.[9] These political and economic processes affect both men and women—their spending practices, perceptions of "urban" and "rural" dwellers, class differences within these communities, how peregrinos use their leisure time, and how this devotional performance maintains and legitimizes Tepeyac.

Public or private, collective or individual, their devotional acts have regenerative effects that transcend the moment of execution. Each Guadalupan gesture and articulation, no matter how ephemeral, contributes to the sanctification of space. The mass movement of women on foot between Querétaro and Mexico City performs several functions: (1) it generates publicity and legitimacy for the Catholic Church and for the cult of Guadalupe;[10] (2) it disrupts and reinforces traditional gender norms; and (3) it stimulates local economies that fall beyond the purview of the region's industrial and service sectors. In addition, collaboration among church actors, state officials, and media correspondents make this an exceptional case study.

To date, a full-length critical interpretation of this tradition has not been realized. While the 1995 documentary *Flowers for Guadalupe/ Flores para Guadalupe,* produced by Judith Gleason with the collaboration of the Colectivo Feminists de Xalapa and Elisa Mereghetti, deftly presents a range of testimonies, it offers, at best, a glimpse of the intricate networks sustaining the annual all-female pilgrimage. Using a phenomenological approach, the next two chapters demonstrate how Guadalupanas' devotional performances—the hypnotic rhythm and repetition of prayer, song, daily mass rituals, and communion, as well as the purchase and subsequent blessing of religious artifacts—sanctify space. It also evaluates secular backstage processes—the organization of food and accommodation issues, health and hygiene concerns—to underline the ritual's complex interfaces across local and regional fronts.

VOTING WITH THEIR FEET

Devotees "vote with their feet" during a pilgrimage.[11] From Mecca to Mexico City, Jerusalem to Santiago de Compostela, Tiruvanamalai to Fatima, individuals make their religious convictions public. Although different belief systems and cultures share elements of this walking ritual, the intricacies of the performance are context-specific—that is, particular to time and environment. In the case of Mexico studies have inferred that preconquest adoration ceremonies bled into Catholic rituals during the early colonial period, thereafter affecting the development of Guadalupan devotional acts.[12] Other scholars, however, challenge the persistence of indigenous culture on contemporary practice.[13] Sidestepping futile discussions, Victor Turner and Edith Turner draw attention to the analytic and epistemological possibilities of studying embodied traditions. They suggest, "One advantage of studying a long term socio-cultural process such as pilgrimage is that one's attention is directed toward *the dynamics of ideological change and persistence,* rather than committed analysis of static ideological patterns and cognitive structures."[14] Pilgrimage is not only an exceptional example of the circulation and transmission of belief and history but also an object of study through which we may clarify shifts and transitions within processes of meaning making. As Diana Taylor reminds us, "Embodied performances have always played a central role in conserving memory and consolidating identities in literate, semiliterate, and digital societies. Not everyone comes to 'culture' or modernity through writing.... [I]t is imperative to keep re-examining the relationships between embodied performance and the production of knowledge."[15]

To understand the regenerative effects of pilgrimage, it is important to comprehend its basic structure. Victor Turner's notions of "communitas" and "social drama,"[16] as well as his definition of ritual as "a *transformative* performance revealing major classifications, categories, and contradictions of cultural processes,"[17] have inspired thoughtful interdisciplinary studies. Although these frameworks continue to be influential, many scholars resist the terms precisely because of their tendency to clarify and compartmentalize the discrepant discourses and environments underwriting each enactment. Simon Coleman and John Eade, for example, argue that employing "social drama" as a conceptual guide "run[s] the risk of taking studies of pilgrimage down a theoretical cul-de-sac, both in its all-encompassing character and in its implication that such travel could somehow (or at least should ideally) be divorced from more everyday social, political, and cultural processes."[18] Challenging the communitas paradigm[19]—spontaneous unmediated interactions occurring during the liminal phase of ritual—Ellen Badone and Sharon R. Roseman suggest, "may be one element of the pilgrimage experience, [but] this social and emotional quality cannot be assumed to exist in all pilgrimages; nor can the concept be used as a master key to unlock the meaning and significance of pilgrimage for all participants in every cross-cultural setting."[20] Co-performatively witnessing the Querétaro pilgrimage has shown that the exchanges Turner proposes do not exist among all 16,000 participants. As I discuss later, the unequivocal presence of socioeconomic-based distinctions and the logistical/practical complications that accompany mass movement deny that theoretical possibility.

This detail does not detract, however, from each individual's ability to claim, inscribe, and "sacralize" space with devotional performances (as opposed to solely relying on an institutional proclamation or divine intervention).[21] Peregrinas articulate their claims through improvised movements, gestures, and rhythms, as well as stylized behavior—a step

forward paired with a familiar glance at a tree where you once con-
fessed along the route, a sigh of exhaustion combined with the sensation of knowing when the road will curve away, looking forward to a
particular *subida* (uphill march) because the *bajada* (downhill march)
will lead you to that day's mass service. These moments of familiarity
function as "mnemonic reserves"—"patterned movements made and
remembered by bodies, residual movements retained implicitly in images or words (or in the silences between them), and imaginary movements dreamed in minds not prior to language but constitutive of it."[22]
Simultaneously recalling and doing, peregrinas ingrain the experience
while also inscribing the space they traverse.

Considering de Certeau's explication of (urban) pedestrian speech
acts further draws attention to the embodied dimensions of the pilgrimage act. De Certeau proposes:

> The act of walking is to the urban system what the speech act is to language
> or to the statements uttered. At the most elementary level, it has a triple
> "enunciative" function: it is a process of *appropriation* of the topographical
> system on the part of the pedestrian (just as the speaker appropriates and
> takes on the language); it is a spatial acting-out of the place (just as the
> speech act is an acoustic acting-out of language); and it implies *relations*
> among differentiated positions, that is, among pragmatic "contracts" in the
> form of movements (just as verbal enunciation is an "allocution," "posits
> another opposite" the speaker and puts contracts between interlocutors into
> action).[23]

With every step, Guadalupanas' actions give substance and shape to
the holy; they not only possess but also circulate it, thereby reaffirming
their relationship with the Virgin and with their environment. James F.
Fernandez suggests in his study of African sacred places, "The qualities
that emerge in sacred places are not all contained implicitly in the place
but are brought to it by performance, the acting out of images. Emergent
qualities arise in the interaction of the images men bring to scenes or
sites with the sites themselves."[24] These articulations, however, are not
static or fixed.[25] A participant may manipulate the content without necessarily changing the form, or, put another way, the ritual has a guiding
structure and regulations, shaped by larger historical, political, and economic currents, but the content is continually in flux, malleable, because
a devotee may modify or reconfigure the tradition on her own terms. A
participant dialectically transforms and adapts the ritual to her individual needs, to the larger socioreligious needs of the pilgrimage community, and to the institutional requirements of the church.

NECESSITY ENGENDERS ACTION

Diocese records claim that this all-female tradition did not begin until Bishop D. Alfonso Toriz Cobián sanctioned the journey in 1958. Oral histories contradict this date. Testimonies suggest that one woman from Querétaro, Herculana Martínez Valdés, initiated the tradition in 1936 when she walked alongside her brother J. Pueblito. Together they secretly followed the all-male pilgrimage en route to Tepeyac. According to the historian América Arredondo Huerta, thereafter Herculana and a circle of fellow *peregrinas* transgressed gender barriers and societal norms and openly defied a church decree (1939–58) prohibiting the act. Among these women were "María Martínez Coronel, Petra Jiménez Villanueva, Celia Chávez Ocampo, Gabina González, Francisca 'Pachita la dulcera,' Maximina 'La Grandota,' Antonia Serrano Martinez, Natalia Ramos Jiménez, Catalina Uribe González, Remedios, Doña Nacha, Ma.de Jesús Chávez, Doña Chayo, Esperanza 'Hija de Pachita' Mercedes Acosta de Pérez, and Magdalena Pérez Acosta."[26]

It is worth noting that these initial journeys involved cross-generational collaborations, for example, Francisca "Pachita la dulcera" and her daughter Esperanza ("hija de Pachita") mentioned above. Although institutionalized in 1958, the journey lacked written documentation until Monsignor Ezequiel de la Isla verified and published the statutes in 1978. At this point, more than ten thousand women had joined the pilgrimage.[27] The majority of the women belong to *decanatos* (subdioceses) located in the state of Querétaro—San Juan del Río, Santa Ana, La Cañada, Santiago, Amealco, Santo Niño de la Salud, El Pueblito, Santa Rosa Jaúregui, Sierra de Querétaro, and Soriano—with fewer than eight hundred women, or 5 percent, representing a diocese in the neighboring state of Guanajuato. In 1979 Pope John Paul II's first visit to Mexico, along with direct encouragement from Bishop D. Alfonso Toriz Cobián, stimulated participation. Fifteen thousand women walked to Tepeyac that year—70 percent adults, 10 percent girls, and 20 percent seniors. In 1981 the tradition reached an all-time high with eighteen thousand attendees.[28]

The sheer number of participants combined with years of tradition and the initial peregrination's feminist roots inspires some Guadalupanas to claim gender equality during the journey. Alejandra, a young mother of two, professed toward the end of the nine-day trip in 2005, "We are better than men in everything. We are smarter, more prepared. . . . This pilgrimage gives us the chance to show that we are equal to them

[men] and even better. That we can take as much as they do!" This participant prefaced her statement by remarking that the men and some of the women with whom she works at an indoor food market in San Juan del Río chided that she would not be able to survive the journey. Alejandra's cousin added tactfully, "Es algo muy bonito que no se puede explicar. Es una experencia muy bonita . . . pues. Todo es alegría, convives con las personas. Todo es felicidad para nosotros" (It is something beautiful that cannot be explained. It is a beautiful experience . . . umm. Everything is joy, living among others. Everything is happiness for us). Once at Tepeyac, however, some women have more to say about sharing gender-specific space. Marta, a seasoned pilgrim, divulged, "Muy bonita. De todo un poco, hay unas muy lloroncitas pero le pedí a mi santísima Madre que me diera paciencia de sorportar unas hermanitas y ya el último, ya nos perdonamos y todo por que veníamos a buscar a la santísima Virgen" (The pilgrimage [experience] is very beautiful. There is a little of everything. There are some women that are crybabies, but I asked my blessed mother to give me patience to bear those little sisters, and at the end we forgave each other, all because we came to find the holy Virgin.) Beyond the vast range of perspectives, one thread held strong: most agreed that sharing, praying, and living with other women is a privilege and something worth experiencing.

Many practitioners also confided that they have difficulty leaving their homes because their husbands may or may not give them permission. On the other hand, as one *veterana* (veteran) told me, organizing her family life to make the journey year after year begins simply with the following announcement: "¿Saben qué? Me voy de peregrina" (Here's the news, I'm leaving for the pilgrimage). Juanita, a forty-year-old homemaker, has her husband's blessing because she prays for his safety. Five years earlier, he was the victim of drug-related violence during which he was shot over fifteen times. Of course, she added, saving money here and there throughout the year and make sure everything is done before her departure—paying electricity, gas, and telephone bills and making arrangements with daughters or neighbors to cook for her children and husband—also ensures an unimpeded departure. Some women do not leave their children at home. Julieta, a peregrina from Jurquilla, shared her pilgrimage experience with her two sons, both of whom were eligible to participate because they were under the age of ten. In this case, the older boy (age eight) started the journey, but his younger brother (age six), who bears a striking resemblance to him, finished the pilgrimage and received the medal of participation. Furthermore, it was common to see mothers pushing baby carriages along the highway, only to see those same strollers, wheels bent and dusty, left on the side of an unpaved road days later.

Once enlisted, each participant anticipates the pilgrimage will follow a set schedule and a specific route, which together dictate the rhythm of the journey. But the ritual's internal logic is inevitably affected by external complications. Indeed, some women articulated disappointment or surprise when the path changed course, even slightly, because of highway construction. They noticed every modification and often discussed differences as they walked. This critical approach allows us to consider how the kinesthetic dimensions of the ritual—the persistence of their embodied memory—determines the sanctification of space as much if not more than the institutional guidelines emphasized in the annual pilgrimage booklet.

The cover of the 2005 schedule features a boldface announcement: "47a Peregrinación Femenina a pie de Querétaro al Tepeyac" (47th Annual All-Female Walking Pilgrimage from Querétaro to Tepeyac) and a photo of Pope John Paul II bowing solemnly before an image of the Virgin of Guadalupe. Two phrases accompany the Pope's profile: "Sin siembra no hay cosecha, sin palabra no hay Eucaristía" (Without sowing there can be no harvest, without the Word there is no Eucharist) above him and "Hoy me puedo sentir mexicano" (Today I can feel Mexican) printed in the lower right-hand corner. The pilgrimage booklet offers a wealth of information: requisite prayers, the formal objectives of the ritual, the role of service organizations such as the Cruz Roja (Red Cross), SESEQ—Secretaría de Salud del Estado de Querétaro (State of Querétaro's Department of Health) and ISEM—Instituto de Salud del Estado de Mexico (State of Mexico's Health Institute), the official walking order, the daily schedule, and the names of administrators appointed to lay and clerical executive committees. The back cover of the pamphlet features the Coca-Cola logo, the official sponsor of the ritual since replacing Pepsi in 1984.[29]

On day 1 of the Santiago de Querétaro pilgrimage, for example, approximately ten thousand devotees know they are to meet in the capital city's historic center to celebrate mass with that year's appointed *director espiritual* (spiritual director). In 2005 Fr. Bernardo Reséndiz Vizcaya presided over the journey. The leaflet alerts participants that peregrinas from the Sierra de Querétaro walk seventeen days while women from San José Iturbide, Guanajuato, and Soriano, Querétaro, walk eleven and ten days respectively. These threads join the procession at specific points along the 210-kilometer route (see map 3). The pamphlet assures them that they will participate in key rituals—attending daily mass services, witnessing the first holy communion ceremony between Arroyo Zarco and Jilotepec on the fifth day, and receiving medals of participation on the seventh day at the Campo Monseñor Salvador Espinoza in Tepejí del Río. They know that members of the *directiva seglar* (lay executive committee) will wake them at either 3:00 or 4:00 A.M. depending on the day's itinerary.

The handbook, however, does not relay the information that each morning a bright light and a woman on a sound system singing "¡Buenos días hermanitas!" (Good morning little sisters!) will awaken participants, that fellow peregrinas will modify the journey each evening with private celebrations ranging from birthday parties to the worship of non-Catholic idols, and the way in which residents in different towns and cities will receive and perceive the women. Negative external perceptions of peregrinas' hygiene and cleanliness in certain towns, for example, modify the timetable printed in the pamphlet. Participants produce an extraordinary amount of refuse during the ritual. One way in which we "contaminated" our path was by relieving ourselves on public spaces like fields and city sidewalks. Also, women menstruate during the pilgrimage, which poses additional difficulties. The biggest issue is not privacy, because everyone wears prairie skirts over pants, but where to discard soiled toilet paper and sanitary napkins. Trash bins are not available on the side of the highway, nor is there sufficient water to keep oneself clean along the walking route or in the pueblos. Most devotees prefer to leave their rubbish behind rather than carry it with them. Further, many participants toss plastic containers and water bottles along the highway and at rest areas. Coordinators try desperately to contain the problem, but there are too many women.

Most Queretanas admit the situation is shameful, especially because the all-male pilgrimage follows their route at certain points. Older Guadalupanas comment that this form of contamination was not such a problem *antes de la época del desechable* (before the era of disposable plates, bottles, etc.). Before throwaway containers became common, the women controlled the problem by attaching one small plate and cup, a spoon, and a fork with string to their belts. They would use these items at every meal and clean them after eating. For most, the presence of trash or waste, however disagreeable or shameful, does not alter their devotion or intentions. These pollution and hygiene issues affect how participants and spectators engage the experience but do not necessarily alter sacred space production. As Mary Douglas reminds us, "Holiness and unholiness after all need not always be absolute opposites."[30]

The differences between what is printed in the booklet and the reality of practice are felt most by those who do not stay in hotels or with family members. For example, the women who sleep nightly in a *maletero* have to search for their truck on the outskirts of town. A maletero is an eighteen-wheel freight truck that transports *maletas* (luggage) from one rest stop to another and functions as a split-level dormitory for participants. I slept seven nights wedged alongside twenty women in the "penthouse." Twenty peregrinas slept below us. Still, the most disenfranchised Guadalupanas sleep underneath the maletero. Despite this class-based segregation tactic, one thing remains certain: all participants are consumers. They are able to purchase goods and services in town, as well as accommodation and showers in a private residence. Some families clear their living rooms of all furniture and rent sleeping space. Local parishes often open their doors, but it is not standard procedure. These unavoidable factors force thousands of participants to exert themselves beyond the ritual's physically grueling requirements.

INSTITUTIONAL STRATEGIES FOR DEFINING SACRED SPACE

Despite erratic timetables, the mobile chapel, or *capilla móvil,* holds the ritual together; it performs as the center of sacred space along the pilgrimage route. It is from this mobile altar that members of the *consejo espiritual,* priests who accompany the women during the pilgrimage, lead the daily mass and blessing ceremonies during the midday descanso. Peregrinas stand, kneel, and sit before this altar. Alone, the portable structure equipped with the requisite materials—a pulpit, the sacramentary, the lectionary, communion chalices, the paten, the ciborium, the corporal, the purificator, the pall, and sanctus bells—is already a powerful symbol of Catholicism, but it becomes spectacular when embellished with balloons, flowers, images of la Virgen de Guadalupe, and colossal portraits of Pope John Paul II (May 18, 1920–April 2, 2005) and Benedict XVI. Hired workers adorn the mobile chapel so that par-

FIGURE 6. Spectacular institutional ties.

ticipants can celebrate the induction of first-time peregrinas and the first Holy Communion ritual in grand fashion. Both events are important because they involve the initiation of younger female generations (ages seven to twelve), who dress as the Virgin of Guadalupe for the ceremony, into pilgrimage culture.[31] In addition to aesthetic strategies to perform institutional resilience and fortitude, the officiating priest used chants to assuage the tough papal transition facing the church. Clergy members and *edecanes* (lay volunteers who assist during religious ceremonies) led the women in a chant articulating Pope Benedict's XVI's authority and dedication to carry on Pope John Paul's legacy of support for the Virgin of Guadalupe. (See figure 6.)

Ecclesiastical officials also use that time and space to verbally reinforce the institutional guidelines printed in the pilgrimage booklet. Abiding by the following ten rules, the women are able to cleanse themselves and thus accumulate and carry the sacred with them to Tepeyac.

1) La norma de toda peregrina sera la CARIDAD FRATERNA, por lo tanto, toda y cada una de nosotras deberemos cultivar esa virtud, solidarizándose mutuamente y con verdadero ESPIRITU CRISTIANO.

2) Toda hermana peregrina deberá adquirir y portar visiblemente su distintivo e integrarse al grupo que le corresponda.

3) La vestimenta adecuada y obligada será la de vestir falda y pantalón, por el recto pudor y decoro que debe tener toda mujer. NO se permite llevar únicamente pantalón.

4) Por el sumo respeto a la gestación a la vida NO SE PERMITIRÁ A NINGUNA MUJER EMBARAZADA realizar la peregrinación.

5) Deberá participar religiosamente y con alegría en las actividades que durante la marcha y los descansos proponga la jefa de grupo. (rezar las cuatro partes del santo rosario, el angelus, cantos de animación, dinámicas y alabanzas)

6) El comportamiento de la peregrina deberá ser con dignidad y respeto. Evítese palabras anti-sonantes, pláticas indecentes, actitudes y posturas que despierten el morbo.

7) Por ningún motivo está permitido, que personas del sexo masculine acompañen esta romería durante el transcurso de las jornadas incluyendo también el lugar de los aposentos. Como excepción a grupos de apoyo debidamente identificados con brazalete otorgado por la Asociación se les permitirá el acompañamiento de varones.

8) No podrán llevar niños varones mayores de 8 años.

9) A toda peregrina le queda prohibido adelantarse sin causa justificada. Pues al abandonar la columna en caso de accidente la Directiva Diocesana no se hará responsable.

10) Es obligación de toda peregrina participar activa y concientemente en la celebración Eucarística diaria.[32]

The first, fifth, sixth, and tenth guidelines require that women experience the pilgrimage together with a sense of caring, virtue, and Christian spirit. They should joyfully participate in all aspects of the ritual, partake in the Eucharist daily, and refrain from conversing during the walk—especially about indecent things or *"actitudes y posturas que despierten el morbo"* (attitudes or dispositions that awaken sexual longing).[33] The second rule explains that each peregrina should visibly display her *distintivo* (pilgrimage badge). In tandem, the ninth rule forbids any peregrina from walking ahead of her place in line. The executive committee cites safety issues to justify this regulation.

The third provision perpetuates stereotypes of what it means to be a proper woman within and outside of the pilgrimage community. It stipulates that women must dress in a respectable fashion, with a skirt worn over pants to maintain propriety and decorum. One must envision sixteen thousand women walking with skirts and sombreros (wide-brimmed hats) adorned with flowers and ribbons to understand the impact of the third rule on gender-image management. The fourth rule prevents any pregnant woman from walking. The last two rules regulate the presence of men or boys. It is prohibited for any male, over the age of ten, apart from those who are offering their services (e.g., priests, Red Cross workers), to accompany the women.

Interwoven and enforced throughout the ritual, these institutional regulations maintain their currency even while women circumvent them. Many peregrinas shop, for example, place calls on their mobile phones, and sleep, sometimes during the mass ceremony. Petty crime is also an issue. The directiva seglar often made anti-robbery pleas over the loudspeaker during the descansos, which often lasted a couple of hours—enough time to participate in the Eucharist, eat, rest, and shop. Toward the end of these breaks it was common to hear the following announcement over the loudspeaker: "Attention peregrinas, if you accidentally picked up a wallet, please return the property to its rightful owner." It was well known, thanks to daily suggestions and cautionary tales, that one should sleep with money and valuables close to one's body, literally touching the skin. These ruptures of indecency or immorality are accepted as part of the quotidian struggle to follow in the Virgin's footsteps. They make the purification rituals—confession and communion—indispensable.

MOTIVATIONS: REPENTING, THINKING, CHANGING

Many devotees are urban dwellers, others live in moderately populated areas, and some reside in isolated communities.[34] The majority of participants speak Spanish, and a fraction, representing regions such as Amealco de Bonfil, speak Otomí. The women work as homemakers, teachers, formal and informal vendors, lawyers, students, nuns, artisans, agricultural workers, secretaries, and domestic servants. They represent different class brackets, age categories, racial statuses (determined less by phenotypic characteristics than by economic and social capital), and each has a family and/or community history that inspires and informs her journey.

Many women leave their communities only once a year. As Genoveva Orvaños Busto suggests in her 1986 study, "The religious phenomenon gives a woman a *justified reason* to leave her community."[35] The journey may provide time away from daily family and social responsibilities, but this does not mean that the women are able to detach themselves from those aspects of their lives. Indeed, scores of women travel alongside family members, and some even continue relationships with deceased family members by performing a manda—repayment for a divine favor—on their behalf. Older women with whom I spoke, especially those who have participated for over a decade, confided that they attend because of tradition or because they are accountable to the Virgin and to loved ones. Without the experience, they inevitably would feel emptiness, regret, and guilt.

One woman traveling on her fourteenth journey explained that her annual participation is a lifelong commitment.

> Vengo a darle gracias. Es que me iban operar de la vesícula y una hernia, entonces pa que no me hicieran triangulo en mi estomago, me la hicieron derecha. Me hicieron un mes de estudio y no me encontraron nada hasta que ya me abrerion el estomago y me encontraron a la creatura de dos meses de embarazo y pos yo, ... decia mi esposo que me curaran pues para me abortaba ... le dije que no, le dije cuantas y cuantas quieren hijos y diosito no se los concede. Y yo que ya estoy vieja, de 42 años, crees que yo voy a tirar esta creatura? Le dije, Dios que me la deje llegar bien, mi Madre Santísima, tengo los que ella diga. Y decía el doctor mire, usted no va a aguantar ni siquiera unos 3 o 7 meses cuando el estamago se va a abrir. ... Pídele a la Virgen. Pídele a la Virgen. Ya, que tanto le pedí a la Virgen y que me concedio a mi hija. Esta sana y salva. Ya anda en el 16 años y por eso vengo a pagar la manda.

> [I come to give thanks to the Virgin. They were going to operate on my gall bladder and a hernia. So they wouldn't cut a triangle into my stomach, they cut a straight line and then they conducted a monthlong study, but they didn't find anything until they opened my abdomen and found a two-month-old fetus. And I, well, my husband suggested they cure me and abort the baby, but I told him no. I told him how many, how many women want to have children but God doesn't grant. And me, now that I am an old woman of forty-two years, do you think that I'm going to throw away the baby? I told him, I want God to help her live, my blessed mother, I'm going to have the children she wants me to have. And the doctor would tell me. You will not be able to take three or seven months of pregnancy before your abdomen opens. Ask the Virgin. Ask the Virgin. I asked her repeatedly, and she gave me my daughter. Healthy and alive. She is now sixteen years old, and that is why I come, to repay the favor.]

Cristina explained further that her daughters would like her to abandon the ritual. "It is too dangerous," they argue. "What if you fall down?" After years of traveling, her response is always the same: "Mientras ella me de vida" (As long as she [the Virgin] gives me life).

Many peregrinas suggest that time away from their loved ones and the people who depend on them at home and in the workplace garners them respect when they return. It raises their devotional capital. As one mother from Santa Rosa Jaúregui, Querétaro, put it, "One year all of my family had lost weight. From that point on, my children and my husband learned to appreciate all that I do for them. *Sí sufrieron mi ausencia* (They did suffer my absence)." Expressing a parallel narrative, Cecilia, an elementary school teacher from Santiago de Querétaro, confided while curing inflamed foot blisters in the maletero's cramped quarters that it was better not to call home because it only weakened her spirit. She admitted actually looking forward to time away from her day-to-day life, but the reality was that she spent the majority of her time during the pilgrimage negotiating a state of sadness and wanting that was previously foreign to her. Before 2005 Cecilia had never been away from her two boys. Living in a two-room apartment but often spending time with her deeply interconnected family—three sisters, five sisters-in-law, and a doting mother and father—the thirty-four-year-old does not have much time alone. She had decided to walk to repay a *promesa* (promise) she made to the Virgin during a problematic childbirth three years earlier. That her aunt and her two sisters-in-law, Victoria and Isabel, both pilgrimage novices, would walk as well inspired her to finally complete her end of the bargain. Her aunt, a well-seasoned participant, walked twenty steps behind her in Group 105.

This family support is exactly what inspired Cecilia's *cuñada* (sister-in-law) Isabel to make her first journey. For many years Isabel had dealt with the death of her only child, Anita, who passed away at the age of eleven. Her daughter's struggle with cancer left Isabel empty, angry, and guilty. Months after losing Anita, Isabel began to have problems with her reproductive system, which led to a hysterectomy. "A parent should not outlive her child," she said quietly as we walked toward Polotitlán one sunny afternoon. "I came to reflect and to ask the Virgin for patience," she commented. "I cannot understand why my daughter had to suffer or why I am still alive." She confided that the sensation of loss accompanies her constantly.

Isabel lives in a spacious two-story ranch house on the outskirts of the state capital designed and built by her husband, who works as a truck driver transporting locally manufactured goods throughout the republic. Three weeks after the 2005 pilgrimage, I reunited with Isabel, Cecilia, and Victoria and their families at this ranch house. We ate breakfast and then took a long walk to see the newborn goats and the landscape. While walking, one brother-in-law, a taxi driver who graciously provided transportation for me while I was in the city, pointed mischievously at railroad tracks that run alongside one edge of the property and informed me, "That train runs to the border, to your hometown [Laredo, Texas], just in case you don't have enough money to get home." The idea of the United States is always close.

That day we spent most of the time telling anecdotes about searching for the maletero after a fifteen-hour walking day, waiting in line for hours to shower and to share a bucket of ice-cold water, making fun of each other's inappropriate or unfortunate wardrobe choices (e.g., Cecilia's platform sandals), and fielding questions from their husbands and brothers-in-law about the journey. "It was all fun and games, wasn't it? Did you have a nice vacation?" Victoria's husband teased. Later in the evening we gathered at Victoria's house to celebrate the reunion with extended family members. Here the anecdotes and joking continued, but there were also generous words that the women later confided were only spoken in private. Indeed, in one husband's words, their absence proved that "the women run the show." Further, he admitted, "They are tougher than I imagined."

During a return visit one year later, I had the opportunity to spend a couple of weeks with other families from Santa Rosa Jáuregui and more time with Cecilia in her home and her parents' home—an urban compound with communal living and eating spaces, five bedrooms, and an internal courtyard. The latter also doubles as the family business, a beauty salon, which is operated by Cecilia's two sisters. It was in those spaces in and around Santiago de Querétaro that the regenerative effects of Cecilia's devotional labor became apparent. Meeting her husband, Armando, an engineer's assistant in an automobile manufacturing assembly plant, not only helped me understand Cecilia's devotion and journey in a deeper way but also inspired reflection of piety beyond Catholicism. He is an Evangelical Christian and spoke at length about a recent road trip to San Salvador, El Salvador, to attend a three-day outdoor festival. Cecilia and the children did not go with him. Armando admitted that being among so many believers was powerful. The experience helped him reflect critically on his way of life, his vices, and the fact that the Bible can help guide us to God's master plan. In addition to this road trip, Armando attends spiritual sessions in Santiago de Querétaro three nights a week. "With my problems," he confided, "this time for myself is like my therapy. It helps me control my temper and to be a better husband and father."

Armando also spoke of living in Canada with Cecilia and their two sons for eight months. They had applied and received refugee status, citing the kidnapping situation in Mexico, which made them fearful on a daily basis (which was only a pretext). After this unsuccessful attempt to make a better life for his family, Armando admitted he had a break-down. Moving back to Querétaro was humiliating, and they had lost everything. He did not know whom to turn to, and Cecilia's faith in la Virgen de Guadalupe did not seem real to him. Reliance on the cult is the typical way people try to solve their problems. He chose to be born again, to follow a different route. This was one reason, Cecilia later admitted to me in private, that she did not fulfill her promesa to the Virgin earlier. She could not count on his support. It was only after Cecilia returned from the pilgrimage, however, that Armando understood her faith in its context. Hearing her describe the embodied elements of the journey, especially her physical sacrifices and public devotional labor, inspired him to make connections with his own belief model. Her enactment of faith did not fade away after the journey; it became a living memory and a shared coping strategy.

Alongside these personal perspectives are institutional interpretations of why women, or what kind of women, make the journey. A diocesan leader related a story she heard during a mandatory organizational meeting at which the presiding priest told them that there are three categories of peregrinas. *Peregrinas brujas* (witches), who seem to fly to each location, make up the first category. They arrive first, eat first, bathe first, rest more, and do so easily, with magic. The second group is the *peregrinas turistas* (tourists). These women stay in hotels or have prearranged accommodations with family or friends. They have their familiars meet them with food at each descanso, and on some occasions they request a portable television set so that they can watch their *telenovelas* (soap operas) on the road. The peregrina turista's efforts are hardly considered a sacrifice but rather more of a vacation. The third and largest group is the *peregrinas de corazón* (of the heart), who walk with the most faith. They sleep wherever they can find a spot (literally underneath trucks or on sidewalks), eat whatever is available, and do not have the purchasing power of the other two groups. This problematic analysis of gender and faith offers two points. It gives us a narrow but telling indication of how the church in Querétaro, from an institutional position, perceives the all-female phenomenon; and second, it opens up for consideration the varying effects consumption practices have on the socioreligious and business-related principles of the journey.

DEVOCIÓN Y NEGOCIO/DEVOTION AND BUSINESS: THE ECONOMICS OF A RELIGIOUS SPECTACLE

Integrating oneself into pilgrimage culture is not cheap. From the distintivo (30–500 pesos/US$21–35) to sleeping accommodations (300+ pesos/ US$21), luggage transportation (300+ pesos/US$21), food (30 pesos a meal/US$2.10), showers (10–20 pesos/US$1), bathroom facilities (2–5 pesos/ US$0.14–$0.35), and daily donations at mass, each element of the trip costs money. Even the food vendors who officially follow the pilgrimage trail pay 50 pesos (US$5) for their authorization to sell. There are also unofficial peregrinas, those who do not register with a diocese and do not pay the requisite participation fee. They walk parallel to the main procession, which creates tense situations. On one occasion, while conducting interviews in the edecanes group at the front of the line, a woman from the directiva seglar screamed at the women traveling on the periphery, "¡Son peregrinas! ¡No son borregas!" (You are pilgrims! Not sheep!). This official nudged me, "Go. Tell them." Tell them what, I wondered? I walked over and spent the rest of the afternoon walking in the parallel columna conversing with peregrinas whose stories were not unlike those told in the main columna. These women confided that they live between villages, places not shown on a map, and do not have the opportunity or the resources to register formally. Silently suffering unkind remarks, these unauthorized travelers articulate their defiance by walking side-by-side with the elite women who, literally, lead the pilgrimage. This frustrates coordinators, because those on the margin may arrive first, eat first, bathe first, and so on. But more important, their presence disrupts the institutional vision of a sacred performance—a seamless collective act demonstrating the group's shared belief in the Virgin of Guadalupe and in a Catholic Mexico.

The current president of the pilgrimage and head of the directiva seglar is Sandra Siliceo Valdespino. She once worked for Kellogg Corporation as an executive director of distribution and production in Latin America but now divides her time between Pepsi in Mexico City and a university professorship in Querétaro. During our conversations, she articulated her vision to unify the women so that they maintain and project a sense of solidarity. She also stressed the importance of practicing spirituality in a safe environment.

> We invite the women to walk together, to sing, pray, reflect, and most of all to hear the Word of God. This is our goal. . . . I also want the women to be happy, to sing, and dance, to enjoy themselves. I have been a peregrina for

more than ten years, and I love to lead prayer and chants. . . . It is our job [the executive committee's] to organize all elements of the journey to make the women as safe as possible and to ensure that they have opportunities to receive the Word of God. This means involving the Red Cross and state officials to care for and protect the women. We must also have the full support of the church to offer the women confession and daily mass.

"My favorite part of the pilgrimage," she added, "is leading chants and dancing that lift the spirit." Participants often performed the high-energy chant *"Cuando un Cristiano baila"* (When a Christian Dances):[36]

Cuando un cristiano baila, baila, baila
Cuando un cristiano ¡baila,baila,baila!
Pies, pies . . . (feet) [women shake their feet and/or skip in place]
rodillas (knees), *cadera* (hips),   [giggling]
cintura pancita (waist stomach),   [woooooo!]
coditos (elbows), *hombritos* (shoulders)
cabeza (head), *ojitos* (eyes)

When pressed about the economic dimensions of the pilgrimage, specifically why there were so many vendors and markets along the route, Silliceo Valdespino responded quickly that the point was not that the ritual welcomes commercialization but that the women should have access to everything they need—food, clothing, and medicine.[37] "And you know how women love to shop," she added. Orvaños Busto also noted this cliché:

From a religious point of view, it really stood out that so many women, who were supposedly walking with a spiritual attitude and disposition, bought the most mundane items such a earrings, necklaces, clothes etc. . . . [T]he women who buy these types of things do so because they live in a place that is so far away from the pueblos or cities where these items are available for purchase. They take advantage of the opportunity to acquire these items on their own terms. They decide the design, the color, the form.[38]

It was impressive how quickly women would shower, change into a different outfit, and explore the *poblado* (town) after waking at 3:00 A.M. and walking for thirteen hours. During these outings, *peregrinas* often purchased gifts, clothes, or products to sell in their home communities. (See figure 7.) On one occasion, *compañeras* (walking partners) from Group 104 bought dozens of little mesh bags at 10 pesos apiece. They planned to embroider them in their homes and give them as gifts or resell them at ten times the original price to neighbors or in their local *tianguis* (market).

FIGURE 7. Leisure time.

Other women use family resources and connections to earn extra income during the pilgrimage.[39] For 300 pesos a person, Teresita, a fruit and vegetable market owner, offers thirty peregrinas sleeping and storage space in her maletero, which she secures using her husband's connections in the transport industry. Potentially, Teresita could earn 9,000 pesos (before paying the driver's salary and gasoline). In addition to financial gain, she garners special attention from participants who want to make certain that they have a spot in the truck. Pursuing informal commercial and service sectors makes economic sense for most participants because women have a foothold in those areas. According to the Instituto Nacional de Estadística y Geografía (INEGI), males dominate the manufacturing (59.7 percent), transport (86.2 percent), construction (92.9 percent), and mining (94.0 percent) industries, but females share employment in service and commercial divisions, at 45.7 and 44.7 percent respectively.[40]

Devotees also contribute to the region's informal economy through donations. Many communities along the route, especially between principal villages, construct provisional altars with a representation of la Virgen de Guadalupe and an image of a local saint (Saint Martha, for instance), flowers, a white sheet, and a makeshift sign asking for money to build a chapel (see figure 8). Women toss *monedas* (coins) onto the sheet

FIGURE 8. Roadside altar.

as they advance, which could add up to 16,000 pesos (US$1,121). Regardless of the amount or the endpoint, peregrinas' pesos circulate within and supplement isolated communities not only in Querétaro but also in Hidalgo, the state of Mexico, and the Federal District (see map 3).

The case of the distintivo is the most telling economic component of the ritual. The distintivo has a standard cost, set by the diocese, of 30 pesos (US$2.10). It marks where one comes from and, more important, where one belongs in line. In 2005, for example, women residing in San Juan del Río walked in Groups 9, 10, 11, and 12; parishioners from Amealco traveled in Groups 81, 82, and 83; and devotees based in Santa Rosa de Lima journeyed in Group 128. The walking order, which is determined by an annual lottery, is a serious matter. First, the women who walk at the front of the line enter the Basílica first, which many consider the ultimate act of faith—leading thousands to the Virgin's home. Also, they arrive at each pueblo first and thus have the opportunity to eat, bathe, and shop before anyone else. There is a two-hour difference between the arrival of Group 1 and Group 150. Second, able participants have the option to pay an additional sum for the privilege of walking ahead of other women. A *peregrina* can buy her way into Group 1 or 2 by paying an extra 300 to 500 pesos (US$21–$35). According to Siliceo Valdespino, this extra money is used to buy necessary items for the group—batteries, flashlights, safety items—or to renovate the *estandarte* (standard) or other group symbols. Considering that a Queretano's average annual salary is 76,186 pesos (approximately US$5,338), paying this amount to gain a superior position allows women to announce their wealth without saying a word.[41]

There is another way to get to the front of the line: knowing someone important. Let me illustrate by explaining the official order in which the groups arrive at Tepeyac. The *carro de sonido* (car equipped with a sound system) leads the four-kilometer *columna*, which, in this scenario, is a Coca-Cola truck. The spiritual advisers and the executive committee are the second cohort to arrive, followed by the edecanes, more priests, security, the *vanguardia* (women who monitor traffic in the front), medical services (Red Cross), and finally the one hundred fifty groups of *peregrinas* and the *retaguardia* (traffic monitors at the back). It is nearly impossible to buy your way into any one of the executive or ministerial groups at the front of the line. It is possible, however, to attain a place in line in one of the service groups, such as the edecanes or vanguardia, if you have a business or personal relationship with a member of the executive committee.

Because they are volunteers, Siliceo Valdespino argued, they pay the standard 30 pesos for their distintivos. Their experience, however, is anything but typical. During midday rest periods when participants attend mass, eat, and sleep, lay volunteers, along with members of the clergy, have the option of eating catered food subsidized with the requisite participation fee. Assuming all participants pay for their distintivos, the executive committee can collect approximately 480,000 pesos (or US$36,554) annually. Edecanes usually stay in the same hotel. In 2005 some members brought two men along to prepare their breakfasts and lunches of fresh fruit, bread, coffee, juice, and other healthy foods. As one woman put it, "We don't want to eat the greasy food they sell on the road." The luxury of not eating quesadillas and *gorditas*—fried tortillas stuffed with meat, beans, and/or cheese—prepared with recycled grease sets them apart from the majority of participants.

These women at the front of the line are known as *güeras* (lit., "fair-skinned women"). As a member of the directiva seglar reminded me the night before the pilgrimage, "You and I are güeras because we are different from the other women. . . . I've always been considered a güera because of my family's reputation. I also work in an office." She added, "You are going to meet a lot of indigenous women who have strange ideas about the ritual. They believe that each *ampoya* [blister]) they get during the walk is a sin. To get many blisters is a positive thing; they are like roses given to them by the Virgin. It means that they are truly repenting for their sins. I don't think like that." But for them, she added, "it is an important part of their experience, of their way of thinking."

The case of the distintivo, in particular, the categorizations it engenders, underlines the ways in which a woman's location within this religious performance says as much about her socioeconomic standing as it does about where she worships on a daily or weekly basis. That officials created an impromptu "migra" force to police the women reveals to what extent one's physical position is a marker of social status. The *migra* (border patrol) ensured that each devotee had purchased a distintivo, that her proof of purchase was always visible, and that she was in the correct group. Moreover, this aspect of the ritual demonstrates that perceptions of race and ethnicity are inextricably linked to class status. This is not to suggest that skin tone does not matter. It is indeed the first and most superficial marker of race and privilege. Yet a participant can be güera without being light-skinned when she displays her purchasing power. Here the anthropologist Mary Weismantel's analysis of race in the Andes provides an interesting parallel. Weismantel proposes:

> If things acquire a race—or bestow one upon their possessor—it is because they are so intimately part of what we are. Like our bodies, our possessions reveal their history—and ours—through their appearance: a wooden handle is smooth and shiny from long contact with the hand that used it; the letters on a keyboard are worn away or soiled by our fingers; a pair of pants begins to sag at the knee. The things we use change us as well: a back takes on a peculiar posture in response to its customary chair, a pair of arms repeat a characteristic motion in response to the balance and heft of the objects they lift each day. Race is indeed socially fabricated—and the construction site is the zone of interaction between our skin, flesh, bones, and the world around us.[42]

The key marker of a Mexican peregrina's identity, after her devotion to the Virgin, is how she consumes the experience—her place in line, her clothes, whether she wears shoes, whether she sleeps on a bed or on a sidewalk, whether she eats fresh fruit or potentially unsanitary food items prepared by vendors. The status that we buy, like the things that we use, mark us.

VISIONS OF HOMECOMING

There is not just one arrival. Tepeyac is the destination, but the women begin to process their experience and envision their homecoming—as a devotee, mother, wife, sibling, laborer—throughout the course of the journey. Consider that each day vendors sell copies of Querétaro's daily newspaper, the *Diario de Querétaro,* which includes a special section titled "Rumbo al Tepeyac" (Journey toward Tepeyac). This insert features color photos of both female and male pilgrimages, articles tracking safety and health issues, and spiritual advisers' remarks defining proper Catholic behavior as well as estimating the place of Catholicism in that year's turbulent Calderón/López Obrador presidential election. "Olvidar ídolos: Obispo" (Forget idols: Bishop [says]), read one such headline.[43] Participants often discuss and debate these issues. Also, many keep a hard copy of the supplement as a keepsake, especially when they or someone they know has appeared in its pages. Consuming this information, *peregrinas* have multiple chances to reflect, react, and negotiate the experience with their insider's knowledge and an indication of opinions circulating in the public sphere. The newspaper prompts the questions: How are we being perceived [back home]? How will we be remembered? It connects them to the everyday and reminds them that their extraordinary devotion draws spectators outside of the pilgrimage ritual. This sparks a consideration of the realities that lie just beyond the journey.

A commemorative videorecording of the ritual also provokes reflection. The directiva seglar solicits a videographer to document each day of the journey, who in turn sells the memento at Tepeyac. The women are able to preview the footage—the evidence of their participation—before beginning that day's jornada. Around four o'clock on the seventh morning, for example, vision blurry from sleep deprivation, my compañeras and I noticed a group of peregrinas huddled around a bright, bluish light that seemed to be floating in the darkness. It was a television screen. Seated on the street curb relishing our breakfast of hot chocolate and a roll, we inadvertently joined a configuration of concentric circles watching them watch the screen. Once in a while, a woman would shout with delight, "¿Me ven? ¡me ven! (Do you all see me? do you all see me!). The footage showed her marching during a previous day's journey, responding to the camera. But in this moment she was smiling and waving at us. "We will be selling this beautiful souvenir for 200 pesos [US$14]," the videographer assured us. "If you do not see yourself, we will be shooting more footage today. . . . Keep a look out."

This snapshot alerts us to issues of identity formation, consumer desire, and what Jane Feurer calls "liveness"—"a charged sense of immediacy, presence, and direct representation that emerges from TV's technological capacity to transmit and receive signals simultaneously, regardless of whether the broadcast in question is 'literally' live or not."[44] The presence of this televised event is not an isolated case. As suggested earlier, some family members who meet peregrinas at different points along the journey bring a portable television sets. And many of the public spaces participants inhabit, whether local residences or even market *puestos* (stalls), inevitably offer a glimpse of life beyond the ritual. The act of watching peers or even yourself performing piety, however, requires a particular reading. On the one hand, the "liveness" mediated by technology and the "liveness" of that moment coalesces to cement peregrinas' collective identity as carriers of Guadalupan faith. This point is especially important when one reflects on the physical intracommunity segregation engendered by institutional and logistical constraints. Group 130, for example, never sees how Group 55 experiences the pilgrimage. Seeing their peers on screen, in a moment that communicates "immediacy, presence, and direct representation," reinforces the idea of an ideologically unified, seamless congregation that is lost in practice. On an individual level, the notion of someone consuming your devotional labor augments the importance of the act beyond your private reasons. In other words, this moment not only serves as a personal touchstone but also is a reminder of the overall efficacy of their actions, specifically, how outsiders will interpret their faith in the throes of arriving and not after they have completed the journey. This point troubles church doctrine's generic conceptual framework, which relies on the idea of one arrival. In this case Tepeyac is the endpoint—the holy place where sweeping realization occurs. Seeing, reflecting, and potentially accepting the televised image's teeming insinuations in the moment of action, however, suggest that peregrinas confront multiple arrivals and moments of integration. They are, in a way, always experiencing the feelings or expectations associated with arriving.

APPROACHING TEPEYAC

At the *acueducto de Guadalupe* (aqueduct of Guadalupe), the last official resting point before Tepeyac, municipal representatives from Delegación Gustavo A. Madero (GAM) greet the women with banners, yellow and white balloons, and refreshments. This warm welcome highlights the city's investment in the annual ritual. Many participants, anticipating their homecoming, put on their best yellow skirts and white blouses, style their hair, and apply makeup. This is not to suggest that the women go without a hairbrush throughout the journey, but upkeep is minimal until we reach Mexico City. Some devotees adorn themselves with a white veil over their floppy hats, to showcase their earned purity. As one woman suggested on arriving at the shrine, "Cumplir a misa, ir a misa. De hecho aqui en el camino es diario. Compartir más y saber valorar a las cosas. Me siento más limpia con la viviencia" (Attending mass, going to mass. We attend daily. Sharing more and learning how to value things, I feel more pure with this experience). In addition to wearing veils, each participant had the opportunity to carry a large poster of the Virgin of Guadalupe embracing Pope John Paul II (provided by the directiva seglar). This same image circulates among devotees at the Second Tepeyac of North America in Des Plaines, Illinois, and other outposts and may be found on home altars.

Some women sing and wave the representation while walking toward Tepeyac. Past the Polytechnic Institute, past quiet shops and sleepy Sunday-morning residences, crowds begin to line the streets shouting their congratulations. It is customary for most pilgrimage groups to approach the shrine on the Calzada de Guadalupe. Queretanas, however, enter through a side entrance, adorned with a welcome banner (provided by municipal officials), which allows them immediate access to the inner sanctum of the Modern Basílica. They are able to proceed directly to the mechanized pathway that gives visitors ten seconds of face-to-face contact with the Virgin's sixteenth-century image. Once the women step onto the airport-style moving walkway, many are overcome by emotion and tears. Some participants, cameras in hand, shook so much that they were unable to take a photo. Others, emotionally overwhelmed and physically exhausted, collapsed. The women come in waves, and each group, each devotee, offers an unrepeatable reaction. These cathartic moments are unlike any other during the pilgrimage. It is not communitas; there is little interaction to speak of. That we completed the journey as a collective hangs solemnly in the air, but this fact quickly becomes part of the backdrop. A sense of personal connection dominates the environment.

Outdoors, Siliceo Valdespino and select members of the executive committee join high-ranking clergy on the Modern Basilica's balcony to celebrate mass. Peregrinas, in turn, sit and wait for mass to begin in the atrium, also known as Plaza de las Américas" (see chapter 1). Many women sleep, most chat, and some greet family members. Cecilia, for example, wept openly when she saw her husband and her two sons, who congratulated her with long hugs and little kisses. "It feels wonderful," she confided, "to have finally completed my promise. I thought about it for years; I would say next year, next year. . . . I really didn't know if I would have worked up the courage without having Isabel and Victoria here."

Seeing the Virgin's image in the Modern Basilica signifies a form of personal closure for many of the women, but the one-hour church service formally concludes the institutional dimension of the journey. But before beginning the closing ceremony, the women demonstrate their religious and regional solidarity with a prayer, "Venimos de Querétaro."[45]

Venimos de Querétaro Virgen bendita
[We came from Querétaro blessed Virgin]

María de Guadalupe fiel madrecita
[Mary of Gudalupe, loyal mother]

Dejamos nuestras tierras y nuestras familias
[We leave our land and our families]

Y vamos a tu casa, hogar de nuestra raza
[And we journey to your house, the place of our race]

> *Que es tu basílica (se repite)*
> [That is your basilica (repeat)]

> *Cuando nos despertamos de madrugada*
> [When we awake in the early hours of the morning]

> *Sentimos tu presencia Virgen bendita*
> [We feel your presence blessed Virgin]

> *Y cuando ya inciamos nuestra jornada*
> [And when we commence our walking day]
> *Delante de nosotros sentimos que caminas*
> [We feel that you walk in front of us]

> *¡Oh bella Indita!*
> [Oh beautiful little Indian!]

Desde distintos ranchos y poblaciones
[From distinct ranches and towns]

De nuestro hermoso Querétaro, Virgen María
[From our beautiful Querétaro, Virgin Mary]

Venimos como hermanas en romería,
[We came as sisters on a pilgrimage,]

Escucha nuestros cantos y nuestras
[Listen to our songs and our]

Oraciones de cada dia.
[Daily prayers.]

Oh Virgencita linda, Reyna del cielo
[Oh lovely Virgin, Queen of heaven]

Escucha como madre oye nuestros ruegos
[Listen like a mother, hear our requests]

Atiéndenos benigna y danos Consuelo
[Look after us merciful [Virgin] and give us solace]

Pues eres forjadora y ardiente defensora
[Well you are a protector and a passionate defender]

De nuestros pueblos.
[Of our towns.]

¡Oh Virgen linda tus peregrinas
[Oh lovely Virgin, your pilgrims]

venimos fatigadas por el camino
[we come weary on the path]

unimos nuestras voces y te pedimos
[we unite our voices and we ask you]

nos des un buen gobierno que lleve
[to give us a good government that leads]

a nuestros pueblos un buen destino.
[our towns to a good destiny.]

Reciting this prayer in front of the Modern Basilica achieves several objectives: (1) it legitimizes Tepeyac as a sacred destination to practitioners, spectators, and impartial tourists; (2) it rhetorically reinforces the notion of a consummate Guadalupan congregation; and (3) it recalls key historical moments in their local and national imaginary. Let us reconsider the last four verses of the prayer: "we come weary on the path. We unite our voices and we ask you to give us a good government that leads our towns to a good destiny." It recalls the pervasive and inextricable link between Catholicism and state/national affairs, even during times such as la Reforma or the Cristero Wars when such a connection was unlawful. Spoken by Queretanas, those phrases acquire a particular valence. In correspondence from the historian William Taylor, I was reminded of Querétaro's political significance and "its militantly Catholic side."[46] On the other hand, Querétaro acquired a reputation as the birthplace of independence because it hosted and supported revolutionaries. At one point during the Mexican-American War, Santiago de Querétaro served as the nation's capital. During these early stages, freedom did not necessarily exclude Catholicism, Spain's primary method of colonization. The Plan of Iguala (1821), which solidified independence, or even earlier when the revolutionary priest Miguel Hidalgo y Costilla issued the *"grito de Dolores,"* the call that incited public resistance, evinces that point. Peregrinas reactivate this legacy as they walk and deliver coded political texts.

During the final Eucharist service, the officiating priest reiterates the guiding principles of the journey and emphasizes personal transformation and purification, the power of sacrifice, coming to know God through the Virgin of Guadalupe (but not placing her above God the Father or Jesus), and emulating her in everyday life. After the ceremony, the priest blesses the women and their families, as well as their purchased goods and keepsakes, before leading the following call and response:

¡México Católico!	Mexico is Catholic!
¡Querétaro Católico!	Querétaro is Catholic!
¡Qué viva la Virgen de Guadalupe!	Long live the Virgin of Guadalupe!
¡Qué viva México!	Long live Mexico!

After the feverish ending, the women disperse in waves. Some of them stay in the city with family or friends until they recover, while others stay at Tepeyac to sightsee or wait for their husbands, brothers, or sons traveling with the all-male pilgrimage. The majority, I found, journey home by car with family members or with their compañeras on a Flecha Amarilla bus, the corporate transportation sponsor of the pilgrimage.

ONWARD TO MICHOACÁN

The Querétaro phenomenon is a polyvalent devotional performance. By gathering the masses once a year, the institution sustains its hold on local traditions and social hierarchies, and maintains its influence and power on devotees' everyday practices and leisure time. The arrival at Tepeyac homogenizes the women; they come to represent a gendered, mobile force that reinforces Catholicism's dominance in Querétaro.[47] Further, their hyper-public performance reiterates that authority through three zones in central México—Hidalgo, the state of Mexico, and the Federal District—and sets the standard for the three other official all-female pilgrimages that travel on foot to Tepeyac from Celaya, Morelia, and Zitácuaro, Michoacán. Approximately 3,000 women journey from Celaya, Guanajuato, and 8,000 from Morelia, Michoacán, travel in early August. A small group, roughly 125 peregrinas travel from Zitácuaro in early October. But, as the intricate socioeconomic micropolitics that pervade the ritual have shown, the women are anything but monolithic.

The spectacle of pilgrimage has the potential to reinforce Catholicism's firm ideological grip on central Mexico, but because the ritual also shapes devotees' consumption practices, it also clarifies how this sacred tradition directly affects the maintenance and growth of local and regional economies as well as intracommunity social relations. As Walter R. Adams points out in his study of political and economic parallels of pilgrimage behavior:

> It is through participation that individuals perform acts which allow them to become aware of the social world of which they are part and which may not be evident in the course of daily living.... [P]erformance does more than remind individuals of an underlying order, it constitutes a public acceptance of the public order.[48]

Contrasting these dimensions not only draws attention to the contingencies and complications that underwrite each performance but also shows that the pilgrimage ritual does not lend itself to one model; it resists paradigm.

This is not to suggest that similarities do not exist between the rituals. Each group produces and custom designs sacred time and space. The act of walking, praying, singing, chanting, confessing, and accepting the Eucharist imbues the spaces they traverse with local elements of the sacred. On a larger scale, their embodied devotion legitimizes the pilgrimage ritual and the cult of Guadalupe within and beyond Mexico's borders. On an individual level, the pilgrimage offers participants the opportunity to contemplate and reflect, feel pain and sacrifice of their own volition, and reinforce family and societal ties through absence. Comparing the institutional, historical, socioeconomic, and sensual ways of knowing present in both Querétaro's ritual and Zitácuaro's reticent tradition alerts us to those complex contingencies.

CHAPTER 3

Feeling History

Calambres, Ampoyas y Sed (Muscle Spasms, Blisters, and Thirst)

With moist skin, rubbery knees and lungs filled with *aire contaminado* (polluted air), and nearing delirium from sleep deprivation, las Guadalupanas from Zitácuaro arrived at Lerma de Villada's central plaza after walking nearly one hundred kilometers over the course of three days.[1] Literally crawling on our knees across a cobbled walkway, the cohort of 120 women reached the front doors of the church. Waiting solemnly, a priest, flanked by two altar boys, blessed us and then proclaimed, "You are all sinners." "This pilgrimage," he continued, "is not sufficient, nor is it significant if you do not receive the sacraments. . . . It is not enough to walk once a year. You must be devout every single day of the year." He went on to simultaneously bless and denounce the women. Positioned near the front of the line, I opened my eyes and looked over my shoulder. All the women sat crouched low to the ground with their eyes clenched tightly, even those carrying *estandartes* (banners) and the Mexican flag. A few peregrinas began to sob quietly. I too shut my eyes, not out of humility or catharsis, but out of irritation.

The priest did not invite us inside the church. Later, in a hall adjacent to the plaza where the group traditionally spends the night, I asked Carmelita, my seventy-four-year-old compañera, her thoughts about the priest's statements. She said that he was right. Carmelita, who has journeyed on this all-female pilgrimage for forty-two consecutive years, confided that for many years she knew that she was a sinner because she had not married in the church; she did not fulfill that religious obligation. She and her life partner, Aurelio, never had enough money to pay a priest to perform the ceremony, much less to travel to their village, located in the *cerro* (hills) surrounding Zitácuaro, to perform the ceremony. It was not until their fiftieth anniversary that their children, now grown and employed, were able to finance the completion of the sacrament. Carmelita's personal experience is not based on "popular" practice. Or put another way, her actions are not antithetical to Catholic precepts, yet they clearly relate an incompatibility between doctrine and practice, specifically, how satisfying institutional requirements is not only a matter of faith or loyalty but also of purchasing power. As unfair as it may seem, this is her reality.

Later, looking over that day's field notes and listening to my taped conversation with Carmelita, I was reminded of a passage from Saba Mahmood's book *Politics of Piety* in which she discusses the real-time implications of an "expanded notion of critique." She writes, "[During fieldwork] I was forced to question the repugnance [a term she borrows from Elizabeth Povinelli] that often swelled up inside me against the practices of the mosque movement, especially those that seemed to circumscribe women's subordinate status within Egyptian society."[2] According to Mahmood, many secular progressives and like-minded people tend to denounce those gender-specific restrictions. But this reaction, she proposes, is suspect. Instead, she prefers to "move beyond a [negative] visceral reaction" in order to comprehend "what makes these practices powerful and meaningful to the people who practice them."[3] Her strategy seems to me to be worthwhile. But it is easier imagined than done, especially while in the thick of things—kneeling in front of a priest alongside dozens of exhausted women. To be frank, I struggled with this issue not only during the pilgrimages but also while conducting fieldwork in Rogers Park. Later, however, when putting the pieces together, I held to one of Mahmood's most productive suggestions.

> What may appear to be a case of deplorable passivity and docility from a progressivist point of view, may actually be a form of agency—but one that can be understood only from within the discourses and structures of subordination that create the conditions of its enactment. In this sense, agentival capacity is entailed not only in those acts that resist norms but also in the multiple ways one *inhabits* norms.[4]

This study is not immune to the urge to place a progressive or feminist interpretation on Guadalupanos' devotional acts, but it refuses to default to the idea of participants being resistant only when they explicitly counter known standards. Instead, it focuses on peregrinas' decisions, how they approach piety, or as Mahmood suggests, how they inhabit it.

The opening vignette and Caremelita's remarks also invite us to reflect on two other important ideas. First, peregrinas' moments of pain and discomfort—walking on blistered feet, proceeding with injured knees and cramped legs, with growling stomachs and salty saliva, with too much light and too little sleep—play a comprehensive role in the ritual's development.[5] Second, it suggests that women's suffering supports not only gender- but also power-based divisions. Although there is a long history of that narrative in Mexico and elsewhere, I am unable to substantiate that claim without knowledge of how institutional/lay power divisions unfold during all-male pilgrimages. However, after co-performatively witnessing the Zitácuaro pilgrimage twice—in October 2004 and October 2005—there is much more to be said about power, suffering as conviction, and how religious histories circulate in spite of failing or falling out of the purview of institutional guidelines.

Below I consider these issues and place them squarely in a transnational context in a way that is quite different from the Querétaro case study. Michoacán's location marks the distinction. Its agriculture economy, unlike Querétaro's industrial model, reduces local economic resources for many of these women, which means that a devotee's small kitchen table sometimes doubles as the pilgrimage altar. It also engenders a sending state environment, in which many men and women travel to the United States, and to the Midwest in particular, to find work and/ or join family members. Some of those relatives are descendants of Michoacanos who migrated as early as 1910. I propose that peregrinas' devotional labor and the physical marks on their bodies—the presence of calluses, scabs, and bruises, suffering however ephemeral—evince their faith, become indelible memories and the center of transnational narratives that inform the development of sacred space in the Chicago area. As de Certeau reminded us early on, "What the map cuts up, the story cuts across."[6]

PILGRIMAGE BEGINS SOMEWHERE

Pilgrimage begins somewhere. The 2004 journey began in October at the Central del Oeste, a bustling bus station that handles most outgoing and incoming traffic between Michoacán, the state of Mexico, and the Federal District (Mexico City). Through the Basilica's Office of Social Communication, I was able to contact and attain permission from

Patricia "Paty" Garcia to walk alongside Guadalupanas from Zitácuaro on their five-day journey to Tepeyac. Born and raised in Zitácuaro, Paty migrated to Mexico City to work as a domestic servant, a trade she learned from her mother, Remedios, while still in *secundaria* (middle school). Her personal pilgrimage experience spans sixteen years. In fact, her employers have come to accept and work around the knowledge that she will take her annual leave the second Tuesday of October—when the all-female pilgrimage traditionally commences. Her uninterrupted participation is contingent on the fact that she is unmarried and childless. Although she lives in Mexico City and has ample opportunities to visit Tepeyac, even daily if she wishes, Paty prefers walking with her Zitácuaro-based relatives and friends because it allows her to maintain a cross-generational family tradition. Her mother has over three decades of experience; her sisters, Rosario, Teresa, and Elena, two of whom are married with children, have traveled on and off for fifteen years. Paty's nieces, ranging in age from nineteen months to nine years, participate when intrahousehold agreements and negotiations make it possible.

During that initial two-hour bus ride from Mexico City to Zitácuaro, Paty revealed many backstage details of the contested tradition. She and Blanca, her fellow planner, organize pilgrimage logistics: accommodation, food, safety, permission and support from civil authorities. The latter, however, is conditional and often unavailable. Blanca, who works at a produce market in Zitácuaro, supervises the first half of the trip and Paty oversees Mexico City–related business, which includes securing an official mass at the Basilica with a donation of 1,000 pesos (approximately US$70). This group contribution, Paty explained, results in a distintivo fee of 60 pesos (US$4.20) for each participant. This amount covers most expenses—luggage transport, accommodation, and the return trip. Contacts along the pilgrimage route provide simple meals—tamales, beans, rice, tortillas or bread, and coffee and champurrado—for the group. Peregrinas with extensive pilgrimage histories, like seventy-four-year-old doña Carmelita, doña Broula, doña Remedios, doña Hilda, and doña Flora, have long since established those dependable relationships.

Paty emphasized how challenging it is for most women to meet the financial costs of the tradition. The majority of participants save all year to walk, and even then, some find themselves relying on the generosity of others. Many do not have adequate clothing—socks, shoes, raincoats, or sweaters—nor do they have sufficient food or blankets.

The acutely impoverished participants—those without shoes or a blanket, for example—mostly live in isolated communities surrounding Zitácuaro; many are unemployed and rely on their husband's underpaid and often undependable seasonal labor to sustain their households. Although Michoacán is most famous for its agricultural productivity—it leads Mexico in strawberry, blackberry, guayaba, melon, and avocado cultivation—social services and the commercial sector offer more stability.[7] NAFTA, signed in 1994, diminished the region's agribusiness prospects by permitting heavily subsidized U.S. products to enter the market. As a result, Michoacán's average annual salary is $50,634 pesos (approximately US$3,548), nearly 30 percent below the national average. The fact that Michoacán ranks second, behind Zacatecas, as Mexico's top sending state to the United States mitigates this reality. Its regional connection with third-ranked Guanajuato and San Luis Potosí contributes to a long migration history to the Midwest.

According to a study conducted by the CONAPO, between 1997 and 2002, for example, approximately 248,000 Michoacanos migrated to the United States. In 2002 only 97,208 had returned.[8] Michoacán is a key participant in the "3 ÷ 1 program"—a (Mexican) government initiative that pledges to match three dollars for every one dollar sent as a *remesa* (remittance). In theory state officials earmark this money for town development. In 2003 laborers working outside the republic contributed approximately $1.7 million to the state's economy, ranking it among the highest areas on the receiving end of remesas.[9] Indeed, both rural- and urban-dwelling participants benefit from money sent via wire transfer or in the concealed pockets of laborers returning from the United States. This extra income may potentially be used to pay for pilgrimage expenses.

More than half the Guadalupanas who make the journey to Tepeyac have husbands, sons, uncles, or friends working in the Chicago area. Some of the women themselves have worked or lived for brief periods in the United States—Illinois, Idaho, Michigan, and California—but have returned to Michoacán to care for their families and to keep their homes. As one woman put it, "Those of us who stay behind try to do two things. One is to save money, and the other is to keep the house and family as pleasant as possible. That way, our husbands will see that their sacrifices in the United States are worth it when they come home to visit." For the majority of participants, the pilgrimage is the only opportunity to leave their caretaker roles and their home communities.

Like their fellow peregrinas in Querétaro, each has a distinct reason for participating, but many said that they use the journey to reflect on their responsibilities and to ask la Virgencita for guidance and protection. They pray for economic stability and healthy marriages, as well as education and employment opportunities for their children. They never fully separate themselves from the realities of matrimony, parenting, or maintaining transnational families.

Families in Zitácuaro and across Michoacán live and worship amid the everyday realities of these binational processes. Paty's immediate family provides a rich example. Her mother, Remedios, a lifelong domestic servant, has six living children—four daughters and two sons, both of whom migrated to Mexico City in search of work. Her Zitácuaro-based daughters and their families live adjacent to her and often frequent her home to share food and childcare. She lives in a humble three-room house with dirt floors and painfully low ceilings, the design of which tells us much about the family's financial struggles and gains. In lieu of wallpaper in one room, for example, clown-themed gift-wrap paper provides an adequate substitute. A water deposit in the center of the courtyard collects rainwater, which Remedios warms on the stove for bucket showers. An unfinished two-story cinder block structure dominates the back portion of the lot. Sparsely furnished with a new bed and vanity, the modern addition with concrete floors is a product of her daughter Teresa's tenure as a domestic worker in California.

Teresa confided that seeking employment outside of Zitácuaro, specifically, looking for work in the United States, interrupted her pilgrimage tradition even before her obligations as a wife and mother complicated the situation. When asked about her devotional rituals away from Zitácuaro, she admitted that she did not have many opportunities to practice formally. The truth was that she had no idea where she was at first. She was certain that she was in California. "Could the place be called Estanton?" she wondered, but she could not read any of the signs or speak English. "Not even one word," she said. This meant she could not find a Guadalupan church or, more urgently, work for quite some time. She needed money desperately to pay the *coyote* (smuggler who led her across the border). Teresa eventually found an evangelical church, but she did not like it because "all they talked about was the Bible," which she thought was an artificial way to worship. She "could not feel it." Instead, she would close her eyes and imagine la Virgencita during the service so that it would feel real. She revealed that since her return she cherishes each time she has the opportunity to walk on the pilgrimage,

FIGURE 9. Women resting in Toluca with *estandarte*.

especially alongside her daughter, her niece, her sisters, and her mother. She also added (half-jokingly) that she and other peregrinas use the ritual to train for the physically grueling journey across the arid borderland between Sonora and Arizona.

Spending time with Paty and her family before the journey not only illuminated the ways in which macroeconomic processes shape their religious practices but also how each woman strives to maintain her individual devotional inclinations in spite of those realities. Doña Remedios, for example, explained that she attends mass daily and has journeyed to the Basilica more than thirty-five times, even while raising six children on her own. Over the years Remedios has developed the tradition of carrying an originally designed estandarte every year, regardless of injury, fatigue, or impoverishment. Traditionally, she constructs the standard from wood or metal; the cloth banner showcases a hand-drawn and adorned image of the Virgin (figure 9). That very summer, however, she had strained her shoulder mopping the terrace of her employer's house before a party. The doctor suggested that she not use the injured arm or carry anything heavy for a couple of months. Disregarding his advice completely, doña Remedios designed and carried an estandarte with an image of Juan Diego whose tilma revealed the Virgin's image. It was evident during the pilgrimage that her devotional labor was the source of much joy and pride among participants. It is this diligence and unwavering desire to continue her pilgrimage ritual and devoutly follow church traditions—daily mass and confession—that provides a model for her daughters and granddaughters.

Conversing with Paty's sisters while they prepared the traditional pilgrimage meal of *tortas de milanesa* (breaded steak sandwiches), they confided, "We always pack too much food, enough for mother, for Paty, us if we were traveling the first jornadas, a hungry peregrina or two, and now for you." Teresa admitted that only Paty and their mother would walk the entire trip this year. She and her sister María would join them at the end of the third day in Lerma de Vilada. María commented that she has walked fifteen times but that now it is hard for her to make the journey because she has too many family responsibilities. And she married a "disagreeable" man. As Teresa and María packed perishable items, Paty and Remedios organized small mountains of bags and bundles—filled with sleeping bags, towels, pillows, cooking items, clothes, and other necessary items. "We always overpack!" Paty said. "That way we can be comfortable and help our *hermanitas* [little sisters]. . . . We always think of everything and then remember something at the very last minute ¡*Pilas!* (Batteries!) ¡*Caramelos!* (Candy!)." Although the target of family ridicule, Paty reassured her siblings that her packing philosophy would remain unchanged.

CLAIMING HISTORY: THE BATTLE FOR RESPECT AND LEGACY

Tradition dictates that the pilgrimage commences from la Parroquia del Señor San José located in central Zitácuaro at 1:00 A.M. It is customary for peregrinas, especially the older women, to arrive up to six hours early to wait with family and friends on the tiled patio outside the church. Three seasoned pilgrimage participants—doña Carmelita, doña Flora, and doña Hilda—all women in their seventies, shared the details of the contested tradition as they sipped coffee, shared bread, and greeted participants. They noted my nervousness and apprehension, both as a first-time peregrina and as a student of the ritual, but they did not attempt to assuage my fears. Instead, they inspired by example. Doña Carmelita looked tough and ready for the walk with her cropped bright white hair and her yellow zip-up jacket. Doña Hilda's glistening eyes and sharp, birdlike movements provided nervous energy, while doña Flor appeared to be perfectly calm in her wool and yarn cap, with its two woven straps loosely tied under her chin. All three were wearing tennis shoes, thin sweatpants, aprons, and at least two sweaters.

Passing a thermos of coffee around, Carmelita explained that this year marked the forty-second anniversary of the all-female pilgrimage from Zitácuaro and surrounding communities. Having walked every year since the pilgrimage's inception in 1962, Carmelita disclosed, with full authority, that this tradition began with a manda. A family crisis compelled a fellow Guadalupana, now deceased, to journey to Tepeyac to ask la Virgencita for help. An annual pilgrimage to the Basilica had been established five years earlier, in 1957, but since it was exclusively male she asked female friends to travel with her. For many years, Carmelita continued, the archdiocese of Morelia acknowledged this group as the only all-female pilgrimage, but an internal conflict among the women in the early nineties split the tradition into two separate expeditions—one from Zitácuaro in October and the other from Morelia, the state capital, in early August. Both excursions follow the route established during the inaugural 1962 expedition (see map 3).

"The women from Morelia have different ideas," Hilda interjected every so often. Flora added, "They conduct the pilgrimage to make money. . . . They do not follow the way things should be." Carmelita suggested that the current president of the Morelia pilgrimage takes advantage of her position: "She sells them everything and at very high prices." Later in the journey Paty and Blanca explained, "We do things differently, and that has led to a decrease in the number of women who travel from Zitácuaro, down from over six hundred peregrinas in 1994." Over the past ten years many Guadalupanas from Zitácuaro have opted to travel with the larger excursion from Morelia because there are more comforts and more encouragement. Local Guadalupanas know of these differences because the president of the Morelia ritual actively recruits Zitácuaro-based devotees.

Basílica records cannot corroborate or contradict their telling of history because the archive lacks any comprehensive documentation of the tradition's beginning stages. They do, however, officially recognize both journeys, despite their apparent differences. After all, each group submits the proper forms and contributes a suitable donation. The physical and ideological separation is a regional affair; Michoacanas negotiate the details among themselves, not with Tepeyac officials. The most telling disparity is that over 8,000 Guadalupanas walk from Morelia, a city with 684,145 residents, while less than 125 devotees journey from Zitácuaro (pop. 136,491).[10] Indeed, the archdiocese of Morelia rhetorically and institutionally undercut the religious identity of Carmelita, Hilda, Flora, Remedios, Paty, Teresa, María, and dozens of participant. In a statement issued to the Basílica's Office of Social Communication in August 2004, for example, Fr. José Córdoba Beltrán, coordinator of the Morelia pilgrimage, proposed:

> Las mujeres son protagonistas en la Iglesia, le dan vida y son forjadoras en su construcción. . . . Para las peregrinas michoacanas, este recorrido físico y espiritual, desde su lugar de origen hasta la Basílica de Guadalupe, representa el culmen de la formación y el apostolado que llevan a lo largo del año en sus parroquias, en las areas de pastoral profética, litúrgica y social.

> [Women are protagonists in the church. They give it life and they reinforce its construction. . . . For female pilgrims from Michoacán, this physical and spiritual journey, from their place of origin to the Basílica of Guadalupe, represents the summit of the training and the apostolate that they carry throughout the year in their parishes, in the prophetic, liturgical, and social pastoral areas.]

Father José's synecdochic interpretation misidentifies the Morelia phenomena as representative of the whole. Further, and more pressing because of its on-the-ground impact, the archdiocese covertly prohibits clergy members from supporting the Zitácuaro-based ritual. Whereas the women from Morelia and Querétaro have priests and nuns who walk alongside them, these peregrinas must persuade a clergyman with transportation costs, a monetary donation, or a sack of avocados.

In addition to articulating the tradition's contested history, ritual practices and relics are a matter of claiming legacy. Margarita, the daughter of the pioneering peregrina, denied Zitácuaro organizers access to the estandarte used during the initial 1962 pilgrimage, as well as to the official documentation that proves the tradition's heritage before the split in the early 1990s. Margarita apparently threatened, "I will not have a problem burning the documents," as a bargaining chip during the estandarte negotiation with Blanca. After almost two years of discussion, she sold/released the original estandarte for 1,500 pesos (US$105).

Both parties recognized that the banner signifies more than the initial manda; it compels acknowledgment and action. As a living symbol, it literally guides peregrinas not only as they perform their faith but also as they prove their collective history. The handling of her mother's legacy highlights an important question surrounding collective memory: how are the material elements of the sacred—the standard, the relics, the pilgrimage route—or the written proof of this devotional act's legitimacy transferred from one generation to the next? One mode of conveyance occurs during the ritual when these women collectively experience the sacred. Another transmission occurs when they interact with key contacts and spectators along the pilgrimage route. They also convey legitimacy and legacy every time they arrive at the Basilica. A fourth method involves relatives and friends living at home and outside of the republic. Via telephone, letters, the internet, and the consciousness of migrants who traverse the border, their experience and history circulate.

The interconnectedness of this small group of women, especially how they collectively approach the sacred journey as a living memory, illuminates complex aspects of the phenomenon in ways that are not present in the Querétaro case study. The main difference between the two, aside from site-specific political and socioeconomic factors, is that one ritual operates with institutional support and the other exists on the periphery. To be clear, peregrinas from Michoacán, although disenfranchised by the Catholic Church, are not ineffectual outsiders; they, like their counterparts in Querétaro, produce sacred space and contribute to Tepeyac's development, maintenance, and legitimization. On the surface their actions may suggest that legitimacy—veritably claiming and celebrating their history—lies just beyond their grasp. But it would be inaccurate to interpret their efforts through this lens. In *How Societies Remember,* Paul Connerton proposes:

> If there is such a thing as social memory, . . . we are likely to find it in commemorative ceremonies; but commemorative ceremonies prove to be commemorative only in so far as they are performative; performativity cannot be thought without a concept of habit; and habit cannot be thought without a notion of bodily automatisms.[11]

These lines resonate not only with action taken in Zitácuaro, but also in Querétaro. Church support, doctrine, and spiritual advisers fortify and legitimize the pilgrimage ritual, but they do not function independently. Embodied commemoration also underpins history. In spite of its low position in the hierarchy, the habit/tradition of walking transmits knowledge, circulates faith, and communicates agency. With or without institutional support, worshiping the Virgin on their own terms, electing to reflect on the place of faith within each aspect of their lives, and choosing to put one foot in front of the other toward Tepeyac—their heaven on earth—is proof enough.

LA PRIMERA JORNADA (THE FIRST NIGHT)

By 10:00 P.M. mounds of boxes, bags, and resting bodies completely covered the brown and tan tiled floor adjacent to the *parroquia* (parish). Carmelita and company continued to sip coffee. Some women chose to cover themselves with blankets to get some sleep, most were relaxing and talking, and others ran out to buy last minute things—"¡Caramelos!" "¡Pilas!" "¡Refrescos!" (Soft drinks!) Arriving peregrinas registered or claimed their prepaid distintivos. Cut from lightweight wood and dangling from a light pink rope, this pilgrimage badge commemorated the year of the Eucharist with a glossy image of Jesus holding a Eucharist in his right hand and a bronze chalice in his left. An image of the Virgin of Guadalupe floating between the two symbols melded that year's call (2004) with the peregrina's personal devotional focus. The other side of the distintivo featured the following prayer:

Contigo voy Virgen pura y en tu	I go with you pure Virgin and in your
Poder voy confiado, pues yendo	Power I trust, so going
De Ti amparado; mi alma volverá Segura	protected by You; my soul will return Safe
Dulce Madre no te alejes, tu	Sweet Mother do not separate yourself,
Vista de mí no apartes, ven	Do not look away from me, come
Conmigo a todas partes y solo	with me everywhere and just
nunca me dejes, pues ya que	never leave me, now that
Me proteges tanto como verdadera	you protect me like a true
Madre, haz que me bendiga	Mother, make it so that I am blessed by
El Padre, el Hijo y el	The Father, the Son, and the
+Espíritu Santo. Amén	+Holy Spirit. Amen

The prayer's message is clear: the women are asking for the Virgin's protection. Although she is the focus of the supplication, peregrinas also reinforce her institutional role as a secondary player. She is not a part of the Holy Trinity—Father, Son, Spirit. This detail echoes the spiritual adviser's vehement yet often disregarded calls during the Querétaro pilgrimage to privilege the Trinity before the Virgin. The point of traveling to Tepeyac should not be to see her but to actively seek out Jesus. Expressing devotion to her is acceptable, but she must remain a vehicle, a mode of communication toward a deeper understanding of God and the church, not the ostensible reason. This institutional precept is frequently undermined in practice, especially with recurrent phrases such as "I am [or we are] going to see the Blessed Mother at her home [Tepeyac]" and "I am walking to fulfill a promise to the Virgin." She is the foremost object of their affection and attention.

The distintivo commemorating the 2005 journey also reinforced this idea. Constructed from the same lightweight plywood, the badge featured a montage of the then recently deceased Pope John Paul II, Juan Diego, the Virgin, and the Modern Basilica. An image of Pope John Paul II, eyes focused and hand outstretched toward the Virgin, hovered in heaven. On earth, Juan Diego, kneeling and cradling his tilma filled with roses, gazed lovingly at the Virgin, who returned his attention. The iconic Modern Basilica added perspective (in the painterly sense of creating background). This image, not unlike those circulated that year in Des Plaines and in Querétaro, legitimizes an alternative notion of the Trinity's God-in-three-persons message. Designing a representation of the Virgin as the middle point of both the pope's and Juan Diego's gaze creates a female-centered narrative, one that helps integrate popular practice into the ritual.

At around midnight, after all the preregistered participants had received their distintivos, Blanca announced that we would soon be on our way. The women began to gather their belongings and walked them over to the maletero that follows our path. The driver, don Alvaro, who has accompanied the women for over thirty years, is the only male we were to interact with on the journey. There was a light drizzle and a fierce chill as we lined up two-by-two outside the church. I had inserted myself awkwardly somewhere near the middle of the line when doña Carmelita summoned me to the front. She requested that I be her compañera. Honored, I made my way toward the estandarte, unaware of all the generational boundaries and intracommunity divisions I was crossing. The order in which we walk is quite hierarchical. Seniority organizes the sequence, unless the peregrina decides otherwise. Doña Broula, for example, whose deep singing voice has accompanied more than forty journeys, prefers to walk toward the end of the line. Although Remedios could position herself at the front, she chooses to walk in the last position behind Broula.

Traditionally, two women lead the procession with the original banner, which features an embroidered image of la Virgen de Guadalupe and the message, "Viva la Virgen de Guadalupe, Salve Morenita Reyna Poderosa Encantadora del Cielo Frondosa. Peregrinación de Mujeres: Zitácuaro, Michoacán" (Long live the Virgin of Guadalupe, Hail the Dark-Skinned, Mighty, Enchanting, Queen of the lush heaven. All-female pilgrimage: Zitácuaro, Michoacán). The Mexican flag and the original estandarte follow. Doña Carmelita and I walked directly behind these symbols, followed by doña Flor and doña Hilda. Approximately eighty women lined up in the drizzle. As we began to march forward, doña Broula began to sing: "Desde el cielo una hermosa mañana, desde el cielo una hermosa mañana. La Guadalupana, La Guadalupana, La Guadalupana, bajó al Tepeyac."

Maintaining the pace and order of this configuration is important; by demonstrating irreproachable pilgrimage organization, the collective secures an outward semblance of respectability. Unlike the Querétaro-based peregrinas, who abide by institutional regulations such as wearing a long skirt and a long-sleeved shirt to impress the idea of propriety on spectators, these women do so by maintaining an orderly walking formation. Even when running through intersections, as we did one morning in the city of Toluca, precision is never compromised. This part of group image management also serves a practical purpose. Because we walk along the interstate, without a Coca-Cola truck or police escort to guide the way, we often duel directly with freight trailers and cars for traveling space. Moreover, walking throughout the night makes visibility an issue. Assuring the safest possible journey requires that we pay attention to these details. During the early hours of the morning, when drowsiness overcomes us, peregrinas link arms so that if one partner falls asleep in one direction, the other can pull her back before she drifts away. This trick prevents embarrassing or potentially dangerous accidents while descending curvy hillside roads.

That first evening was surreal. Walking hours on end under a starry sky took its toll physically. Throughout the early part of the morning journey, praying and singing praise songs such as "Buenos días Paloma Blanca" enhanced the meditative quality of the devotional act. But as dawn approached, two songs in particular—"Alabaré" (Sing Praise) and "Padre Abraham" (Father Abraham)—kept participants alert and engaged (see Appendix):

Alabaréalabaré	Sing praise, sing praise
Alabaréalabaré	Sing praise, sing praise
¡ALLAA-baré a mi señor! (repeat)	Sing praise to the Lord!
Todos unidos, alegres cantamos	Everyone united, happy we sing
Gloria y alabanzas al SE-ñor;	Glory and praise to the Lord;
¡Gloria al padre!	Glory to the Father!
¡Gloria al hijo!	Glory to the Son!
Y ¡Gloria al espíritu de Amor!	And Glory to the Spirit of Love!

Repeating these lyrics kept many peregrinas (including me) from dishonoring the Virgin. It also served a practical purpose. Some women joked that drivers would be able to hear us before they saw us walking toward them in the darkness. They seek to claim space with their voices not to boast but to survive. Everyone proceeds under the Virgin's auspices. Moreover, after years of walking, most have learned to trust the ritual.

BOSENCHEVE: PAIN AND PRACTICE

At around noon we reached the first rest stop—an elementary school in Bosencheve—just beyond the Michoacán/Estado de México border. Leaning against a cinderblock wall, the women passed around Lala yogurt containers full of rice and beans. Meanwhile, doña Broula sat next to her mobile *comal* (a flat earthenware pan) heating tortillas for the group. Passing around enormous avocados and one plastic spoon completed the scene. Just over the wall, some of the schoolchildren noticed our presence and attempted to involve us in an ambitious game of catch. But it was too sunny to look up with sleep-deprived eyes. Also, most participants were too tired to oblige despite their semisweet pleas.

Bosencheve is where the physical consequences of the devotional ritual began to reveal themselves. Soon after sitting down, *calambres*—muscle spasms comparable to a series of intense charley horses—immobilized Carmelita. As she writhed in pain on her yellow jacket, the women murmured about the problem and possible remedies. Meanwhile Carmelita was unable to express what part of her leg hurt or even how it hurt. The action of rocking back and forth, her eyes wet and wide with frustration, her hands gripping for relief, communicated what she could not verbalize. Someone suggested a foot and calf massage; others said she needed to stretch. Everyone agreed that she must use alcohol on the area. Rubbing alcohol is the fix-all solution on a pilgrimage. You may use it to massage sore muscles, to wake someone after they have passed out, and to disinfect your hands before you eat and after you relieve yourself. I volunteered to rub Carmelita's feet and legs with alcohol for several reasons, the most important being our burgeoning relationship as compañeras. At first, it seemed that I was making the situation worse as I kneaded the throbbing blue veins running laps below her left knee. She would violently retract her leg in pain, and all I could do was hold on and gently feel for the most sensitive spots.

The cramps ceased within a couple of minutes, but Carmelita was exhausted. Some of the women cleared a larger spot in the shade for her to lie down. Hilda sat by her side and smoothed her hair. It became apparent there and on subsequent days that this experience requires unimaginable endurance and that survival is a group concept. The physical dimensions of the pilgrimage cannot be overstated.

Peregrinas attempt to embrace their pain throughout the journey. Hours of walking with blisters, thirst, too much light or cold rain, with sore muscles, hunger, sleep deprivation, and limited descansos take their toll. Like Carmelita's calambres, these elements of the journey deny a written description; pen and paper cannot contain the action. Recognizing the inexpressibility of pain draws attention to that which it potentially engenders—envisioning and reinforcing their collective identity.[12] Although each organism experiences pain in a unique way, these women share the spiritual and physical framework that gives rise to communal corporal suffering.

As previously mentioned, the tradition's place outside the boundaries of official church documentation and budgetary concerns discourage Zitácuaro-area priests and doctors from accompanying the women. Blanca and Paty, however, circumvent this restriction at the elementary school in Bosencheve. A local priest, who receives transportation, a group collection, special attention from participants, and a sack of ripe avocados for his troubles, travels to Bosencheve as a consultant (one could argue). This is the only time during the five-day journey when the peregrinas are able to participate in a mass service. Father Santiago does not perform his duties on traditionally sanctified space. He uses one of the classrooms to provide time for confession so that the women can be prepared to receive communion. He officiates mass outdoors using the sound system from Blanca's pickup truck and the altar, which is actually Remedios's small collapsible kitchen table. (See figure 10.) The women gathered around him use rocks and patches of grass as their pews. That year Father Santiago encouraged the women, but he articulated several times that they should recognize their position as sinners. "Adhere to the sacraments," he preached. "We need them to overcome the sins we commit every day." By authoritatively insisting on the importance of the seven sacraments—Baptism, Penance, Eucharist, Confirmation, Holy Orders, Matrimony, and Anointing of the Sick—institutional parameters maintain their currency even in informal settings.

FIGURE 10. Improvised altar en route to Tepeyac.

SURMOUNTING DISGRACE: THE DIFFICULT ROAD
BETWEEN "EL 91" AND LERMA

After mass at Bosencheve, the group is able to rest for several hours before continuing on toward "el 91" at midnight. Leaving a rest stop is always more laborious than arriving. In addition to packing sleeping bags and food, leaving the place clean is mandatory as it ensures next year's accommodation. Older peregrinas, like doña Hilda, appoint themselves to these duties as part of their sacrifice. Indeed, that first evening I found Hilda vomiting behind the maletero. "I've just cleaned the bathrooms," she explained, "and the women did things they weren't supposed to do." Not wanting to hold the pilgrimage up, she rinsed her mouth with water and literally ran to the front of the line.

That evening was not unlike the previous night's journey. The repertoire guided our rhythm; singing, praying, and chanting "¡Qué viva México! ¡Qué viva la Virgen de Guadalupe! Michoacán Católico! Zitácuaro Católica!" Twilight came and went, but we continued to walk, resting for twenty minutes or so every four hours. Along this leg of the journey a man tried to sell us pies *de queso* (cheese pastries) and pies *de piña* (pineapple pastries) while we were walking through a forested area along a dangerous winding road. He pitched, "These pies are fresh.

They will take away your hunger. Just smell them." A couple of women bluntly told him while marching past that we would not buy anything. This vendor, however, was persistent. Unluckily, he tried to sell his product to the wrong group of peregrinas. Not only did the women shun him on the road, but they also ignored him when he attempted to sell his goods at the next rest stop. It is customary, during the Querétaro pilgrimage, for example, to disrupt the marching formation to purchase food or fill water bottles with *agua potable* (drinkable water) from large mobile tanks waiting alongside the highway. Here, purchasing something from a vendor would signify commercialization of the ritual, which is the primary reason these women separated themselves from their counterparts in Morelia. This is not to suggest that peregrinas do not purchase food or water along the route. The difference is that they do so strictly during rest periods. In addition, it is taboo for participants to speak with males, especiallly unfamiliar ones. Keeping a strict gender division is another way these women perform propriety. This rule is not spoken, nor is it written down; it is a way of knowing that is transmitted by example. Also, safety concerns ensure that participants avoid distracting opportunistic locals. If a peregrina were to pause while walking, she might cause a pile-up of women or cars, or both. Moreover, if one were to wander off too far, some women warn, she could be raped. While there is the occasional need to get out of line, the rule is that we take care of business during rest periods.

Arriving at "el 91" along uphill roads on a brutally sunny day took longer than expected. Not quite dragging our feet, we arrived at an isolated farmhouse at mile-marker 91. Rosita, the owner of the house, motioned the group toward a large covered area and encouraged us to line up for plates of rice, beans, tortillas, and *carne guisada* (stewed meat). Between finishing every last morsel on our plates and being serenaded by three boisterous cows, who seemed to be disoriented by the sudden apparition of women en masse, there was little room for conversation. The rest of the afternoon unfolded quietly. Most participants took turns showering near the cattle stalls and then settled in to rest. Later, sleeping beside Carmelita, Hilda, and Flora, I awoke to find a woman and a man staring at us. Just behind them stood Blanca, Paty, and Raquel—Blanca's daughter—looking agitated and worried. The woman introduced herself as Lucy, the president of the Morelia pilgrimage, and the man as a physician, whom she brought to ensure that the women, especially the older peregrinas, were in proper health to continue the journey. As the doctor checked Flora's blood pressure, Lucy explained (loudly so that most participants could hear):

> I know how hard it can be during these journeys. And I also know that you don't have a lot of resources and certainly not medical care. . . . I was in the area, and I thought it would be kind of me to bring a *certified medical doctor* [emphasis mine] here to see you. I provide this service for my peregrinas. I can provide them with these services because I have many contacts with city officials and doctors all across this area.

Lucy did not hesitate to add, "Of course, all of you are welcome to join the Morelia pilgrimage. We walk in August, and it is always a beautiful journey with lots of singing and laughing. We walk, but we also make things comfortable. I will be bringing the doctor around to see who needs medical attention. You can tell me if you are interested then." Only a few of the women requested the doctor, but Lucy was able to speak with a number of Guadalupanas. Her visit was short but seemed to send a shock wave through the community. Blanca, above all, was livid and used the few precious hours of rest that remained tearfully rehashing the story with the elders—Broula, Carmelita, Remedios, Hilda, and Flora—who offered little in the way of sympathy but did express their confidence in the tradition.

Performing and proclaiming devotion to la Virgen de Guadalupe without external support during 8:00 A.M. rush hour traffic in Toluca the next morning also incited confrontational situations. (See figure 11.) Several times, the walking community literally had to run across busy intersections to dodge impatient motorists. Commuters honked and cursed at us. Participants heard the following phrases sporadically throughout that strip of the journey: "¡Mujeres locas!" (Crazy women!) "¡Váyanse a sus casas, huevonas!" (Go back to your homes, lazy women!) "¡Si quieren chismear, háganlo en sus casas! (If you want to gossip, do it in your own homes!) These derogatory comments are clearly gender-specific—lazy, gossipers, your place is in the home—and play on tropes of women as inferior and weak-minded. When discussing these events, most participants disregarded the insults, while others explained that some people show respect and others do not. Nevertheless, a few women, in the moment, challenged unsupportive spectators to get out of their cars or trucks. "¡Le pego con el estandarte!" (I'll hit him with the banner), said Carmelita at one point, much to the delight of teenage Guadalupanas. More experienced devotees murmured knowingly, "He

FIGURE 11. Women on foot from Zitácuaro, Michoacán, to Tepeyac in Mexico City.

threatened us, but he didn't get out of the car, *no se bajó.*" At one point, Blanca's daughter actually jumped on the hood of a car to prevent it from hurting the women. Reciting the prayer printed on their distinti-vos—"contigo voy Virgen pura y en tu poder voy confiado, pues yendo de Ti amparado; mi alma volverá segura"—while running across dangerous intersections helped them cope with the stressful clash of sacred and secular agendas.

FAMILY, A T-SHIRT, AND DEVOTIONAL CAPITAL

Several studies have shown that gender and belief inform a person's status within his/her family and community.[13] Devotees implicitly understand that their practices reflect their personal values as well as community mores. And, as articulated earlier, contemplating and acting on belief engenders devotional capital within and outside the ritual. As the pilgrimage scholar Beatriz Barba de Piña Chán points out, "Pilgrims acquire a higher social status because they have completed a religious obligation that has produced benefits for the whole community."[14] The benefits differ from community to community, but women who complete the journey acquire respect, admiration, and capital that may give them access to socioeconomic benefits and opportunities.

Conversely, a peregrina's family and daily realities shape pilgrimage behavior. One woman performed as a messenger for family members, male and female, who could not participate in the pilgrimage. Sara, a twenty-three-year-old participant, wore a white T-shirt or layered it over a sweater throughout the journey. Many of her relatives and friends had written short notes asking for protection and help on the shirt with either felt or ballpoint pens. Three notes, in particular, were legible toward the end of the journey.

[1] *Virgencita de Guadalupe*	Little Virgin of Guadalupe
Te pido cuides a mis hijos	I ask that your protect my children
Y me bendigas	and that you bless me
Por que salga bien	so that it turns out well
[2] *Ayúdanos*	Help us
y cuídanos	and protect us
LUPE	Virgin of Guadalupe
[3] *Virgencita de Guadalupe*	Little Virgin of Guadalupe
Te pido por mi hijo Cayetano	I ask for my son Cayetano
Y protégelo de todo mal	protect him from all wrong
Gracias	Thank you

This young woman acknowledged her body as a vehicle not only for her own belief but also for her brother's, her father's, and her mother's spiritual aspirations. By taking on the responsibility of transmitting intimate information, she fulfilled the social role of good daughter and the spiritual role of good Guadalupana. This evocative example suggests how acts of devotional labor—walking, singing, and suffering—not only grants security but also produces regenerative effects.[15] All the prayers and names on her T-shirt were born of the simple action of putting pen to cloth. On Sara's return to Zitácuaro, however, those actions and aspirations return transformed to their senders. Recipients, in turn, use the idea of that change in their own lives in both sacred and secular realms. The memory of performance lingers, and forcefully so.

The arrival of Paty's sisters and their daughters at the parish hall in Lerma also substantiates this point. Their late appearance might be viewed as evidence of an incomplete or insincere journey. In this situation, however, Remedios's and Paty's unwavering commitment to the pilgrimage community helped them earn their place in the ritual. This is not to suggest that their participation over the last two nights would somehow count less. On the contrary, the five-hour uphill walk from Lerma to Cuajimalpa along Highway 15 is an excruciatingly painful and precarious jornada. The serpentine interstate caters to incoming traffic from Michoacán to Mexico City. And that Friday evening, cars and trucks recklessly speeding toward the metropolis combined with narrow walking space made this leg of the pilgrimage a high-risk event.

Although exhausted, sleep deprived, and emotionally on edge, the period spent at Cuajimalpa was one of transformation. It was here where the women began to reflect on the journey and to collectively acknowledge their sacrifice. Like their counterparts in Querétaro, these women experience multiple arrivals—physical, mental, and emotional. After eating and resting, the majority of participants began to ready themselves for the final jornada. Although they did not coordinate a standard skirt, blouse, and veil, these peregrinas did put on their best clothes, combed their hair, and, in some cases, applied makeup. A couple of women and I took photos to celebrate the fact that we were all still standing. Carmelita always posed in profile because it is her "best side" (see figure 9).

At midnight, we set off toward Tepeyac to ensure arriving on time for our 6:00 A.M. mass inside the Modern Basilica. This last night was quite different from previous ones. First and foremost, municipal police officers escorted the group as we changed course from Highway 15/ Toluca-México to the Avenida Paseo de la Reforma. Walking toward Tepeyac on Reforma, an avenue inspired by the Champs-Élysées in Paris but which now recalls Benito Juárez's nineteenth-century reform policies, offers a particular perspective of the city. On the ground, streams of people, cars, and *peseros* (mini-buses) travel along Reforma to the historic center and perhaps to Calzada de Guadalupe, which cuts north toward Tepeyac. Both of these historic pathways discursively and materially divide Culture from culture in the capital. Post-1950 industrialization processes in the northern regions of the metropolis gave way to a reputation that marks the landscape as an impoverished/anti-tourist area, whereas along Reforma and in the south, especially in *colonias* (neighborhoods) such as Chapultepec and Coyoacán—Frida Kahlo's and Leon Trotsky's old stomping grounds—Culture engenders innocuous tourism.

Walking along the avenue offers the opportunity to see some of Mexico City's most emblematic statues—Cuauhtémoc, Christopher Columbus, the Angel of Independence, and the Roman goddess Diana—all representative of how the capital organizes history. Further, the avenue runs past grand hotels and embassies, luxurious pockets that pose problems for pilgrimage participants. Singing *alabanzas* may not be a common public practice in that part of town. For many spectators, however, witnessing the group stop for a bathroom break in front of the Iraqi embassy may have seemed outlandish. Although we held up blankets to maintain modesty, it was impossible to ignore snickering pedestrians. The environment changed significantly as we marched toward la Calzada de Guadalupe. La Plaza de la Tres Culturas (the Plaza of the Three Cultures) in Tlatelolco (the location of the infamous student massacre on October 2, 1968) and la Villa, in addition to less visible pyramid ruins, are the only cultural landmarks north of downtown. La Villa, a jewel amid the neglected landscape of northern Mexico City, is a place where the city feels comfortable remembering.

PEREGRINACIÓN CUMPLIDA (COMPLETED PILGRIMAGE)

After five days of hardship and sacrifice, our arrival is a joyous and overwhelming event. Spectators line either side of the walkway leading to la Villa's gates. Further, thousands of devotees, embarking on, returning from, or supporting a fellow Guaadalupano, fill the atrium of the sacred space. The annual international *antorcha* (torch) walking pilgrimage, which begins at Tepeyac and ends at St. Patrick's Cathedral in New York City on December 12, commenced that Sunday morning.[16] In addition, there are family members and friends awaiting the arrival of approximately a dozen other groups. Most of these spectators attend the mass scheduled for 6:00 A.M., which is held in honor of the peregrinas from Zitácuaro.

Aside from the occasional peregrina vomiting or threatening to pass out (me included), it is quite a beautiful experience to wait for the official blessing and mass in front of door number 5 of the Modern Basilica. This set of doors is decorated with stained-glass cornucopias, grapes, leaves, a sun, and a moon. At the door, doña Broula led the women with voice quivering:

Buenos días Paloma Blanca,	Good morning White Dove
Hoy te vengo a saludar,	Today I have come to greet you
Saludando a tu belleza	Saluting your beauty
En tu reino celestial.	In your heavenly kingdom
Eres madre del Creador	You are the mother of the Creator
Que a mi corazón encanta:	Which my heart loves
Gracias te doy, con amor.	I give you thanks, with love
Buenos días, Paloma Blanca	Good morning, White Dove[17]

Standing at the gates puts accumulated pain into relief. Once inside the Modern Basilica, the focus becomes catharsis and pride. As the official recipients of the celebration, the women take their seats front and center in the VIP section of the floor. More important, the officiating priest welcomes, blesses, and acknowledges the group by name—las Guadalupanas de Zitácuaro—throughout the ceremony. His speech acts reassure the women of their tradition's legitimacy. He congratulates participants for demonstrating their faith in such a powerful manner. He insists, and emphatically so, that the Virgin of Guadalupe only illuminates the path to God; she is not God. Overall, his remarks are less demeaning than those spoken by the priest in Bosencheve or Lerma. He reminds the women that this extraordinary annual practice cannot and should not replace daily piety. But he acknowledges their experience as one that helps them resolve their moral shortcomings.

The journey culminates during communion. Accepting the body of Christ in the Modern Basilica—the Virgin's home, the place that protects her image and her legacy—is their most institutional demonstration of piety. This fifty-five-minute ceremony bestows legitimacy on their commitment and on the cult of Guadalupe. It is a verification that is felt locally and transnationally.

THE JOURNEY HOME

Unlike the Queretanas' open-air mass in which the priest blesses relics purchased along the pilgrimage route and leads a relatively lengthy call and response, this Eucharist ends promptly at 6:55 A.M. Basílica personnel must ready the space for the next officiate, the next group, and the next ceremony. This logistical detail does not affect the peregrinas. Returning to Zitácuaro is now a top priority. With less than an hour before the return journey, the women have just enough time to find a bathroom and purchase food items—bottled water and *tortas*. Those few who choose to stay in Mexico City with friends or family say their good-byes and disappear into the bustling street life of *"el DF"* (the Federal District). There are two ways to get back: squeeze in with twelve other weary peregrinas in the back of a pickup or make the trip (standing room only) in the back of the enclosed maletero. Both options require further endurance, sacrifice, and patience from the exhausted women.

On the way back to Zitácuaro, it is customary to stop for a half hour on the side of the road to cheer on male Guadalupan pilgrims on bicycles traveling from different regions in Michoacán to Tepeyac. All the women got out of the small cargo truck and out of the back of Blanca's truck to clap, jump, wave, and whistle as the men cycled by. After this short break, the rest of the trip unfolded quietly. We arrived in Zitácuaro at around 3:00 P.M. There was no ceremony, no food, and no welcome committee. There were some family members present but not many. The women efficiently gathered their belongings from the maletero and began the process of assimilating the pilgrimage experience on their soil.

FOLLOWING DEVOTEES: GUADALUPAN TIES BETWEEN MICHOACÁN AND ILLINOIS

As stated early on, the Marian shrine known as Tepeyac has been a center of transmigration networks since the sixteenth century. The Zitácuaro and Querétaro all-female pilgrimage traditions are not only a product of the cult's legacy but also an extension; they form part of that narrative. Specifically, Guadalupanas' dynamic repertoire—variations of chants, songs, prayers, penitence traditions, and gesticulations—sustain transnational ties between central Mexico and the U.S. Midwest. Enacted at various sites, their devotional performances facilitate the transposition of sacred space and the expansion of the cult of Guadalupe, with all its possibilities and limitations, across national borders.

In the following chapters we return to the Chicago area to take another look at how Guadalupanos circulate practices and idioms. But this time we shall focus our attention on the neighborhood known as Rogers Park on the city's Far North Side. Rogers Park shares the same migration history as some of Chicago's more well known "Mexican ports of entry" such as the Back of the Yards, which received an influx of migration from Michoacán and other states in central/western Mexico in the early twentieth century. But it has followed a substantially different trajectory. Michoacán's presence has always been strong in Chicago, but it is no longer the dominant sending state.[18] In Rogers Park the majority of migrants hail from Michoacán and Guanajuato, but many also vividly remember Veracruz, Nuevo León, Jalisco, Guerrero, and San Luis Potosí. Together adherents built a public shrine in response to a 2001 apparition of the Virgin of Guadalupe, which united them across their regional affiliations but it did not erase all differences. The cult of Guadalupe inspired ethnoreligious community formation, but it did not prevent intracommunity tension. In this respect, this last leg of the journey complements many of the themes explored thus far, but it will also remind us of the importance of attending to Guadalupan devotion in a site-specific way in order to appreciate the intracommunity dynamics that shape sacred space production.

PART THREE

Conquering

CHAPTER 4

Devotion in the City

Building Sacred Space on Chicago's Far North Side

On July 3, 2001, a woman originally from Guanajuato, Mexico, who may or may not be accounted for by census data, stood on a street in Rogers Park—a multiethnic urban area on Chicago's Far North Side. This is the only part of the narrative that remains consistent across gender, sexuality, race, class, or citizenship status. Some neighborhood Guadalupanos believe that she was waiting on the corner of Rogers and Honere behind Pace Bus Stop #290 with her young daughter, Guadalupe, when she heard her name called. Others report she felt a tap on the shoulder, which alerted her to la Virgencita's presence. Another account suggests she merely felt compelled to look behind her toward the tree where she saw the Virgin of Guadalupe's image ingrained.

The Virgin's apparition produced more of a trace of an image than an exact replica. On the tree, approximately six feet above the sidewalk, an oval the size of my palm protrudes from the bark. It is not textured like the rest of the bark but smooth. In the center one can see an outline of the Virgin's figure. Shadows, not hard edges, add depth and delineate where the Virgin's veil meets her body. From the original photo (taken the day of her appearance), one can see hints of blue and pink, the Virgin's signature colors. There are no facial features to speak of; her hands folded palm to palm in front of her abdomen are not apparent. But it is she. Guadalupanos living in Rogers Park at the time attest to this fact. This original representation of her presence remains forever immortalized in a photo that has since circulated throughout the

FIGURE 12. Initial manifestation of shrine in Rogers Park, spring 2002.

neighborhood and beyond on commemorative T-shirts and pamphlets. The actual mark on the tree—the hard proof of her apparition—is no longer discernible. But this does not mean that the apparition scenario faded away. On the contrary, longing for the evidence created a fervent desire to produce what they could no longer see. Constructing a shrine offered a suitable solution. (See figure 12.)

Although the sacred tree was never officially embraced by St. Jerome's—the neighborhood Catholic institution—Guadalupanos/ Católicos across generations, occupations, and ethnic affiliations immediately mobilized around it. Well into the early hours of Independence Day (2001), curious neighbors pondered the significance of the apparition, while devotees, the majority of whom are Mexican nationals, vigilantly protected the representation. They did so not only with their physical presence but also with their repertoire of devotional performances, especially with the well-known and oft-used song "Las apariciones guadalupanas." Let us rehearse the song one last time.

DEs-del ci-e-lo U-na Ermosa ma-Nia-na
One beautiful morning from heaven

DEs-del ci-e-lo u-na Ermosa ma-Nia-naaa
One beautiful morning from heaven

*La Gua-da-lu-pa-na, la Gua-da-lu-pa-na, La Gua-da-lu-pa-na bajO
alTe-pe-yaac*
the Virgin of Guadalupe,
the Virgin of Guadalupe,
the Virgin of Guadalupe
descended to Tepeyac

Su-pli-cante juntaba las manos
She clasped her hands together pleadingly (repeat)

Y eran mexicanos, y eran mexicanos, y Eran mexicanos su porte y su faz
Her bearing and her face were Mexican, and they were Mexican, and
they were Mexican

Guadalupanas/os use of this and other performative acts in Rogers Park to develop a place of worship on public property, as opposed to institutionally sanctified space, offers fertile ground for further theorization of diasporic ethnoreligious community formation. As we have seen, Guadalupan devotees rely on this song in different locales across North America to solve what Karen McCarthy Brown calls a "cosmologistical problem"—"how to practice religion that is tied to place when one is no longer in that place and when travel to that place can be difficult or prohibitively expensive."[1] Most adherents in Rogers Park do not have the option to visit Guadalupan shrines located in their region of birth— Michoacán, Guanajuato, and Nuevo León, for example—much less Tepeyac in Mexico City. Immigration restrictions deny them that possibility. This reality, however, does not limit their access to the Virgin of Guadalupe. She will be anywhere they can be.

Guadalupanas/os in Rogers Park established religious space betwixt and between traditional devotion in their homelands and the individual realities of immigrant life in urban space. Initially, their performances strengthened intracommunity ties and showed outsiders that their religious expressions were at once singular and diversely connected. Even non-Spanish-speaking residents in Rogers Park—demographically a Chicago anomaly, with 10 percent Asian and 30 percent white, black, and Latino residents respectively—were able to understand the lyrics, *"y eran mexicanos, y eran mexicanos."* But that street corner in West Rogers Park, resident Guadalupanos' "axis mundi,"[2] also unveiled underlying prejudices and xenophobic attitudes within the multicultural urban landscape and elucidated fraught state-community relations, particularly with local law enforcement officials.[3] The tension engendered by the Virgin's presence in Rogers Park was a veneer beneath which deeper conflictive sentiments of race, class, nationality, and the use of public urban space were at play. In speaking of and making visible la Virgencita's presence through communal action, devotees opened a precarious space of contestation, resistance, and hope. Singing, dancing, chanting, holding nightly prayer meetings, maintaining the shrine, and organizing celebrations featuring *mojigangas* (giant dancing puppet figures) or live *conjunto* bands—"making themselves over-present"— brought intolerance and prejudice to the surface of that multiracial neighborhood.[4] As Joseph Roach aptly proposes, "Performances tend to reveal, whether the performers intend to or not, the intricately processual nature of relationships of difference."[5]

A handful of nonbelievers, for example, propose that the image spoken of by the "Spanish" in the neighborhood is not real—that it neither represents legitimate religion nor justifies the use of public space for private purposes. As one senior white woman who has lived in the neighborhood before it became "Spanish" and "black" wearily suggests, "People see what they want to see." She adds xenophobic undertones to her remarks by recalling the days when people in the neighborhood pronounced the street name "correctly": "Honer-ee" instead of "On-e-ray." Regardless of what constitutes the true story, these accounts of the apparition have become a part of social memory and the underbelly of neighborhood conflict.

A mere month after la Virgencita's apparition, the tree was burned in an "accidental fire" or a deliberate act by *"los que no tienen fe"* (those who do not have faith). The fire, which was set/occurred in the middle of the night, disfigured the Virgin's image and destroyed the humble beginnings of the sidewalk shrine. Some neighborhood residents suggest that one of the candles must have toppled over; Guadalupan devotees, however, believe that the incident was an intentional and malicious act. It depends on whom you ask. For many, it seems it is unjust that neither the Chicago police department nor the media conducted a rigorous investigation of the "accident." Most feel that the Virgin has given them the highest blessing by appearing near them; her physical presence not only sustains their faith but also brings them closer to a way of life they left behind in Mexico. The irreparable damage is a constant reminder of the emotional violence they saw in the incident. One recent immigrant from Michoacán, for example, told me that seeing the vandalized shrine troubled her deeply. "It is as if someone physically harmed my flesh-and-blood mother. I feel shame every time I walk by the shrine," she explained. Yet, as one man confided, the collective effort to sustain the shrine is proof that "they will never destroy our faith. Someone will always be present to repair the damage."

For adherents in Rogers Park, especially those who had left their natal land, this shrine became a space in which they remembered, recounted, and performed rituals taught to them by grandparents, siblings, and other cherished familiars in another time and on different soil. To better understand those exchanges and to set the stage for the last leg of our own transnational journey, we must return to Chicago's industrialization and deindustrialization histories. The emphasis here is not on the production of suburban-based sacred space (the Second Tepeyac), nor will it be on the city's traditional ports of entry (e.g., the Back of the Yards) that many scholars default to when speaking of "Mexican Chicago." We will step into the past to consider the development of one of Chicago's most complex multiethnic neighbourhoods vis-à-vis the city's changing labor force, intracity migration circuits, and postwar property politics—processes that affect devotees' day-to-day realities and their ability to produce, maintain, and legitimize sacred space in a multiethnic neighborhood. In those terms, Rogers Park's particular religious history challenges monovalent conceptions of "urban religion." As Orsi reminds us, "'Urban religion' in the singular is a convenient misnomer; the term should be understood to refer to the complex, contradictory, polysemous range of religious practices and understandings shaped by different groups of urban residents in engagement with the conditions of specific urban environments at particular moments in the environmental, political, and social histories of the cities."[6]

BUILDING CHICAGO/CLAIMING ROGERS PARK

In 1916 Carl Sandburg, a first-generation poet/journalist of Swedish immigrants, depicted the relationship among race, labor, and industrialization in Chicago with the publication of the *Chicago Poems*. In "Chicago" he wrote:

> Under the smoke, dust all over his mouth, laughing with
> white teeth,
> Under the terrible burden of destiny laughing as a young
> man laughs,
> Laughing even as an ignorant fighter laughs who has
> Never lost a battle,
> Bragging and laughing that under his wrist is the pulse.
> and under his ribs the heart of the people,
> Laughing!
> Laughing the stormy, husky, brawling laughter of
> Youth, half-naked, sweating, proud to be Hog
> Butcher, Tool Maker, Stacker of Wheat, Player with
> Railroads and Freight Handler to the Nation. [7]

Sandburg's protagonists are white ethnic males. They are Irish, Swedish, German, Luxembourgian, Russian, and Hungarian. This section of the poem reveals much about Chicago's era of industrialization. Sandburg brilliantly acknowledges, albeit with much sentimentality, the physical labor behind this process that affected not only the city of Chicago but the entire Midwest as well. But he also homogenizes the ethnic, class, and linguistic differences among these communities. This portrayal suggests that factories and plants, the places of labor, helped to create a shared sense of community among these workers. Indeed, they unified some laborers. The Haymarket Riots in 1886 attest to this. But these industrialized spaces also divided workers, especially when immigration from particular areas—specifically, southern Italy, Latin America, and the black American South—darkened the labor force. The relationship between progress and labor in Chicago has always been a racial affair. This effects of those varied migration histories were always visible but became more so after Chicago's deindustrial turn. [8]

Those first waves of German, Swedish, Irish, and Luxembourgian agricultural workers Sandburg wrote about developed the vicinity of Rogers Park, officially incorporated as a village in 1878 and annexed by the city of Chicago in 1893. [9] As these white ethnic laborers were drafted into the first and second world wars, Mexican migrants, displaced by racially biased land reform policies and economic hardship during Porfirio Díaz's extended presidency, the Mexican Revolution, and the Cristero War, made their way to the Midwest via transnational rail lines. Further, the race politics embedded in the Immigration Act of 1917, in particular, alongside ongoing agricultural development and industrial expansion, created employment opportunities for mobile, low-wage labor from Latin America. They did not settle in Rogers Park but in areas that were previously inhabited by Italian, Greek, Jewish, Irish, and Polish workers—the "Back of the Yards," the Near West Side, and South Chicago—because of their proximity to rail yards and factories. Chain-link migration patterns engendered by these processes shifted with timely deportation policies, including the systematic expulsion of Mexicans, Mexican Americans, and Central Americans during the Great Depression and after the termination of the Bracero Program (1942–64).[10] Post-1965 immigration policies offset these adjustments.[11]

Classic economic frameworks often misinterpret these processes. The neoclassical "push-pull" model, for example, elides a discussion of prejudiced circuits of power, unequal economic development, political manipulation, and military interventions particularly by the United States across Mexico and Central America in the nineteenth and twentieth centuries.[12] This model positions the migrant laborer as an opportunistic agent who voluntarily migrates to pursue enticing "pull" factors only found in the first world. As Pierrette Hondagneu-Sotelo rightly asserts, "The voluntarist assumptions embedded in this [push-pull] paradigm ignore the contingent social structural factors that shape migration, so that individual calculus occurs in a vacuum devoid of history and political economy."[13] Equally influential is the "guest worker" arrangement, which locates the laborer as a "target-earner" who does not integrate himself socially or culturally into the host country—does not assimilate, does not learn the language, and so on— and is only interested in economic advancement.[14] These frameworks, theorized from the perspective of the receiving country, fail to engage the complex social and cultural components of labor and economy— how many times this guest laborer leaves and returns, the different forms of social and economic capital he accumulates and distributes with each journey. Further, this viewpoint does not account for the worker's choice to settle permanently in the host nation or to sponsor, formally or informally, family members. Extensive anthropological and sociological scholarship has shown that kinship networks established in the early twentieth century now sustain and encourage contemporary transmigration circuits from Latin America and across the globe.

As Douglas Massey suggests, migration processes cannot be "turned on and off like a faucet."[15]

ROGERS PARK: CHICAGO ANOMALY

Unlike classic "port of entry" neighborhoods, Rogers Park did not undergo significant demographic changes until after deindustrialization, when urban restructuring processes shifted multiethnic workforces throughout the city. Strategic urban renewal projects such as the construction of the Eisenhower Expressway and the development of the University of Illinois campus, which forced nine thousand residents of the Near West Side to relocate between 1960 and 1970,[16] shifted laborers across the city and into the suburbs. Moreover, the politics behind city housing, especially the age and declining value of housing stock, shaped intracity migration circuits, and in the anomalous cases of Albany Park and Rogers Park diversified city space. [17]

A building boom in the 1920s covered most of Rogers Park, for example, with small businesses, apartment buildings, and houses, and additional construction after World War II filled remaining empty spaces and lots.[18] Buildings from the former period now constitute what in 1964 the Chicago Real Estate Board called "gray areas"—"older and less-well-maintained housing [that] will become increasingly difficult to market to rising-income families. As a result, the housing in many of these so-called 'gray areas' will gradually shift to the market for either complete redevelopment or occupancy by lower-income groups, particularly nonwhites."[19] Rogers Park experienced the regenerative effects of these processes most powerfully in the 1980s when subsidized housing tenants in "gray area" buildings peaked and renters registered at 84 percent, the highest among renters in the city.[20]

These intracity political and economic factors, which contextualize the presence of undocumented Mexican migrants living on Chicago's Far North Side, aid our understanding of actions and reactions to a culturally specific happening. By placing the intangible occurrence and the ethnic makeup of the neighborhood in dialogue, however, I am not suggesting that only Mexican or Spanish-speaking residents inherently understand or know the cult of Our Lady of Guadalupe. Devotional acts at the Second Tepeyac of North America instantiate that point. Many people, regardless of ethnicity, sexual preference, class, or citizenship status, could have recognized her iconography, could have seen her image on that tree.

Historically, in fact, adherents from various denominations have circulated doctrine as well as popular practices and reworked them on the ground for local site-specific struggles in that neighborhood. In doing so, residents created an environment where recognition was often necessary to determine the who, the what, and the why of a certain city block. According to the Rogers Park/West Ridge Historical Society's records, the vicinity was always religiously diverse. The English Evangelical Church, St. Jerome's Church, Loyola Church, Temple Mizpah (a Reform synagogue), and the Congregation B'nai Zion (a conservative synagogue established in 1910), among other religious centers, continue to serve the area.[21] What I am proposing is that in order for the cult to flourish—for ideas to be practiced, sacred space constructed and maintained, rituals celebrated, time and energy invested—took a particular form of mobilization that entails a specific religious history that was previously unobserved outside of Chicago's traditional Mexican neighborhoods such as Pilsen and Little Village. Further, continuing to provide the historical and sociopolitical context of the apparition shows its position as a nexus of local and international networks. Not unlike its counterparts in Des Plaines and Mexico City. The presence of la Virgencita in Rogers Park is a result of the transnational movement of people, ideas, performances, capital, and labor—a space where the circulation of religious idioms and practices collapse some boundaries and reinforce others. Along these lines, Manuel A. Vásquez suggests:

> In the time-space compression brought by the current episode of globalization, the Third World implodes into the first and the core exhibits substantial "peripheralization." The result of these transformations is a "proliferation of border zones," zones of cross-fertilization and struggle that require a different kind cognitive mapping than that provided by modernization, dependency theory, or even Wallerstein's world-system approach. . . . [R]eligion plays a major role in the emerging border zones, marking difference and hybridity.[22]

Rogers Park is one such zone of cross-fertilization.

Guadalupan devotion in Rogers Park will also trouble conceptions of American pluralism.[23]

> The "pluralism" model of American urban culture seems to imagine ongoing exchanges among people of different cultures who find themselves living alongside each other in urban settings. My [Orsi's] experience and

understanding suggests otherwise: proximity more often heightens tension, particularly in the context of late-capitalist ideas of a zero-sum economic and social reality.[24]

I would add that the unconventional, supernatural, and divine characteristics of the occurrence in Rogers Park, alongside the class- and race-based politics informing the production of sacred space, further troubles any attempt to read negotiations and entanglements between communities as exchanges based on equal footing and mutual respect.

Public documents both endorse and challenge this perspective. In 1967, as reported by the *Chicago Tribune*, for example, residents witnessed a racial shift in the religious needs of the community: "One hundred Rogers Park religious and community leaders publicly welcomed Negroes into the community. Within the next few months, black families moved into the area without incident, opening the door for peaceful integration."[25] In the 1980s the neighborhood again showed signs of increasing diversification. Ethnic groups, including Assyrians, Indians, Koreans, Haitians, Mexicans, Jamaicans, and Belizeans, changed the religious needs of the neighborhood.[26] At that time Rogers Park had 60,231 residents—around 70 percent white and around 10 percent each black, Latino, and Asian.[27] Many of the Jewish, German, and Irish inhabitants migrated west or to the suburbs during this period. In the words of one resident:

> When we moved here in 1976, the neighborhood was filled with big houses that were primarily owned by German and Irish-Catholic families with lots of kids. However, within a few years, people began to move away as their children grew up. The houses were too big for them, and the neighborhood seemed less safe. In the 1980s, there was an increase in subsidized housing and a number of halfway houses opened nearby. Some neighborhood residents panicked and left.[28]

Ironically, many Jewish residents had moved to Rogers Park from "racially changing" Lawndale in the 1950s.

In 2004 the number of residents and the neighborhood's diversity index, 30 percent white, black, and Latino, remained stable but gentrification processes—commercial investment, the remodeling of multiunit apartment buildings, and condominium projects—were changing the neighborhood. A few blocks north of the apparition site where Clark Street divides East and West Rogers Park, for example, a shopping center accommodating a Bally's fitness club, a Jewel Osco supermarket, and a Marshall's department store cast a Scumpeterian gaze over the makeshift altar. Loyola University, located on the neighborhood's south-eastern end, attracts chain restaurants and new commerce, but a range of markdown variety and clothing shops, exploitative check-cashing/money transfer businesses, family-owned food markets, and a string of West African, Jamaican, Belizean, Peruvian, Mexican, and Indian restaurants continue to dominate the area.

In terms of an overarching social-political identity, Rogers Park has seen more independent politicians than any other Chicago neighborhood. For example, David Orr, now state of Illinois Cook County Clerk, previously Rogers Park's independent councilman during the 1980s, and Alderman Joe Moore mark the neighborhood's semi-independence from the Daley machine.[29] Because of this, some residents herald it as a progressive neighborhood. Katy Hogan, co-owner of the Heartland Café, a local restaurant established in the 1960s, said, "The neighborhood has aged well. I think that the significant thing has been the success of independent politics in 1979.... I agree with the idea of Section 8 housing. It brings people together who are willing to be together. This neighborhood is moving towards becoming the paradise I hope to live in, where everybody lives together and where we overcome barriers."[30] Rogers Park, however, is far from being a multicultural utopia. It remains vulnerable to racial tension, sociopolitical hierarchies, and uneven economic development. La Virgen de Guadalupe's apparition and ensuing public devotional performances have revealed these deeper conflicts.

SUMMER 2001: ACTIONS AND REACTIONS TO THE INEFFABLE

Concentric support circles formed around la Virgen de Guadalupe immediately following her apparition in July 2001, and especially after the tree was set/caught on fire. There was a feeling of collective ownership of the shrine—a sense of religious and patriotic communitas.[31] The *Chicago Tribune* interviewed "Latino Catholics" who had flocked to the shrine. "It's a miracle," commentators claimed, "we think things will change here. No more gangs. No more shootings." Luis Hurtado, forty, pointed to the Virgin's image on the knot of the tree and said, "That's my mother."[32] The media—newspaper, television, radio—did not continue coverage of the shrine's evolution after the apparition, despite the fact that the ineffable significantly altered the social fabric of that community.

For weeks, hundreds of curious spectators and devotees from across the city flocked to the tree. Spectators from all over the city plus local actors on their daily rounds witnessed and contributed to shrine activity well beyond that initial summer. In fall 2002, for example, two women of Polish origin commented one afternoon that the dark-skinned statuette of the Virgin sitting atop one of the glass cases reminded them of the Black Madonna of Częstochowa. They asked, "Is she the Virgin Mary?" "She is an incarnation," I replied. "She is beautiful," the older woman commented as she gently ran her fingers along the hem of the Virgin's dress. Because the apparition occurred along Pace Bus Stop #290 en route to Des Plaines, even suburb-bound commuters were privy to the slightest modifications.

The only actors to explicitly distance themselves from the apparition were those affiliated with the neighborhood Catholic church. Many Guadalupanas/os with whom I spoke suggested that local officials did not want parishioners to practice noninstitutional Catholicism. Many considered the devotional practices sustaining the shrine incommensurate with doctrine based on the fact that the Catholic Church rarely sanctions apparitions. Basílica officials in Mexico City, for example, articulate nine points on which the church bases its authorization. Most important, an ordained official must preside over a formal investigation. If an apparition does not fully meet all of the criteria, the institution will not recognize it. Esequiel Sánchez, director of the Hispanic Ministry of Chicago, echoed his Mexican colleagues in his estimation of the apparition in Rogers Park. The *Chicago Tribune* reported that "he [Sánchez] and the Roman Catholic Church are skeptical of such visions and are in no rush to declare an apparition authentic. . . . Such a sighting is judged by six guidelines, including the psychological health of the person who witnessed it."[33] This is not to suggest that because the establishment does not sanction an occurrence it becomes less real. Institutional parameters do not bound principles or practice. Actions that follow such happenings, often referred to as popular devotion, may not adhere to set guidelines, but they augment not only the sanctity of the cult but also its cultural and sociopolitical currency.

I spoke with several neighborhood residents who witnessed this initial period. One core group devotee explained, "Everyone brought candles, flowers, rosaries, photos, and someone kept watch at all times." The sentiment underlying these informal discussions was that they wanted first to protect the sacred tree and second to claim the physical space for her. In turn, the shrine became a tangible manifestation of their loyalty, faith, and, above all, thankfulness to the Virgin for she had appeared in Rogers Park for them. Although the cult of Guadalupe in many ways espouses the idea of Mexican nationhood, emphasizing this point did not become a priority until after a core group of devotees had emerged from the community. I also spoke with non-Mexican/non-Guadalupan neighbors. One woman, who lives half a block from the tree, felt the sustained activity surrounding the shrine was bothersome and irritating: "One could hear the women [Guadalupanas] singing on the corner at four o'clock in the morning, every morning. They wouldn't let anyone sleep!"

The ownership/appropriation of forty square feet of sidewalk space by a specific ethnic group for particular socioreligious reasons divided this multicultural neighborhood into several factions. These factions were not static or fixed; membership changed according to the context or situation. The first group consisted of city institutions and public actors: the Chicago Police Department (specifically, the Chicago Alternative Policing Strategy, or CAPS, organization), the alderman's office, and the media. Individuals representing these entities witnessed the events from afar and only became involved at their convenience.

The second group, the largest, contained all the residents who lived within a three-block radius of the tree. They were all witnesses, willing and unwilling, because of their geographic location. We may divide these residents into four groups. First, there were those non-Guadalupan residents, both Latino and non-Latino, who chose not to involve themselves in the conflict. This is not to say that they did not have an opinion about the phenomenon, or that the situation did not affect them, but they did not take an active role in the proceedings. Another group consisted of Guadalupan devotees who participated in special rituals but did not support the informal organization of sacred space. One woman in particular, who was an active member of the neighborhood's Catholic church, criticized the ways the core devotee group organized public rituals. On many occasions she called for devotees to pray the rosary instead of chit-chatting/gossiping with one another over coffee and sweet bread. The most antagonistic characters made up the third intraneighborhood faction—non-Guadalupan, non-Latino residents who fought public devotional rituals by calling the police or by blaring music.

The last and most active party, a core group of Guadalupan devotees consisting of six men and two women, reconstructed the fire-damaged shrine. Using a Chicago Transit Authority (CTA) bus stop directly in front of the tree as a mounting point, they covered the eight-by-five-foot area with a white tarp to protect the tree. One devotee, who works in the landscaping industry, acquired this covering from his workplace. Another Guadalupano obtained the supporting materials—metal poles and fixtures—to construct the protective structure. Devotees used the walls of the bus stop to post messages for pedestrians about upcoming fund-raising events and community planning meetings. Another core member paid $50 a month to obtain access to electricity from two antagonistic actors who owned the property directly behind the tree. These two women, life partners, informed the core group's perception of gender and sexuality. Because this couple did not particularly embrace their devotional practices, many Guadalupanos/as, when referring to them and their informal economic transactions, prefaced their remarks with a joke or a derogatory comment about their sexual preference. Nevertheless, they always acknowledged that the extension cords running from their house to the shrine provided a necessary light source for devotees who frequented the place of worship after dark. This detail also added another element of security to the shrine and to that street corner.

After building this physical structure and organizing the lighting scheme, the group placed two handcrafted cases built of wood and glass near the tree. These cabinets protected several images of la Virgen de Guadalupe and other saints, as well as devotees' prayers scribbled on scraps of paper, statuettes of the Virgin, braids of hair, and photos of loved ones—alive and deceased, from Chicago and far away.[34] Several members of this burgeoning ethnoreligious community donated chairs, small tables, and brooms to make the space hospitable. But more important, they maintained the appearance of the shrine with painstaking attention to detail.

BACKSTAGE LOGISTICS OF SACRED SPACE PRODUCTION

One of the community's collective hopes was to build an archway across Rogers Street to replicate the archway on Twenty-Sixth Street in Little Village, recognized across Chicago as a quintessential Mexican neighborhood. They envisioned this structure as a type of portico, as a marker of la Virgencita's presence on the North Side of the city, and as an excellent way to signify Rogers Park as a Mexican locality despite the fact that it does not come close to sharing Little Village's demographic and historical realities. They often discussed hypothetical design strategies for the archway. They would estimate the height and width of the structure, what materials to use, color schemes, and different symbols. Everyone was well aware that public expression of their collective religious and cultural identity would require a considerable amount of money, community mobilization, and political support, in particular, from alderman Joe Moore. Resident Guadalupanas/os, however, had little or no contact with the elected official; a bilingual secretary mediated all their political relationships. Moore would sometimes have a cameo role at public celebrations, the block parties commemorating the Virgin's appearance, for example, but he never engaged the primarily Spanish-speaking crowd. Because of this touch-and-go relationship, swaying Moore and other key municipal officials was never very likely.

Moreover, as *indocumentados,* their resources are limited—many work for subminimum wages, and only then, fairly recently, with the acceptance of the *matrícula* (Mexican identification cards), have these laborers been able to use banks. Most affiliates rely on informal economic networks to survive and to send remittances to their families and communities in Mexico. Statistically, Mexico benefits the most from these transactions. In 2003 remittances contributed $14.5 billion to the Mexican economy, and this figure rose 20 percent in 2004 to total over $17 billion. This, of course, is the official estimate. Analysts projected that migrant laborers would send $30 billion to family and communities across Latin America in 2005.

Indeed, many shrine-related activities blurred the boundaries between the formal and informal economies.[35] One evening after a prayer meeting, for example, a devotee offered to provide me with a green card at a price of $50 courtesy of a local vendor. When I told him that I have U.S. citizenship, he offered me a cash-payment job as truck dispatcher with a friend who needed a bilingual employee. This is just one example of the ways in which devotional labor can produce regenerative effects, especially for mobile, disenfranchised communities.

Some devotees with whom I worked have lived in that neighborhood for more than five years, while others had been residents for only a few months. And many of them, out of necessity, seek out alternative or informal ways to survive socially and economically. "The condition of ascriptive low-wage labor," John Betancur and his colleagues suggest, "has prevented Latinos [in the Chicago area] from developing the human capital and the political and economic power necessary for adapting to or benefiting from changes in labor demand."[36] Many newly arrived and established immigrants, as well as citizens, used that sacred space to assemble, network, mobilize, share coping tactics, and overcome totalizing notions of illegal identity. In Rogers Park adherents acquired tips on how to access affordable childcare and housing, employment, medical care, legal advice, translation services, as well as immigration and tax information; what neighborhoods to avoid; the state of law enforcement and police "interventions." They did so not with monetary capital but with their embodied devotional labor—how often and in what ways a devotee would lead prayer for the community, how frequently one would sweep the sidewalk in front of the shrine, wash the silk roses, replace the altar's candles, or how efficiently one could gather the tools and materials to repair the shrine's canopy and wooden cases. Devotees used embodied performance to build their reputations as well as trust within the community. If you were in good standing with la Virgen de Guadalupe, you were in good standing with your fellow devotees you acquired devotional capital and thus could reap the material benefits of your wide and intricate network of community members.

Core group members cultivated this aspect of sacred space production after organizational meetings and at various local "offices"—a neighborhood Dunkin Donuts and a local Chinese Buffet. Otherwise, most meetings occurred after the nightly rosary service. Sometimes Araceli—the woman who saw the apparition—and her husband, a green card–holding resident who works as a personal driver for Loop businessmen and their associates in the suburbs, would host meetings in their garage. That private space was often filled with food and other dry goods. That they offered everyone two or three jugs of orange juice from the buy-in-bulk emporium Costco, considered a luxury to many, alerted core group members to their financial stability. Moreover, they leased not an apartment but a house; one filled with furniture, appliances, and hundreds of hand-carved wooden images of the Virgin. Araceli, inspired by her vision on July 3, 2001, spends those days replicating the representation she saw on the tree.

Discussion at these meetings often involved the group's primary goal—buying the property directly behind the sacred tree, which was then valued at around $360,000 (2002). Core group members raised money at nightly prayer services, dances, and block parties—where they would sell food, beverages, T-shirts, and religious items. Although the house was not officially on the market, an English-speaking devotee spoke with the female owners about a possible purchase. He reported to us during a garage meeting that the women set the price of the house at $300,000 and promised they would give the group preference. Another devotee immediately suggested the women were trying to take advantage of us. He found, through independent research, that appraisers put the value of the house between $240,000 and $250,000. "How are we to explain a $60,000 difference to the rest of the community?" he questioned. These economic realities as well as external factors such as ongoing gentrification contributed to intragroup tension.

The next year (2003), in particular, made devotees anxious. Whispers and rumors circulated that the shrine was ruining the appearance of the neighborhood and its capacity for attracting businesses that would "revitalize" the area as well as the aforementioned construction of a Bally's Fitness Club and a Marshall's department store less than four blocks away. This chain of events lowered the community's morale but did not deter their community-building efforts.

MAINTAINING SACRED SPACE/OVERCOMING OBSTACLES

Despite, or perhaps because of, their less than desirable day-to-day prospects, neighborhood Guadalupanas/os gathered nightly at eight o'clock to pray the rosary at the shrine. These rituals occurred on and off for two and a half years (August 2001–November 2004). Multilingual conversations simultaneously spoken in Spanish, English, and even French Creole were common. Mexican nationals accounted for the majority of participants. Before prayer service, female devotees would light all the candles, sweep the sidewalk, dust the display cases, and replace flower water. Devotees kept one rosary in the smaller of the cases. Once at least ten devotees arrived, the volunteer prayer leader for that evening would slide the glass up and collect the sacred string of beads. We would begin and end the rite by greeting and then offering "peace" (a handshake or a hug) to everyone who had gathered—men, women, and children. Most evenings we would disband at nine o'clock, but on a few occasions, gang violence, signaled by the sounds of people rifting through trashcans and breaking glass bottles, forced us to abandon the shrine earlier.

These weeknight gatherings thus functioned simultaneously as time and space where neighbors could talk about many subjects: community issues, their children, the status of their documentation, their jobs, unemployment, gang violence, joke and share memories of their families in Mexico, or offer counsel. One Guadalupano, originally from the Mexican state of Nuevo León, arrived at a prayer meeting totally inebriated and determined to repent for his infidelity. Crying hysterically and apologizing profusely to his wife, who was not present, and to the Virgin, he advised a fellow devotee to take over his *helados* (ice cream) cart before repeatedly running into oncoming traffic. A couple of men physically restrained but also attempted to comfort him with what seemed like empty justifications. After about twenty minutes of halfhearted attempts to take his life he sat down near the altar, burying his head in his hands. None of the female devotees uttered an insult or a consolation.

This scene was not a common occurrence. Devotees mostly used postprayer time to discuss each individual's sociopolitical or economic woes. Traveling into the city, that is, downtown, was often a topic of discussion. One woman, a friend of a core group member who was not an active participant at the shrine, had to appear in court at the federal plaza, located in downtown Chicago. She was summoned to clear up debt she owed to the hospital after the birth of her daughter. Although a legal resident and insured, she was liable for the entire balance because birth-related costs, according to her insurance company, were not included in her plan. A Spanish speaker and fearful of her precarious position as a recently minted resident, she found it extremely daunting to use public transportation, find the right building, talk to lawyers, and appear before a judge. At that meeting we talked about her situation and concluded that two core group members should accompany her on the journey to her destination inside the Loop. These interactions only strengthened the shrine's currency and each Guadalupanas/os' devotional capital.

Given the financial, legal, and institutional obstacles devotees faced on a day-to-day basis, core group members had to search for creative or unorthodox ways to garner community support and resources. In many ways, their organizational tactics resembled those of the cofradías of the early colonial period in Mexico. But as in most organizations and networks, participants scrutinized each other's efforts and decisions. During an intense meeting in March 2003, for example, one devotee commented that some neighbors inquired about the money collected during fund-raisers. "How much do we have saved?" "Who is keeping track of the money?" "Is more than one person looking at the books?" She said people suspected they were *"chingando el dinero,"* or, politely put, swindling the money. The devotee who kept the money in a private bank account assured her that all the money was there. "At this point," he said, "after the block party and monthly expenses, we have about $7,200." He was in charge of saving the money because he is a legal resident and speaks English. These factors made it possible for him to maneuver easily through institutional regulations and requirements. Further, it was his wife who first saw the apparition. He never claimed to be the leader of the group but always exercised a certain authority because of that fact. This last detail created deep intragroup tensions and eventually led to the shrine's collapse. As that point makes clear, I am not promoting an idealized analysis that attributes the shrine's physical demise solely to external/non-Guadalupan forces. Those factors definitely played a role, but conflictive internal dynamics also prevented the development of a long-term sacred space. But before anatomizing the dismantling of the shrine, let us consider how devotees legitimized this sacred space with public celebrations—time and space where Guadalupanos and non-Guadalupanos interacted.

COMMEMORATIVE BLOCK PARTY: ACQUIRING LEGITIMACY WITH FRIENDS AND FOES

Physical devotional labor, especially before block parties, the main commemorative event that often attracted devotees living beyond Rogers Park's borders, imbued the space with a sense of legitimacy. Adherents were self-reflexive; they noted the time and labor each person contributed to the altar. Year-round, it was not common for neighborhood devotees to gather on Saturday or Sunday. Instead, many maintained their institutional ties by attending church services; some would even travel to the Second Tepeyac in Des Plaines on special cultural holidays such as Día de la Raza or Christian feast days. It was only in preparation for special events or holidays that we met over the weekend. We would wash all of the silk roses, replace old candles, sweep and scrub to ensure the shrine would make an impression on believers and nonbelievers alike. Anniversary block parties, in that respect, modified how the sacred space performed; the thought of different eyes, different kinds of spectators, challenged the core group to create an environment that was beyond reproach.

This was certainly a key objective when preparing for the first anniversary of the Virgin's apparition. At 5:45 A.M. on July 4, 2002, every restaurant—Mexican, Belizean, Jamaican, and Chinese—every food market, money exchange and dollar store, along Clark Street in Rogers Park was dormant. Only the *panaderías* (bakeries) bustled. I peeked into the panadería Ayutla and saw a woman and a man arranging the freshly baked *pan dulce* (sweet bread) in the wall-length glass cases. I knew that a devotee had ordered sweet bread for the celebration from this bakery.

As I walked north along Clark Street, I thought about all the planning that went into this commemorative celebration. In addition to preparing the shrine, the most influential devotee had gotten permission from the city to barricade the street and a band permit a month before the festivities. Much to everyone's surprise, the city donated an inflatable jumping dragon for the kids and agreed to set up a stage for the musicians. The city later retracted their offer to set up a sound stage, explaining they could not pay laborers holiday overtime.

As I turned the corner on Rogers Street, my stomach lurched, as it sometimes did when I approached the tree. There were approximately twenty-five people gathered. Some devotees leaned against the park fence across the street; others sat solemnly on the chairs surrounding the shrine. Everyone seemed to be waiting for someone to take charge. The mariachi players were already fifteen minutes late to start the celebration, so one of the core devotees got on his cell phone. The foggy dawn light framed his chubby body as he paced up and down the sidewalk waving his thick hands for effect. Within minutes, eight mariachi musicians tumbled out of a van. The devotee led them proudly toward the shrine, the sun now at his back. The light gave the makeshift parade a peculiar glow as they walked toward the tree playing "Las mañanitas." The piercing sound of the horns and violins paired with the deep voices of the singers invigorated the crowd, which at this point had grown to 150 spectators. The band, which charges $400 an hour, played for an hour and a half. Many pedestrians, in cars and on foot, stopped or slowed to witness this early morning celebration. Their presence reminded me of one woman's admonition during a devotee meeting: "It doesn't matter what people think. They will always find something wrong if they are looking for it."

The same man who had summoned the mariachis produced another surprise for the crowd. He walked toward the makeshift altar carrying a hand-sewn silk estandarte, which he had commissioned from a contact in Mexico. It featured a portrait of the Virgin similar to the original 1531 image displayed in Mexico City: rays of light extending from her posed body, hands folded, and a solemn but caring face gazing downward. The community received the gift with thunderous applause. As the musicians played on, the same devotee led a small but impressive procession toward the shrine. Two giant female *mojigangas* (puppets)— *la morena* and *la güera*—mesmerized the crowd. A neighborhood devotee constructed these dolls *"en el estilo de Guanajuato"* (using the methods of doll makers in Guanajuato). These dolls upstaged the mariachi band and perhaps even la Virgencita, attracting great attention from devotees and pedestrians alike as they kissed and danced.

Following the spectacle, a female community member translated the formal blessing from Father Dominic—the Vietnamese pastor of St. Henry's Church. He urged people to attend his parish because the church accepted all God's children: "We come from Vietnam, from Mexico, Jesus and the Virgin Mary loves us very much." After he presided over the rosary, most of the crowd dispersed, but others stayed to talk and enjoy more sweet bread and coffee. Meanwhile, core members prepared for the afternoon festivities by tracking down the owners of all the parked cars in the area. We swept the street, rigged the sound system for the bands, and set up food and beverage tables. Once we accomplished these tasks, the women went off to their houses to make *flautas, tortas de jamón, tostadas de puerco, horchata,* and lemonade while the men stayed outdoors to prepare the barbecue grills for the *carne asada.*

I helped Margarita, a core group member, make the flautas in a multiunit building near the shrine where she, her husband, her brother, and her three children share a spotless two-room apartment. We talked about our families while she fried the tortillas and I chopped onions. I told her that I am the eldest of two brothers and one sister and that I also have one half brother, one half sister, and other siblings I have never met. "My father is disgraceful," I explained. She offered that she had come to the United States from Michoacán more than ten years ago because Mexico had little to offer her. But her home country was good, she added, because "you will not be evicted if you do not pay your rent. Here they will evict you." She lamented the fact that she had not seen her family since she left, and she especially missed her older sister in Mexico (whom I had the opportunity to meet two years later while living in Mexico City). She also confided that her brother, who recently migrated from Michoacán, walked for days across the arid regions of the Sonora-Arizona border. We then began to talk about the "costs of opportunity" but then realized that we were very late taking the food down.

Core members unanimously put me in charge of selling tickets and taking care of the money (because "they did not trust each other"). We sold the flautas and the tortas for $2 and the tacos de carne asada, tostadas, horchata, and lemonade for $1. In addition, we sold commemorative T-shirts with the original photo of la Virgen de Guadalupe's pre-fire image on the tree. Throughout the course of the day, around five hundred people gathered to eat, network, and dance. The only incident that put a damper on the festival occurred when an older white neighbor called the police to complain about the noise level. The only other bilingual core member was not present when the officers arrived at 3:30 P.M., so the group urged me to speak with them in his place. The lead police officer suggested we turn down the volume or face penalties. He softened the warning by admitting that he did not want any trouble and that he would be at the party if he were not on duty.[37] We lowered the volume slightly, just enough to satisfy them for the moment. They did not give us a citation, but their presence did intimidate the crowd. Later, other white residents reprimanded the woman who had initially phoned the police. "Why can't you just enjoy the party? It's the Fourth of July!" I heard them say.

JULY 4, 2003: THE SECOND (AND FINAL) ANNIVERSARY BLOCK PARTY

Devotees celebrated la Virgencita's second year in Rogers Park with many of the same rituals—the morning serenade by the mariachi band, the blessing from Father Dominic, prayer, food, dancing, and music. Yet the festivities were different because the sacred space had undergone several transformations. In April 2003 the wind had blown off the shrine's protective canopy. Neighborhood Guadalupanos ineffectually reattached and patched up the tarp with scrap pieces of material they took from their jobs, but there was little they could do at this point except to replace the covering altogether. They urged the core member who kept the shrine's funds to remedy the situation, but he never cooperated. This, in turn, increased distrust and suspicion among devotees in the neighborhood. The situation deteriorated in May when the CTA removed the waiting area structure supporting the shrine. I phoned numerous times to inquire. A representative explained that the CTA was in the process of replacing the structures throughout the city with modern stops inspired by the Parisian public transportation system. Although the corner of Rogers and Honere still functioned as a bus stop, the transit authority never replaced the physical structure. This left the sacred space vulnerable to vandalism and weather damage and ultimately led to a chain of events that affected the larger Guadalupan community's perceptions of the core group's financial decisions.

These events, however, did not deter devotees from commemorating the Virgin's apparition that year. An increase in devotional activities differentiated the way that core group members planned the second anniversary party. At 9:00 A.M., the mariachi group Tenochtitlán serenaded

FIGURE 13. *Matechine* dancers, summer 2003.

la Virgencita. Around midday, a second group, mariachi Durango, performed in front of hundreds of spectators, including many nondevotee attendees who had positioned themselves across the street at Pottawatomie Park. These same spectators witnessed the troupe of *matechine* dancers that followed the musicians (figures 13 and 14).[38] Recalling and deploying Mexico's indigenous past through embodied devotional performance made the production of sacred space in Rogers Park even more dangerous; the "indigenous" costumes, choreographed dance moves, drumbeats, feathered headdresses, and use of copal (incense) further exoticized the shrine. For Mexicanas/os in the crowd, this less than authentic but familiar performance helped them claim and shape safe space away from home. For others, perceptions of the spectacle ranged from charming to baffling to enigmatic. This ethnoreligious community was no longer just a group of people celebrating their spirituality. The incorporation of indigenous ritual clearly moved the celebration out of the realm of religion and into the arena of nationalist politics. This shift perhaps inspired the "aural warfare" between believers and nonbelievers that all but spoiled the celebration that year.

Many anticipated that there could be complaints during this block party commemorating the second anniversary of la Virgen de Guadalupe's apparition in Rogers Park.[39] Hundreds of people were planning

FIGURE 14. Watching the dancers/watching the altar, summer 2003.

to appropriate not only public space but also Independence Day to honor Mexico's patron saint. But we never expected the aural warfare that was to unfold that day. Two white women, disparagingly referred to as *"las lesbianas"* by some neighborhood Guadalupanos, were the most vociferous in their resistance to the celebration. These were not the same women who dealt with Guadalupanos' need for electricity. Core members asked me to have a word with the couple when they complained that the street band's music was shaking the walls of their house, preventing them from working on their taxes, and compromising their eighty-five-year-old mother's health.

The women invited me into their two-story home as soon as they realized that I spoke English. I sensed they took for granted that I would understand their position. I did. That is, until one of them commented, "Just because there are more of them [Mexicans] than there are of us does not mean that they can take over the neighborhood. We have to fight fire with fire." They then proceeded to set up four Peavey amplifiers in each of the windows to drown out the conjunto band. Apparently, these two women were in a folk/rock band, so they had all this equipment in their living room. They blasted what I recognized as heavy metal and placed a microphone in front of one of the speakers to create deafening feedback.

I left shocked by their pettiness but soon returned. I needed to make a point: "If your argument was that the noise level harmed your mother's health, why are you increasing her discomfort by blasting the music so loudly?" They answered that their mother was fine now because they had put airplane headphones on her, blocking out all the noise. I looked over and saw the elderly woman sitting bewildered and silent on a couch, her hands clasped together on her lap, and her ears protected by a plush, black contraption. They informed me they "would not be taken advantage of." I answered quickly, and tersely, that this event was not a personal attack against them. But determined to keep relations diplomatic, I changed my tone and told them that we would not be able to resolve the problem today. I suggested we should organize a meeting where all the residents could talk. They ignored my comment and said they were going to sue. "Sue whom? If you sue anyone it will be the city of Chicago. They are the ones that authorized the block party," I countered. "We know people," one of them replied, "important people who can make things happen." "They should have notified us that they were going to have this party," her partner added. "They put up flyers," I said. "Only in Spanish," they responded. "No, they distributed flyers in Spanish and in English." "We didn't get one," one of them said, ending our discussion. At this point, she walked to the front door, stepped outside, and started dancing on her stoop.

Burlándose (making fun) of the spectators, she waved her arms fluidly up and down and took giant wobbly steps toward devotees gathered on the sidewalk. Making her way to the oil-stained dance floor on the far end of the street, she seemed to be celebrating the fact that the unintelligible soundscape she and her partner had created was louder than the band's music. As I watched from the stoop of her house, an older male devotee approached her. Smiling, he stood in front of her, took her in his arms, and began to dance conjunto style as the crowd laughed and cheered at the paradoxical sight. She followed his lead at first but soon became flustered and quickly boogied her way back to the house.

Both groups continued to blast music until two police officers arrived around 3:00 P.M. As it was July 4 and they had to attend to important calls, they listened halfheartedly to us as we argued our respective points. Like the year before, we managed to turn down the volume enough to appease them. With pained expressions, the women, along with their elderly mother, left their house. Relieved, core devotees offered each of the officers a heaping plate of tacos of fire-grilled meat on corn tortillas,

FIGURE 15. Newly vandalized shrine, spring 2004.

with extra pico de gallo—diced tomato, onions, and jalapeño pepper soaked in lime and salt—and a soda pop, which they quickly accepted. The negotiating power of food is undeniable.

The anxiety surrounding this cultural performance remained; it was tangible, especially during such public rituals when diverse migrant and constituent groups from across the city witnessed both the passionate actions and reactions that gave meaning and life to the sidewalk shrine.[40] The aftermath of such events took many forms—increased tension among core group members, less cooperation within the larger community, and more vandalism. (See figure 15.)

OTHER POINTS OF CONFLICT: DEVOTIONAL PERFORMANCES AND POLICING STRATEGIES

Circuits of municipal power affected Guadalupanas/os collective efforts to establish sacred space in this urban landscape. Because devotional mobilization—nightly prayer meetings, block parties, and special holiday celebrations—provided officers with a potential source of information about undocumented life, the Chicago Police Department and the CAPS program monitored community activities closely.

In 1993 the city of Chicago created CAPS in response to, among other issues, immigration: "The influx of immigrants and the corresponding changes in the racial and ethnic composition of the Nation's population have placed significant demands on the infrastructure of the Nation's public service sector, particularly the criminal justice system."[41] CAPS officers were then trained to accommodate the on-the-ground needs of community residents; they learned "problem-solving techniques and models" and implemented them in Chicago's 279 beats.[42] According to a report issued by the U.S. Department of Justice and Northwestern University, beat meetings "serve as a forum for exchanging information and prioritizing and analyzing local problems."[43] I found this sweeping statement problematic in light of my experiences with CAPS officers and Mexican nationals in Rogers Park.

During the first meeting we attended in the twenty-fourth district, police officials used different methods from those described in the Department of Justice research report. Although the tree is located in the twenty-third district, core group members attended this meeting because CAPS officers wanted to discuss the shrine and gang activity. The head CAPS official, whose mother lives near the shrine, informed us that the force was having many problems with the gangs, specifically, the Latin Kings, "who use the shrine to drink and smoke." To remedy the situation, he wanted us to be in constant communication with CAPS officers—inform them where gang members congregate, where they live, who they know, and so on. If not, he cautioned, CAPS would consider cutting down and relocating the tree to a proper place, St. Jerome's Church, for instance. His blatant threat troubled many devotees because these "gang members" could well be their sons, brothers, friends, and nephews.

After this initial gathering we agreed to meet the following week in the twenty-third district at Pottawatomie Park. During the week, the police department unilaterally transformed the scheduled meeting into a protest march; CAPS officials invited devotees to participate in a *"marcha en contra* [sic] *las gangas"* (protest march against the gangs). They distributed flyers with the following message: *"Juntese con su comunidad. Disfrute de la solidaridad hispana. Conozca a sus vecinos. Demuestre que NOSOTROS somos los dueños del parque"* (Join together and enjoy solidarity with your Hispanic community. Know your neighbors. Demonstrate that WE are the owners of the park). Police officers waited by their vehicles in the Pottawatomie parking lot, but no one came.

Two core devotee members and I met with CAPS officials in the park house an hour after the scheduled protest. Angered and humiliated, the officers now claimed that the shrine definitely "increased neighborhood gang violence." They argued that the Latin Kings hid their guns and drugs behind la Virgencita's flowers and candles, and the only solution, from a policing strategies perspective, was to cut the sacred tree down. Devotees' "disregard for community issues" had forced them to consider this alternative approach. An inconclusive but intense discussion ensued in which CAPS officers created a singular immigrant identity by conflating the spiritual practices of these "noble," "custodians of ancient religion" with the "animalistic," "disease"-ridden, "terrorist" activities of their savage Latin King counterparts.[44] Using generic analyses, police officials justified their threats to "cut down the tree and put it where it belongs" if the core group did not comply and act as informants. Although they never acted on this threat, the culture of fear they created remained.

OUR FINAL MEETING: THIS IS NOT A ROMANTIC STORY

On a rainy night in late November 2003, about thirty Guadalupanos, including all core members, huddled together around the sacred tree. La Virgen de Guadalupe's image on the tree, the mark of her apparition, was hardly visible. The remains of her santuario—dirty silk roses, aging *promesas* (promises), braids of hair, rosary beads, and broken display cases—were stuffed and piled in industrial-sized garbage cans. It appeared as if someone had strewn the contents of one garbage can over the city street and haphazardly smashed them into the containers. Neighborhood Guadalupanos suspected that three male core group members had embezzled the money and had dismantled the shrine to end inquiries and involvement. In fact, one devotee pointed out that one of the men who took the money already had a reputation as a "rata" (lit., "rat" but here swindler/thief) in his native Michoacán. We waited for an explanation or reassurance that someone would rebuild the shrine but received neither.

After two and a half years of devotion, one fire, various acts of vandalism, two block parties, and two Chicago winters, the community faced irreparable collective loss, the physical removal of their spiritual, political, and economic labor. In an attempt to ease tension created by doubt and pain (and the disappearance of the community's funds), the three male devotees who tore down the altar suggested that everyone agree to transfer the shrine, and its accompanying savings account, to Michoacán. In Michoacán, they argued, "she would be safe." This suggestion raised

FIGURE 16. Remains of the dismantled shrine, spring 2006.

many questions and concerns within the larger Guadalupan devotee group: Why transfer the shrine to a community in Michoacán and not Guanajuato, a state from which most had migrated? Why move the shrine to Mexico if la Virgencita appeared here in Chicago, for them?

The majority of the group wanted to give up on the impossible dream of constructing a permanent shrine and, instead, donate la Virgencita's money, which most agreed should be more than $5,000, to a hospital or a charity. The devotee with the bank account said only $1,500 remained. An intense verbal battle ensued in which devotees pointed fingers and defamed one another. In the end, the community never resurrected the shrine and the money never materialized. Although rumors continue to circulate, today there is only a decorative wreath on the sacred tree. Flowers alert pedestrians to the Virgin's representation on the tree. (See figure 16.) Most of the bark remains charred after that fire in August 2001, but the Virgin's image is smooth because of numerous hands touching it for protection. Jagged points remain where devotees took pieces of bark to their home altars. Almost all the core group members have left the neighborhood. One family returned to Michoacán and then to Los Angeles—their original port of entry. Two moved to another neighborhood in the city, four relocated to the suburbs, and one devotee, who has dual citizenship, returned to Guanajuato, Mexico, to take care of a family matter. The Virgin's presence in Rogers Park is not any less significant because of their diaspora. Their acts of piety continue to render the ineffable visible in that built environment.

In lieu of a conclusion, I would like to return to Lefebvre and to the idea of conquering. He proposes:

> In reality, social space "incorporates" social actions, the actions of subjects both individual and collective who are born and who die, who suffer and who act. From the point of view of these subjects, the behaviour of their space is at once vital and mortal: within it they develop, give expression to themselves, and encounter prohibitions; then they perish, and that same space contains their graves.[45]

Lefebvre's use of "vital" and "mortal" here—which suggests subject to death, constantly threatened with erasure, disappearance—captures the mix of permanence and fleetingness that characterized the development of the sidewalk shrine and the surrounding social dynamics. Devotees in Rogers Park inscribed their identities, their dreams, and their inconsistencies on that street corner. A physical trace hardly remains, but that does not mean that they failed. They may not own property. They may not have overpowered any one debilitating socioeconomic factor or political obstacle, but they produced sacred space on their own terms—space that is at once "vital and mortal," even if a physical structure remains elusive. In that respect, I propose that devotees not merely survived but conquered that space. For many, adoring the Virgin was also a matter of pride, of leaving a mark on that neighborhood. Demonstrating that they are alive, present, indeed sometimes overpresent in an unfriendly and often unforgiving environment produced more than one triumphant moment. And sometimes that is enough (for now).

Conclusion

Making Space Sacred

Performances of piety in Des Plaines, Mexico City, Santiago de Querétaro, Zitácuaro, and Rogers Park are not simple stories of sacred space production. Guadalupan coping strategies and devotional acts constantly shift and transform, thereby challenging any overarching analysis of how ethnoreligious communities make their beliefs tangible. There is not one set path toward the sacred. Guadalupanos across North America, out of convenience or necessity, often advance their spiritual objectives by co-opting institutional proclamations and/or sidestepping, going around, under, or over socioeconomic and political deterrents. Acknowledging their daily "ways of operating," or how they pursue "innumerable and infinitesimal transformations of and within dominant cultural economy in order to adapt it to their other interests and their own rules," deepens our understanding of the complications, triumphs, and antagonisms that accompany sacred space production.[1] Further, attention to the dynamic backstage elements supporting each site—long-standing transnational networks and local circuits of power, for example—shows that political economy shapes worship practices as much as religious doctrine. These modes of inquiry illustrate how Guadalupan devotion is a pervasive force in North American history, how devotees' labor is often spatially and temporally polyvalent, how Guadalupan shrines in central Mexico and the Chicago area are transnationally linked by doctrine, tradition, aesthetic/physical replication, and early-twentieth-century labor circuits. Moreover, these analytic guideposts substantiate how the Virgin of Guadalupe is a symbol that exceeds national boundaries.

There are certain elements of the cult—in particular, the apparition scenario—that link sacred spaces across the United States and Mexico. Praying, chanting, and embodying the sixteenth-century master narrative sustains the cult of the Virgin of Guadalupe. Devotional performances allow geographically disparate Guadalupan spaces to live in concert across borders. Even then, those practices produce results that are numerous and varied. The cultivation of devotional capital, for example, is one such product. But like other developments, its shape and reach is contingent on a particular spatial and temporal context. The creation of devotional capital is site-specific. Peregrinas from Michoacán and Querétaro may share the apparition scenario, prayers, chants, and dogma. Both groups form alliances outside the walls of the church during time spent on access roads—the highways, unmapped dirt paths, and potholed city streets that take them toward Tepeyac. Some ties last year-round; others are reactivated during the next pilgrimage. But their day-to-day realities are vastly different, and thus their worship environments are distinct. A peregrina's approach and experience is singular; peregrinas make walk side by side and toward the same physical space, but each woman is pursuing her own spiritual journey toward the Virgin and establishing her own devotional capital.

Devotional capital thus offers an optic through which to consider faith-based actions and reactions as more than collective representation or symbolic reciprocity. It recognizes devotional labor as a series of site-specific interchanges (either between the Virgin and a devotee or among Guadalupanos) that operate on multiple levels. This aspect yields the most promise and provocation. Among other aftereffects, pious exchanges can shape intracommunity power circuits and status positions. During festivals and other moments of worship-centered interaction, adherents have the opportunity to perform for the Virgin and for each other. The more one participates, the better one's status. Through shrine maintenance—cleaning, creating, and displaying religious objects; adoring the Virgin through dance, prayer, and festival—devotees in Rogers Park, for example, simultaneously revitalize sacred space and secure their place in the community. Moreover, their seemingly "disinterested" exchanges generate devotional capital, which helps them make practical connections with other Guadalupanos. [2]

Although we have seen similar exchanges unfold at hyper-public feast day celebrations in Des Plaines and Mexico City, as well as in private domestic spaces in Rogers Park, Querétaro, and Zitácuaro, the relationships and advantages generated by devotional labor are particular to the space in which they are negotiated. The socioeconomic benefits received in urban and rural areas of Querétaro—networking and business opportunities among women from the same *rancho,* for example—may have commonalities with those circulated in Rogers Park or Des Plaines, but this is not a case of replication through doctrine or tradition. Devotees living in the Chicago area deal with distinct problems and thus their devotional performances proffer precise advantages such as learning which areas of the city are friendlier to undocumented individuals, where to find employment, how to find certain goods and reliable immigration advice.

Using performance as an object and method of study, which lends particular attention to gesture, tone, sound, body language, the choreography of everyday life, clarifies how Guadalupanos create, exchange, and circulate devotional capital as they produce sacred space. Also, looking through and learning from acts of pilgrimage, song, prayer, and shrine replication and maintenance at the Second Tepeyac, for example, alerts us to the processes by which histories, mythologies, and cultural production strategies persist and thrive. In the process of conceptualizing sacred space, devotees in Des Plaines relied on the apparition scenario to transpose elements of Tepeyac, but they also politicized San Juan Diego's legacy to champion their human/immigrant rights agenda. This dimension of cultural production in the Midwest was often spoken about, but it was also communicated through performative acts and the juxtaposition of symbols—a dimension of space production that Lefebvre calls "representational spaces."[3] In that respect, certain modes of communication and ways of behaving unveil the permeability and impermeability of social boundaries. "Performances," Roach advises, "are so rich in revealing contradictions: because they make publicly visible through symbolic action both the tangible existence of social boundaries and, at the same time, the contingency of those boundaries on fictions of identity."[4] A performance optic helps refocus our attention toward the places and times where power wordlessly changes hands—interactions that often define a community. Recognizing the contingency of boundaries and connections is what the study of everyday and extraordinary performances renders. It lets us see how embodied action exceeds the moment of execution; how devotional labor, alongside economic and sociopolitical factors, produces sacred space.

THE SACRED AND SPACE PRODUCTION

From the beginning stages of this project, highly expressive public devotional performances such as pilgrimage and the communicative power of coded exchanges provoked a set of key questions that determined how to approach two key issues: the sacred and space production. They are (1) When is space sacred? (2) How do we determine its boundaries? (3) How is it sustained and legitimized? (4) How do conceptions of sacred space in the United States and Mexico differ from place to place, from community to community vis-à-vis urban, suburban, and rural settings?

In order to address the first question, this materialist-oriented study grappled with diverse understandings of what constitutes the sacred, perhaps the most contested notion in the study of religion because of various shifts over the nineteenth and twentieth centuries. Two scholars influenced by Enlightenment ideals—Edward Burnett Tylor (1832–1917) and James George Frazer (1854–1941)—modified religion's place and conceptualizations of the sacred in the modern world's hierarchy of knowledge.[5] In addition, the work of "reductionist" scholars such as Karl Marx (1818–83), Emile Durkheim (1858–1917), and Sigmund Freud (1856–1939) and "irreductionist" thinkers such as Rudolf Otto (1869–1937) and Mircea Eliade (1907–86) play a fundamental role. Some scholars suggest, "Reductionists are those who insist that religion is best understood by going outside of religion to explain it. In various ways their theories are concerned to show that a religious phenomena—let us say, belief in God, or an act of ritual—owes its existence to nonreligious causes."[6] In contrast, Otto argues that "religion is not exclusively contained and exhaustively comprised in any series of 'rational' assertions; and it is well worth while to attempt to bring the relation of the different 'moments' of religion to one another clearly before the mind, so that its nature may become more manifest."[7] These academic boxing matches ultimately expand the study of religion.[8] We, however, must understand that the reductionism/irreductionism debate should not lead us to an either/or conclusion; we do not have to choose. This study has taken elements of both debates to understand how the sacred is a dynamic, organic, and complex impression of one's spiritual world. Combining resources helps us acknowledge the multiple ways in which devotees conceptualize and set boundaries around sacred space.[9] Recognizing both trajectories makes clear, for example, that the all-female pilgrimage from Zitácuaro, Michoacán, although not sanctioned by the dioceses, is in fact a sacred act. Indeed, every step the peregrinas take not only reinscribes the sacred onto that terrain but also legitimizes Tepeyac in Mexico City, which has remained an axis mundi for millions throughout centuries of colonial and postcolonial change.

At various points during this journey, like some women in central Mexico, we veered off course to consider not only the "popular" practices that may exist alongside more formal ways of approaching the sacred but also those acts that rise up when devotees have exhausted all other options. At those times we took note of Manuel A. Vásquez's suggestion that focusing on sacred and/or canonical texts creates a "hierarchy between authentic originative experiences, which are expressed in the grand religious narratives, and today's 'degenerate' religious practices."[10] On the contrary, we took seriously their creative reimaginings of Guadalupan devotion—using kitchen tables as altars, replicating the sacred hill of Tepeyac in Des Plaines with two bronze statues instead of seventeen, and using mojigangas in a multiethnic neighborhood to entertain and remind a group of devotees of modes of worship practiced in western Mexico. This analysis insists that "degenerate moments"— apparitions that remain unsanctioned by the Catholic Church and mostly rural-based female devotees in Querétaro who conduct their pilgrimage parallel to but far away from registered Guadalupanas, for example— tell us as much as sacred texts, if not more, about the circulation and transformation of religious life in the Americas. Moreover, this project reaffirms that religious doctrine and practice do not circulate separate from secular forces. They inhabit the same spaces.

Although many ecclesiastical officials with whom I spoke at Tepeyac and elsewhere would insist that the sacred or the numinous is so because of a divine favor, this study contends that notions of holiness are continually affected by circumstance. In that respect, proposing a consummate definition or theory of what constitutes "the sacred" is outside the purview of this project. I can only offer pathways.[11] Devotees' tired tongues, tense shoulder muscles, scraped knees, and calloused feet—in communication with metaphysical or transcendental forces—dictate what is sacred for each individual. Their ways of interacting with the divine also modify the spaces in which they reside—an idea that is central to this study.

But how are these types of spaces actually sustained and legitimized? This project argues that the Virgin of Guadalupe's influence as a religious, historical, and cultural icon and her malleability—a devotee's prerogative to adore her individually or collectively to advance a wide range of objectives—brings people and institutions together to a particular location. But embodied practices do the work of maintaining and acknowledging a place as holy. Pilgrimage, public celebrations, and prayer services draw individuals to a space; people's blood, sweat, and sacrifices, however, qualify the idea that *"un grano de arena"* is all that is needed to consecrate a place. After all, when the women from Michoacán via Pilsen articulated that perspective, their almost frozen hands were selling tamales (which are quite laborious to prepare) to reinforce their connection with the Virgin, but their devotional labor also gave spiritual meaning to the physical space known as the Second Tepeyac. More important, their oblations prevent the space from becoming antiquated.

These types of claims lead us to the second principal idea that underpins this study: space is not absolute; the environments in which we coexist are susceptible to change because, as the story of sacred space production in Rogers Park demonstrated, "space is at once vital and mortal: within it they [users] develop, give expression to themselves, and encounter prohibitions."[12] In this respect, Lefebvre's work, which challenges scholars to pursue the inconsistencies and "prohibitions," as well as the role of embodied practices, conceptual frameworks, and coded exchanges, has helped us understand that the inextricable links among belief, embodied practice, physical markers, and legitimacy turn placemaking into dynamic enterprise.[13] But it is his provocative questions that have guided this analysis toward one of its main contributions to Guadalupan studies: a critical exploration of the material foundations of sacred space production.

> What is an ideology without a space to which it refers, a space which it describes, whose vocabulary and links it makes use of, and whose code it embodies? What would remain of a religious ideology—the Judaeo-Christian one, say—if it were not based on places and their names: church, confessional, altar, sanctuary, tabernacle? What would remain of the Church if there were no churches? The Christian ideology carrier of a recognizable if disregarded Judaism (God the Father, etc.), has created the spaces which guarantee that it endures.[14]

Lefebvre's message is clear. Belief needs a receptacle; ideology desires a vehicle. Sites of practice—Tepeyac, the Second Tepeyac, pilgrimage routes, the corner of Rogers and Honore on Chicago's Far North Side—are repositories for the sacred. Adherents' devotional performances, the Virgin's iconography, and the coded symbols that adorn shrines are conduits.

Multiple players revitalize the Virgin of Guadalupe's currency across North America as they imbue environments with the divine, but as Lefebvre proposes, they may also impress her spaces with social, political, and ideological convictions.[15] The objective of examining the various layers of action and belief grounding sacred space production through historical and materialist optics is to acknowledge that peregrinas "feel history" through the act of pilgrimage, that lawyers offering their services to devotees in Des Plaines do not make the Second Tepeyac any less sacred, and that Guadalupanos in Rogers Park using the sidewalk shrine to claim a collective sense of Mexican identity is a result of intracity labor migration circuits as much as of the Virgin of Guadalupe's appearance on a tree.

These materialist-oriented theories of space production, especially aspects that deal with practice, dovetail nicely with the overall performance studies focus to which this project subscribes. The rubric of performance in religious studies allows us to consider "how performative actions produce a culturally meaningful environment as opposed to simply communicating ideas or attitudes,"[16] but that belief does not create a univocal reality. As we have seen, conceptions of sacred space in the United States and Mexico differ from place to place and from community to community. A temporary roadside altar in Querétaro meets that particular family's spiritual and social needs as well as a single red rose does for a Guadalupan community whose shrine has outgrown its physical presence. Paying attention to those processes—some long-standing, some ephemeral—that inform, modify, and link these very different spaces to one another helps us understand the ease with which religious ideals and practices adapt themselves to urban, suburban, and rural environments.

Finally, a performance studies framework approaches the question of methodology, which will always be an interdisciplinary venture. Using performance as an object and a method of study throughout this project required an embodied engagement with the polyvalence of religious practices. To do this, one must pursue "an understanding of the knowledges of the body in the culture, a clear sense of what has been embodied in the corporeality of the people who participate in religious practice, what their tongues, skin, ears, 'know.'"[17] Having a sensibility of what the body knows is not a task that we can accomplish by reading textbooks, merely observing ritual practices, or participating sometimes.[18] As this study has shown, we acquire a deeper understanding by co-performatively witnessing or placing our bodies in the immediate context of devotional practices.[19] Twenty-four-hour engagement—walking, praying, singing, bathing, eating, and sleeping alongside women in central Mexico—as opposed to conducting interviews, taking photographs, and then writing notes in private, was key. This performance-oriented methodology has clarified details that often remain unnoticed: the intercommunity differences between "formal" and "popular" religion, day-to-day coping tactics, as well as the way devotion may positively or negatively influence intracommunity gender, race, and class relations. Further, practicing alongside devotees while paying attention to historical and material factors allowed me to make multilayered connections within each community. More important, however, pursuing dialogue, debates, and exchanges using this method of engagement has created ties that exceed the parameters of the project.

Pilgrimage Repertoire

From the song booklet, Sin siembra no hay cosecha, sin palabra no hay Eucaristía *(Querétaro: Directiva Seglar de la 47ª Peregrinación Femenina a pie de Querétaro al Tepeyac, 2005).*

LAS APARICIONES GUADALUPANAS	THE VIRGIN OF GUADALUPE'S APPARITIONS

From *Sin siembra no hay cosecha, sin palabra no hay Eucaristía,* pp. 52–54.

Desde el cielo una Hermosa mañana
Desde el cielo una Hermosa mañana   One beautiful morning from heaven

La Guadalupana,
La Guadalupana,
La Guadalupana,   the Virgin of Guadalupe
Bajó al Tepeyac,   descended to Tepeyac

Suplicante juntaba las manos
Suplicante juntaba las manos   She clasped her hands together
    pleadingly

Y eran mexicanos,
Y eran mexicanos,
Y eran mexicanos   Her bearing and her face were
    Mexican,
Su porte y su faz.   and they were Mexican, and they were
    Mexican. . . .

Su llegada llenó de alegría
Su llegada llenó de alegría   Her arrival filled with happiness

De luz y armonía
De luz y armonía
De luz y armonía   with light and harmony
Todo el Anáhuac   all of Anáhuac

Junto al monte pasaba Juan Diego
Junto al monte pasaba Juan Diego.   Juan Diego passed by the hill

Y acercóse luego,
Y acercóse luego
Y acercóse luego   and later he approached
Al oir cantar.   when hearing singing

Juan Dieguito la Virgen le dijo,
Juan Dieguito la Virgen le dijo.   the Virgin told little Juan Diego

Este cerro elijo
Este cerro elijo,
Este cerro elijo
Para ser mi Altar.   I choose this hill to be my altar

Y en la tilma, entre rosas pintadas
Y en la tilma entre rosas pintadas. and in the cloak among painted roses

Su imagen amada,
Su imagen amada,
Su imagen amada   Her beloved image
se dignó dejar.   She deemed worthy to leave

Desde entonces para el mexicano,
Desde entonces para el mexicano.   And since then for the Mexican

Ser Guadalupano
Ser Guadalupano
Ser Guadalupano   To be a devotee of Guadalupe
Es algo escencial.   is something essential

En sus penas postrado de hinojos,
En sus penas postrado de hinojos.   Kneeling down in sorrow

Eleva sus ojos,
Eleva sus ojos,
Eleva sus ojos   Raises his eyes
Hacia el Tepeyac.   Towards Tepeyac

BUENOS DÍAS, PALOMA   GOOD MORNING, WHITE
BLANCA   DOVE

From *Sin siembra no hay cosecha, sin palabra no hay Eucaristía*, pp. 67–68.

Buenos días paloma blanca,   Good morning White Dove
Hoy te vengo a saludar,   Today I'm coming to greet you

Saludando a tu belleza	Saluting your beauty
En tu reino celestial.	In your celestial kingdom
Eres madre del Creador	You are the mother of the Creator
Que a mi corazón encanta:	which my heart loves;
Gracias te doy, con amor.	With love, I give you thanks.
Buenos días, Paloma Blanca	Good morning, White Dove
Niña linda, niña Santa	Lovely girl, saintly girl
Tu dulce nombre alabad,	your sweet name be praised
Porque sois tan sacrosanta	Because you are so holy
Yo te vengo a saludar.	I'm coming today to greet you.
Reluciente como el alba,	Gleaming like the daybreak,
Pura, sencilla, sin mancha;	Pure, simple, without stain;
¡Qué gusto recibe mi alma!	What pleasure my soul receives!
Buenos días, Paloma Blanca	Good morning, White Dove
Felíz guía del marinero,	A sailor's favorable guide,
Eres la estrella del mar;	You are the ocean's star;
En la tierra y en el cielo,	On earth and in the sky,
Yo te vengo a saludar.	I am coming to greet you.
Sapientísima Señora	Most wise Lady
En Ti pongo mi esperanza,	I place my hope with You,
Bella, reluciente aurora	Beautiful, resplendent dawn
Buenos días, Paloma Blanca	Good Morning, White Dove
Pues que fuiste concebida	As you were conceived
Sin la culpa original,	Without original sin,
Desde tu primer instante	From your first moment
En tu reino celestial.	in your heavenly kingdom.
Virgen celestial, princesa,	Celestial Virgin, princess,
Virgen sagrada María;	Sacred Virgin Mary;
Desde tu primer instante	From your first moment
En tu reino celestial	in your heavenly kingdom.
Virgen celestial, princesa,	Celestial Virgin, princess,
Virgen, Sagrada María,	Sacred Virgin Mary;
Yo te alabo en este día	I praise you today
Saludando a tu belleza.	Saluting your beauty,
¡Oh gracias niña pura,	Oh thank you pure girl,
hermosa perla oriental!	beautiful pearl of the orient!
Que a todo el orbe iluminas	You illuminate all of the world
En tu reino celestial	in your heavenly kingdom.
Hecha con grande primor	Made with extreme care
De Dios la suma grandeza	of God the utmost greatness
Porque exaltas en tu amor	Because you uplift with your love
Saludando a tu belleza	Saluting your beauty

Líbranos de todo mal,
Yo te pido gran Señora;
Tú serás mi protectora
En tu reino celestial

Free us from all evil,
I ask of you great Lady;
You will be my protector
In your celestial kingdom

En la tierra y en el cielo
Cantemos dulce alabanza;
Repitiendo con anhelo:
Buenos días, Paloma Blanca.

On earth and in heaven
We sing sweet praise;
Repeating longingly;
Good morning, White Dove

Tú serás nuestra madrina
En el juicio universal;
Oyenos graciosa Niña,
En tu reino celestial.

You will be our godmother
on judgment day;
Hear us graceful girl,
in your celestial kingdom.

ALABARÉ

ALABARÉ

From *Sin siembra no hay cosecha, sin palabra no hay Eucaristía*, p. 17.

Alabaré, alabaré
Alabaré a mi señor,
Alabaré, alabaré
Alabaré a mi señor.

Sing praise, sing praise,
sing praise to the Lord.

Juan vio el número de los redimidos

John saw the number of the saved
ones

Y todos alababan al señor;
Unos cantaban, otros oraban,
Y todos alababan al señor.

and everyone praised the Lord;
Some sang, other prayed,
And everyone praised the Lord.

Todos unidos, alegres cantamos,
Gloria y alabanzas al señor;
¡Gloria al padre! ¡Gloria al hijo!
Y ¡Gloria al Espíritu de amor!

Everyone united, happily we sing,
glory and praise to the Lord;
Glory to the father! Glory to the son!
And glory to the Holy Spirit!

Somos tus hijos Dios padre eterno

We are your children, Lord Father
eternal

Tú nos has creado por amor;
Te alabamos, te bendecimos
Y todos cantamos en tu honor.

You have made us because of love;
We praise you, we bless you
And we all sing in your honor.

PADRE ABRAHAM

FATHER ABRAHAM

From *Sin siembra no hay cosecha, sin palabra no hay Eucaristía*, p. 25.

Padre Abraham tenía muchos hijos
Muchos hijos tenía el Padre Abraham
Tu eres uno yo también
Por eso vamos alabar a nuestro Dios.

Father Abraham had many kids
and many kids had Father Abraham
Because you are one, and so am I
and because of that we will praise our
Lord.

Mano derecha	Right hand
Mano izquierda	Left hand
Pie derecho	Right foot
Pie izquierdo	Left foot
La cabeza	the head
La cadera	the hip
Media vuelta	half turn
Vuelta entera	full turn
Se acabo.	It's done.

Notes

INTRODUCTION

1. For examples and explications of co-performative witnessing, see Dwight Conquergood, "Performing as a Moral Act: Ethical Dimensions of the Ethnography of Performance," *Literature in Performance* 5, no. 2 (1985): 1–13; "Health Theatre in a Hmong Refugee Camp," *TDR: The Drama Review* 32 (1988): 174–208; "Performance Studies: Interventions and Radical Research," *TDR: The Drama Review* 46 (2002): 145–56; and "Rethinking Ethnography: Towards a Critical Cultural Politics," in *The Sage Handbook of Performance Studies,* ed. D.S. Madison and J. Hamera (Thousand Oaks, CA: Sage, 2006), 351–65. See also E. Patrick Johnson, *Sweet Tea: Black Gay Men of the South* (Chapel Hill: University of North Carolina Press, 2008); Margaret Drewal, "The State of Research on Performance in Africa," *African Studies Review* 34, no. 3 (1991): 1–64; and D. Soyini Madison, "Co-performative Witnessing," *Cultural Studies* 21, no. 6 (2007): 826–31.

2. For an in-depth discussion of the numerous labels surrounding migrant communities in the United States, see Frank D. Bean and B. Lindsay Lowell, "Unauthorized Migration," in *The New Americans: A Guide to Immigration since 1965,* ed. Mary C. Waters and Reed Ueda (Cambridge, MA: Harvard University Press, 2007), 70–82.

3. For studies of Mexican migration to the Midwest, see Gabriela F. Arredondo, *Mexican Chicago: Race, Identity, and Nation, 1916–39* (Urbana: University of Illinois Press, 2008); Paul S. Taylor, *Mexican Labor in the United States: Chicago and the Calumet Region* (Berkeley: University of California Press, 1932); Francisco A. Rosales, "Regional Origins of Mexicano Immigrants to Chicago during the 1920s," *Aztlán: International Journal of Chicano Studies Research* 7 (Summer 1976): 187–201; Francisco Hinojosa, *Mexican Chicago*

(Mexico City: CONACULTA, 1999); Mark Reisler, "The Mexican Immigrant in the Chicago Area during the 1920s," *Journal of the Illinois State Historical Society* 66, no. 2 (Summer 1973): 144–58; and Rob Paral, Michael Norkewicz, Madura Wijewardena, and Christina Diaz Peterson, *Mexican Immigration in the Midwest: Meanings and Implications* (Chicago: Chicago Council on Global Affairs, 2009).

4. Key texts in the study of geography, especially after 1970, have shown us that "absolute" space is a positivist ahistorical fallacy. For supporting arguments, see Henri Lefebvre, *The Production of Space*, trans. Donald Nicholson-Smith (Oxford: Basil Blackwell, 1991); Michel Foucault, "Of Other Spaces," *Diacritics* 16, no. 1 (1986): 22–27; David Harvey, *The Urbanization of Capital: Studies in the History and Theory of Capitalist Urbanization* (Baltimore, MD: Johns Hopkins University Press, 1985); David Harvey, *The Condition of Postmodernity* (Cambridge, MA: Blackwell, 1990); David Harvey, *Justice, Nature, and the Geography of Difference* (Oxford: Blackwell, 1996); David Harvey, *Spaces of Hope* (Edinburgh: Edinburgh University Press, 2000); Saskia Sassen, "Spatialities and Temporalities of the Global: Elements for Theorization," in *Globalization,* ed. Arjun Appadurai (Durham, NC: Duke University Press, 2001), 260–78; Yi-Fu Tuan, *Space and Place: The Perspective of Experience* (Minneapolis: University of Minnesota Press, 2001); Dolores Hayden, *The Power of Place* (Cambridge, MA: MIT Press, 1995); and Setha Low and Denise Lawrence-Zúñiga, eds., *The Anthropology of Space and Place: Locating Culture* (Malden, MA: Blackwell, 2001).

5. Henri Lefebvre astutely proposes, "It is not the work of a moment for a society to generate (produce) an appropriated social space in which it can achieve a form by means of self-presentation and self-representation—a social space to which that society is not identical, and which indeed is its tomb as well as its cradle. This act of creation is, in fact, a process." Lefebvre, *The Production of Space,* 34.

6. See Conquergood, "Performance Studies," 145.

7. "Master symbols," Eric Wolf suggests, "provide the cultural idiom of behaviors and ideal representations through which different groups of the same society can pursue and manipulate their different fates within a coordinated framework." See Eric Wolf, "The Virgin of Guadalupe: A Mexican National Symbol," *Journal of American Folklore* 71 (1959): 34.

8. The debate over the truth of the apparitions or the existence/nonexistence of Juan Diego is for all practical purposes a moot point. It bears mentioning, however, that a long since established debate continues to mold the ideological base of the cult. The anti-apparitionist Francisco de la Maza, for example, coined the phrase "four evangelists" to describe the scholars who have played a fundamental part in verifying the legitimacy of the cult of la Virgen de Guadalupe. The first evangelist, Miguel Sanchez, published the first history of la Virgen de Guadalupe's apparition, *Imagen de la Virgen María, madre de Dios de Guadalupe, milagrosamente aparecida en la ciudad de México* (1648). The *Nican mopohua,* which recounts the apparition narrative in Náhautl, followed in 1649. Initially accredited to Luis Lasso de la Vega, this text is widely regarded as the work of Antonio Valeriano. The third evangelist, Luis Becerra Tanco, wrote

Origen milagroso del santuario de Nuestra Señora de Guadalupe (1666), and Francisco de Florencia penned *La estrella del norte de México* (1785). For a critical viewpoint, see Francisco de la Maza, *El guadalupanismo mexicano* (Mexico City: Fondo de Cultura Económica, 1981).

9. Negotiations during the twelfth and fourteenth centuries among the Triple Alliance of Tenochtitlán, Texcoco, and Tlacopan set the groundwork for the establishment of the Aztec empire in 1325, which stretched from the Atlantic to the Pacific coasts, northward to the desert region and into the southern areas of present-day Oaxaca. See Bernal Diaz del Castillo, *The Discovery and Conquest of Mexico, 1517–1521,* trans. A.P. Maudslay (New York: Harper, 1928), 271–88; and Miguel León-Portilla, *Aztec Thought and Culture: A Study of the Ancient Nahuatl Mind,* trans. Jack Emory Davis (Norman: University Oklahoma Press, 1963). For a fascinating performance-oriented study of Aztec culture, see Dávid Carrasco, *City of Sacrifice: Violence from the Aztec Empire to the Modern Americas* (Boston: Beacon, 1999).

10. See Miguel León-Portilla, *Bernardino de Sahagún: First Anthropologist* (Norman: University of Oklahoma Press, 2002); and Miguel León-Portilla, Jorge Klor de Alva, and Lysander Kemp, *The Broken Spears: The Aztec Account of the Conquest of Mexico* (Boston: Beacon, 2006).

11. Horacio Sentíes Rodriguez, *La villa de Guadalupe: Historias, estampas, y leyendas* (Mexico City: Portico de la Ciudad de México, 1991), 3.

12. See Antonio Pompa y Pompa, *El gran acontecimiento guadalupano* (Mexico City: Editorial Jus, 1967), 18; Francisco Miranda, *Dos cultos fundantes: Los remedios y Guadalupe, 1521–1649; Historia documental* (Zamora: Colegio de Michoacán, 1998); Gustavo Watson Marrón, *Los templos del Tepeyac* (Mexico City: Arzobispado de México, 2001); and Horacio Sentíes Rodriguez, *La villa de Guadalupe: Crónica centenaria* (Mexico City: Gobierno del Distrito Federal/Delegación Gustavo A. Madero, 1999).

13. Sebastián García, *Guadalupe en Extremadura en América* (Madrid: Gráficas Don Bosco. Arganda del Rey, 1991), 71; for a list of Extremaduran bishops in New Spain/America (1500–1850), see p. 97.

14. For a discussion of the Extremaduran cult in New Spain, see Jacques Lafayé, *Quetzalcóatl and Guadalupe: The Formation of National Consciousness, 1531–1813,* trans. Benjamin Keene (Chicago: University of Chicago Press, 1976), 217–24; and Alyshia Gálvez, ed., "'She Made Us Human': The Relationship between the Virgin of Guadalupe, Popular Religiosity and Activism among Members of Mexican Devotional Organizations in New York City," in *Performing Religion in the Americas: Media, Politics, and Devotional Practices of the 21st Century* (New York: Seagull Books, 2007), 142–45. For a commemorative approach, see Matilde Muro Castillo, *Guadalupe: La llamada de la luz* (Guadalupe: Junta de Extremadura, 2007). For a historical study of the town of Guadalupe, see Sebastían García Rodríguez, ed., *Guadalupe: Siete siglos de fe y de cultura* (Madrid: Ediciones Guadalupe, 1993).

15. Dávid Carrasco and Scott Sessions, *Daily Life of the Aztecs: People of the Sun and Earth* (New York: Greenwood Press, 1998), 53; Robert Ricard, *The Spiritual Conquest of Mexico: An Essay on the Apostles and the Evangelizing Methods of the Mendicant Order in New Spain: 1523–1572* (Berkeley:

University of California Press, 1966); and Miguel León-Portilla, *Tonantzin Guadalupe: Pensamiento náhuatl y mensaje cristiano en el Nican Mopohua* (Mexico: Colegio Nacional and Fondo de Cultura Económica, 2000).

16. Gloria Anzaldúa, *Borderlands/La Frontera: The New Mestiza* (San Francisco: Aunt Lute Books, 1987), 49–50. For more on precolonial gender roles, see Rosemary A. Joyce, *Gender and Power in Prehispanic Mesoamerica* (Austin: University of Texas Press, 2000).

17. Octavio Paz, for example, winner of the 1990 Nobel Prize in literature for *Labyrinth of Solitude,* suggests in that highly acclaimed book, "In contrast to Guadalupe, who is the Virgin Mother, the *Chingada* [doña Malinche/the mistress of Cortés] is the violated Mother. Neither in her nor in the Virgin do we find traces of the darker attributes of the great goddesses: the lasciviousness of Amaterasu and Aphrodite, the cruelty of Artemis and Astarte, the sinister magic of Circe or the bloodlust of Kali. Both of them are passive figures. Guadalupe is pure receptivity, and the benefits she bestows are of the same order: she consoles, quiets, dries tears, calms passions. The *Chingada* is even more passive. Her passivity is abject: she does not resist violence, but is an inert heap of bones, blood, and dust." Octavio Paz, *The Labyrinth of Solitude and Other Writings,* trans. Lysander Kemp (New York: Grove Press, 1985), 85. Paz, who is well known for his problematic conceptualization of Mexican consciousness, places men in an irreproachable position of power—literarily on top of women.

18. See Jeanette Rodriguez, *Our Lady of Guadalupe : Faith and Empowerment among Mexican-American Women* (Austin: University of Texas Press, 1994).

19. The *Nican motecpana* offers a short account of Juan Diego's life and the *Nican tlantica* reviews the history of the cult of Mary in the New World.

20. Another version of the legend proposes that the Virgin appeared five times. The fifth apparition, in this scenario, occurred on December 12 in the house of Bishop fray Juan de Zumárraga.

21. See, e.g., Norma Alarcón, "Chicana's Feminist Literature: A Re-Vision through Malintzin/or Malintzin: Putting Flesh Back on the Object," in *This Bridge Called My Back: Writings by Radical Women of Color,* ed. Cherríe Moraga and Gloria Anzaldúa (New York: Kitchen Table/Women of Color Press, 1983), 182–90; Yvonne Yabro-Bejarano, "The Female Subject in Chicano Theatre: Sexuality, 'Race,' and Class," in *Performing Feminisms: Feminist Critical Theory and Theatre,* ed. Sue-Ellen Case (Baltimore, MD: Johns Hopkins University Press, 1990): 131–49; Alicia Gaspar de Alba and Tomas Ybarra Frausto, *Velvet Barrios: Popular Culture and Chicana/o Sexualities* (New York: Palgrave Macmillan, 2003); Theresa Delgadillo, "Forms of Chicana Feminist Resistance: Hybrid Spirituality in Ana Castillo's 'So Far From God,' " *Modern Fiction Studies* 44, no. 4 (1998): 888–916; Ana Castillo, ed. *Guadalupe: Goddess of the Americas/La diosa de las Américas; Writings on la Virgen de Guadalupe (*New York: Riverhead, 1996); Sonia Saldívar-Hull, *Feminism on the Border: Chicana Gender Politics and Literature* (Berkeley: University of California Press, 2000); and Diana Taylor, *The Archive and the Repertoire: Performing Cultural Memory in the Americas* (Durham, NC: Duke University Press, 2003), 90–93.

22. Sandra Cisneros, "Guadalupe the Sex Goddess: Unearthing the Racy Past of Mexico's Most Famous Virgin," *Ms.* (July–August 1996): 45.

23. Here I refer to Ignacio de la Mota's interpretation of "Guadalupismo": "Devoción hacia la Virgen de Guadalupe, incluso por encima de los sentimientos puramente religiosos, pero sin renunciar a ellos, intergrándolos o fundiéndolos con los del nacionalismo mexicano, por considerar su presencia inicial y su asistencia continuada en todos sus procesos, incluyendo el independentista, como el acontecimiento más importante de su historia, que se prolonga a través del tiempo con el mismo fervor, sin perder su característica de bandera y símbolo de la nación" (Devotion toward la Virgen de Guadalupe, inclusive of and in conjunction with pure religious sentiments. Guadalupan devotion merges, without sacrificing this pure religious element, Mexican nationalism on the basis of its initial and continual presence in all processes, including independence— the most important event of its history. This devotion will extend across time, with the same amount of fervor, without losing its characteristic as flag and symbol of the nation). See Ignacio de la Mota, *Diccionario guadalupano* (Mexico City: Panorama Editorial, 1997), 122.

24. Pompa y Pompa, *El gran acontecimiento guadalupano*, 19.

25. Esteban Martinez de la Serna, *Los santuarios de la virgen de Guadalupe* (Mexico City: Editora Escalante, 2003), 7; Jorge Durand and Douglas S. Massey, *Miracles on the Border: Retablos of Mexican Migrants to the United States* (Tucson: University of Arizona Press, 1995); Jacqueline Orsini Dunnington, *Guadalupe: Our Lady of New Mexico* (Santa Fe: Museum of New Mexico Press, 1999); Elvira Araiza Velázquez, "La Virgen de Guadalupe de México: Para América," *Boletín Guadalupano* 2, no. 34 (2003): 8–10; and Gálvez, "'She Made Us Human,'" 141–57.

26. Harvey, *Spaces of Hope*, 23.

27. Michel de Certeau, *The Practice of Everyday Life* (Berkeley: University of California Press, 1984), 129.

28. The literature on transnationalism has grown exponentially over the past decade. There are some texts, however, that provide key insights. See Linda Basch, Nina Glick-Schiller, and Cristina Blanc-Szanton, *Nations Unbound: Transnational Projects, Postcolonial Predicaments, and Deterritorialized Nation-States* (Langhorne, PA: Gordon and Breach, 1994); Ulf Hannerz, *Transnational Connections* (London: Routledge, 1996); Sidney Mintz, "The Localization of Anthropological Practice: From Area Studies to Transnationalism," *Critique of Anthropology* 18, no. 2 (1998): 117–33; Michael Peter Smith and Luis Eduardo Guarnizo, *Transnationalism from Below* (New Brunswick, NJ: Transaction, 1998); Aihwa Ong, *Flexible Citizenship: The Cultural Logics of Transnationality* (Durham, NC: Duke University Press, 1999); and Peggy Levitt, *The Transnational Villagers* (Berkeley: University of California Press, 2001). For recent perspectives, see Robert Alvarez, *Mangos, Chiles, and Truckers: The Business of Transnationalism* (Minneapolis: University of Minnesota Press, 2005); Aminah Beverly McCloud, *Transnational Muslims in American Society* (Gainesville: University Press of Florida, 2006); François Pierre-Louis, *Haitians in New York City: Transnationalism and Hometown Associations* (Gainesville: University Press of Florida, 2006); Sarah England, *Afro Central Americans in New York*

City: Garifuna Tales of Transnational Movements in Racialized Space (Gainesville: University Press of Florida, 2006); Shari M. Huhndorf, *Mapping the Americas: The Transnational Politics of Contemporary Native Culture* (Ithaca, NY: Cornell University Press, 2009); and Benjamin Johnson and Andrew R. Graybill, eds., *Bridging National Borders in North America: Transnational and Comparative Histories* (Durham, NC: Duke University Press, 2010). For an overview of transnational theory and its application across disciplines, see Peggy Levitt and Sanjeev Khagram, eds., *The Transnational Studies Reader: Intersections and Innovations* (New York: Routledge, 2007).

29. Rana P.B. Singh and others suggest that the transposition of sacred space entails "the re-establishment of religious patterns at a different place and different scale from the original." Rana P.B. Singh, "Sacred Space and Pilgrimage in Hindu Society: The Case of Varanasi," in *Sacred Places, Sacred Spaces: The Geography of Pilgrimages,* ed. Robert H. Stoddard and Alan Morinis (Baton Rouge, LA: Geoscience Publications, 1997), 194. For an excellent case study, see Karen McCarthy Brown, *Mama Lola: A Vodou Priestess in Brooklyn* (Berkeley: University of California Press, 1999).

30. David Ricardo, *Economic Essays,* ed. E.C.K. Gonner (London: G. Bell and Sons, 1923).

31. See Karl Marx, *Capital: A Critique of Political Economy* (Chicago: Charles H. Kerr & Co., 1919), 269; and Karl Marx and Friedrich Engels, *Karl Marx and Friedrich Engels on Religion* (New York: Schocken Books, 1964).

32. Pierre Bourdieu, *The Logic of Practice,* trans. Richard Nice (Stanford: Stanford University Press, 1980), 120–21; *Outline of a Theory of Practice,* trans. Richard Nice (Cambridge: Cambridge University Press, 1977); and *Distinction: A Social Critique of the Judgment of Taste,* trans. Richard Nice (Cambridge, MA: Harvard University Press, 1984).

33. For more on "winks and twitches" and "backstage/front stage," see Clifford Geertz, *The Interpretation of Cultures* (New York: Basic Books, 1973), 27–28; and Erving Goffman, *The Presentation of Self in Everyday Life* (Garden City, NY: Doubleday, 1959).

34. Written from Latin American, North American, and European perspectives, texts include Ernesto de la Torre Villar and Ramiro Navarro de Anda, eds., *Testimonios históricos guadalupanos* (Mexico City: Fondo de Cultura Económica, 1982); Virgil P. Elizondo, *La Morenita: Evangelizer of the Americas* (San Antonio, TX: Mexican American Cultural Center, 1980), and *Guadalupe: Mother of the New Creation* (Maryknoll, NY: Orbis Books, 1997); De la Maza, *El guadalupanismo mexicano;* Carmen Aguilera and Ismael Arturo Montero García, eds., *Tepeyac estudios históricos* (Mexico City: Universidad del Tepeyac, 2000); Stafford Poole, *Our Lady of Guadalupe: The Origins and Sources of a National Symbol, 1531–1797* (Tucson: University of Arizona Press, 1995); William B. Taylor, "The Virgin of Guadalupe in New Spain: An Inquiry into the Social History of Marian Devotion," *American Ethnologist* 1(1987): 9–24; William B. Taylor, "Mexico's Virgin of Guadalupe in the Seventeenth Century: Hagiography and Beyond," in *Colonial Saints: Discovering the Holy in the Americas,* ed. Allan Greer and Jodi Bilinkoff (New York: Routledge, 2003), 277–98; Xavier

Noguez, *Documentos guadalupanos: Un estudio sobre las fuentes de información tempranas en torno a las Mariofanías en el Tepeyac* (Mexico City: Fondo de Cultural Económica, 1995); Richard Nebel, *Santa María Tonantzin Virgen de Guadalupe: Continuidad y transformación religiosa en México* (Mexico City: Fondo de Cultura Económica, 1996); Victor Turner and Edith Turner, *Image and Pilgrimage in Christian Culture: Anthropological Perspectives* (New York: Columbia University Press, 1978); Luis D. León, *La Llorona's Children: Religion, Life, and Death in the U.S.-Mexican Borderlands* (Berkeley: University of California Press, 2004); and Timothy Matovina, *Guadalupe and Her Faithful: Latino Catholics in San Antonio, from Colonial Origins to the Present* (Baltimore, MD: Johns Hopkins University Press, 2005).

35. Here I follow Manuel A. Vásquez and Marie F. Marquardt's lead in *Globalizing the Sacred: Religion across the Americas* (New Brunswick, NJ: Rutgers University Press, 2003). See also Anna L. Peterson and Manuel A. Vásquez, *Latin American Religions: Histories and Documents in Context* (New York: New York University Press, 2008).

36. Timothy Matovina and Gerald E. Poyo, eds., *¡Presente! U.S. Latino Catholics from Colonial Origins to the Present* (Maryknoll, NY: Orbis, 2000); Hector Avalos, ed., *Introduction to the U.S. Latina and Latino Religious Experience* (Boston: Brill, 2004); and David A. Badillo, *Latinos and the New Immigrant Church* (Baltimore, MD: Johns Hopkins University Press, 2006).

37. Frank J. Korom, *Hosay Trinidad: Muharram Performances in an Indo-Caribbean Diaspora* (Philadelphia: University of Pennsylvania Press, 2003); Thomas Tweed, *Our Lady of the Exile: Diasporic Religion at a Cuban Catholic Shrine in Miami* (New York: Oxford University Press, 1997); R. Marie Griffith and Barbara Dianne Savage, *Women and Religion in the African Diaspora: Knowledge, Power, and Performance* (Baltimore, MD: Johns Hopkins University Press, 2006); Elizabeth McAllister, *Rara! Vodou, Power, and Performance in Haiti and Its Diaspora* (Berkeley: University of California Press, 2002); Robert A. Orsi, ed., *Gods of the City: Religion and the American Urban Landscape* (Bloomington: Indiana University Press, 1999); and Peggy Levitt, *God Needs No Passport: Immigrants and the Changing American Religious Landscape* (New York: New Press, 2009).

38. For excellent exceptions, see Katy Gardner, *Global Migrants, Local Lives: Travel and Transformation in Rural Bangladesh* (Oxford: Clarendon Press, 1995); and Kathryn Burns, *Colonial Habits: Convents and the Spiritual Economy of Cuzco, Peru* (Durham, NC: Duke University Press, 1999).

39. Geertz, *The Interpretation of Cultures*, 16.

1. VIRGEN DE LOS MIGRANTES

A version of this chapter was published in *American Quarterly*. See Elaine Peña, "Beyond México: Guadalupan Sacred Space Production and Mobilization in a Chicago Suburb," *American Quarterly* 60, no. 3 (2008): 721–47.

1. "¡Juan Pablo, Hermano, Ya eres Mexicano!" *Católico* 17, no. 9 (September 2002): 13–14.

2. Jacques Lafayé, *Quetzalcóatl and Guadalupe: The Formation of National Consciousness 1531–1813,* trans. Benjamin Keene (Chicago: University of Chicago Press, 1974); Stafford Poole, *Our Lady of Guadalupe: The Origins and Sources of a National Symbol, 1531–1797* (Tucson: University of Arizona Press, 1995); Paz, *The Labyrinth of Solitude and Other Writings;* Rodriguez, *Our Lady of Guadalupe; Flowers for Guadalupe/Flores para Guadalupe,* VHS, produced by Judith Gleason with the collaboration of the Colectivo Feminists de Xalapa and Elisa Mereghetti (New York: Filmmakers Library, 1995); Anzaldúa, *Borderlands/La Frontera;* and Deidre Sklar, *Dancing with the Virgin: Body and Faith in the Fiesta of Tortugas, New Mexico* (Berkeley: University of California Press, 2001).

3. Matovina and Poyo, *Presente!* 147.

4. Vásquez and Marquardt, *Globalizing the Sacred,* 45. For a case study on the utility and necessity of sacred space replication, see Colleen McDannell, *Material Christianity* (New Haven, CT: Yale University Press, 1995), 132–62.

5. Lefebvre, *The Production of Space,* 33–39.

6. Ibid., 33.

7. Ibid., 38.

8. Ibid., 59.

9. Chicago was at a crossroads of international and national political negotiations when German, French, Slovakian, Irish, and Swedish laborers, among others, ignited the city's unprecedented population and economic boom. Mid-nineteenth-century westward expansion to Oregon Territory and the riches of California as well as shifts in trading routes from North-South to East-West initiated the area's century of progress. The year 1848 was pivotal for U.S. capital accumulation and development, primarily as a result of the Treaty of Guadalupe Hidalgo, which made possible the country's unprecedented land expansion. It was also the year that the Galena and Chicago Union Railroad Company replaced the steamboat transportation industry with the construction of the first rail line in the city. Chicago's natural proximity to the Great Lakes and the construction of the Illinois-Michigan canal, which connected the city waterways to the Mississippi River, added further to the area's allure as a transportation and commercial center. By 1856 ten railroads were operating within the area. The city's population increased tenfold to 300,000 residents and the city's meatpacking and steel industries were prospering during this initial stage. The industrialization machine was so effective that it efficiently rebuilt the city after the Great Fire destroyed many urban areas in 1871. By 1910 Chicago had achieved the status of the second largest city in the United States and until the 1940s held the title of the industrial capital of the nation. Migrants often worked from and lived in the actual boxcars at various points along the route, which made labor recruitment quick and efficient. These laborers settled in areas that were previously inhabited by Italian, Greek, Jewish, Irish, and Polish workers—the "Back of the Yards," the Near West Side, and South Chicago—because of their proximity to rail yards and factories. John Betancur, Teresa Córdova, and María de los Angeles Torres, "Economic Restructuring and the Process of Incorporation of Latinos in the Chicago Economy," in *Latinos in a*

Changing U.S. Economy: Comparative Perspectives on Growing Inequality, ed. Rebecca Morales and Frank Bonilla (Newbury Park, CA: Sage, 1993), 109; and Gregory D. Squires, Larry Bennett, Kathleen McCourt, and Phillip Nyden, *Chicago: Race, Class, and the Response to Urban Decline* (Philadelphia: Temple University Press, 1987), 26. For more on race and migration, see Thomas A. Guglielmo, *White on Arrival: Italians, Race, Color, and Power in Chicago, 1890–1945* (Oxford: Oxford University Press, 2003); John Joseph Parot, *Polish Catholics in Chicago, 1850–1920: A Religious History* (De Kalb: Northern Illinois University Press, 1981); Stephen J. Shaw, *The Catholic Parish as a Way-Station of Ethnicity and Americanization: Chicago's Germans and Italians, 1903–1939* (New York: Carlson, 1991); Manuel Gamio, *Mexican Immigration to the U.S* (Chicago: University of Chicago Press, 1930); and Paul S. Taylor, *Mexican Labor in the United States: Chicago and the Calumet Region* (Berkeley: University of California Press, 1932).

10. See Rita Arias Jirasek and Carlos Tortolero, *Images of America: Mexican Chicago* (Chicago: Arcadia, 2001), 94; Anita Edgar Jones, "Conditions Surrounding Mexicans in Chicago: A Dissertation" (Master's thesis, University of Chicago, 1928), 131–35; and Louise Año Nuevo Kerr, "The Chicano Experience in Chicago, 1920–1970" (Ph.D. diss., Univeristy of Illinois at Chicago, 1976), 56.

11. Geoffrey Johnson, "A Common Altar: Chicago's Immigrant Catholics," *Chicago* (September 2005): 79.

12. Pierrette Hondagneu-Sotelo, Genelle Gaudinez, Hector Lara, and Billie C. Ortiz, "There's a Spirit That Transcends the Border: Faith, Ritual, and Postnational Protest at the U.S.-Mexico Border," *Sociological Perspectives* 47, no. 2 (2004): 137.

13. Karen Mary Davalos, "The Real Way of Praying: The Via Crucis, *Mexicano* Sacred Space, and the Architecture of Domination," in *Horizons of the Sacred: Mexican Traditions in the U.S. Catholicism*, ed. Timothy Matovina and Gary Riebe-Estrella (Ithaca, NY: Cornell Univeristy Press, 1993), 41–68; and Robert Stark, "Religious Ritual and Class Formation: The Story of Pilsen St. Vitus Parish, and the 1977 Via Crucis" (Ph.D. diss., University of Chicago Divinity School, 1981).

14. Davalos, "The Real Way of Praying," 48.

15. Ibid., 42.

16. Gregory D. Squires and his colleagues address the function and motives of four institutional actors who manipulate neighborhood space—banks and savings and loan institutions, municipal zoning regulations, government agencies, and real estate companies. These players determine who receives and does not receive mortgage money, housing plans in certain metropolitan areas, where racial groups will be "steered," and the enforcement or relaxation of federal guidelines. See Gregory D. Squires, Larry Bennett, Kathleen McCourt, and Phillip Nyden, *Chicago: Race, Class, and the Response to Urban Decline* (Philadelphia: Temple University Press, 1987), 93–94; and Dwight Conquergood, "Life in Big Red: Struggles and Accommodations in a Chicago Polyethnic Tenement," in *Structuring Diversity*, ed. Louise Lamphere (Chicago: University of Chicago Press, 1994),138–39.

17. Nicholas De Genova and Ana Ramos-Zayas, *Latino Crossings: Mexicans, Puerto Ricans, and the Politics of Race and Citizenship* (New York: Routledge, 2003), 38.

18. For a recent opinion on the effect of O'Hare International Airport on the suburbs and Chicago politics more generally, see Bob Herbert, "Op-Ed: Stifling an Opportunity," *New York Times,* March 16, 2009, A27. See also Betancur, Córdova, and de los Angeles Torres, "Economic Restructuring and the Process of Incorporation of Latinos in the Chicago Economy," 124.

19. According to the 2000 census, Illinois's Hispanic population increased by 69.2 percent, from 625,816 residents to 1,530,262 between 1990 and 2000. This pan-ethnic group now makes up 12.3 percent of the state's population. This growth has directly affected the city of Chicago's population, which registered its first increase since deindustrialization in the 1950s, as well as her suburbs, which constitute 42 percent of Illinois's total population. All six Chicagoland counties—Cook, Du Page, Kane, Lake, McHenry, and Will—recorded a rise in their Hispanic populations over the past decade. Cook County, home to Chicago and Des Plaines, for example, experienced an increase from 13.7 percent in 1990 to 19.9 percent in 2000. Similarly, Du Page County, just west of Chicago, doubled its numbers, from 4.4 to 9.0 percent. Although the overall percentage is significantly lower than Cook County's numbers, it represents the demographic and racial shifts occurring outside of Chicago's city limits and across the state. Northwest suburbs such as Rolling Meadows and Palantine Village, both of which have presences in the Tepeyac community, have experienced a similar if not greater growth pattern. Northbrook, Park Ridge, Morton Grove, and Glenview, areas that devotees link with Des Plaines and the shrine through consistent Sunday service attendance, however, officially retain low percentages. Rolling Meadows's Hispanic population, for example, almost doubled from 11.16 percent in 1990 to 19.20 percent in 2000 and Palantine Village's numbers tripled, from less than 5 percent of the population to 14.55 percent. Northbrook registered 1.84 percent, or 616 Hispanic residents, in 2000. Cicero popularly considered a settling area among Mexican immigrants and a key player in the Second Tepeyac's development is an anomaly with 66,299 Hispanic residents, or over three quarters of the total population. Although helpful, these statistics do not account for the dynamic fluxes and interchanges engendered by informal economic networks, shifts in industrial, agricultural, and domestic service labor realms, and waves of chain-migrants from Latin America, among other regions of the world, arriving in the Chicago area on a daily basis.

20. Badillo's study of religious spaces in select suburbs of Chicago nicely demonstrates this point. See David A. Badillo, "Suburbanization and Mobility in Catholic Chicago," in *Latinos and the New Immigrant Church,* 120–53.

21. See Joseph Roach, *Cities of the Dead: Circum-Atlantic Performance* (New York: Columbia University Press, 1996), 54–55. For a broader history of suburban development, see Dolores Hayden, *Building Suburbia: Green Fields and Urban Growth, 1820–2000* (New York: Pantheon Books, 2003).

22. In 2002 Maryville's youth home operation received negative media attention when the state removed 130 wards on charges of negligence and misconduct, specifically, in relation to the suicide of a teenage girl and two alleged sexual

assaults on campus. Illinois's governor Rod R. Blagojevich publicly denounced the academy, discredited Smyth, and pursued a defunding agenda. Elite members of Chicago's political and social organizations including the Chicago Bears veteran Chris Zorich, government officials—Senator Dave Sullivan (R-Park Ridge), state Senator Dan Cronin (R-Elmhurst)—and other public figures such as Cook County commissioner Liz Gorman showed their support for Reverend Smyth during a rally held on the campus in late September 2003. Karl Maurer, "Hundreds Rally to Protest Maryville Closing," www.Catholiccitizens.org (accessed October 2003). This high-profile gathering did not reverse the state's decision, nor did it alleviate the Academy's or Smyth's tarnished public image. In December 2004 Sister Catherine Ryan, a Franciscan nun, former Maryville board member, and juvenile justice lawyer, replaced Smyth as executive director of the Academy. Maureen O'Donnell, "Franciscan Nun to Run Maryville," www.Catholiccitizens.org (accessed February 2005).

23. Sentíes Rodriguez, *La villa de Guadalupe: Historias, estampas y leyendas*, 142–43.

24. Edmundo O'Gorman, *Destierro de sombra: Luz en el origen de la imagen y culto de Nuestra Señora de Guadalupe del Tepeyac* (Mexico City: Universidad Nacional Autonoma de México, 1991), 281–82.

25. Sentíes Rodriguez, *La villa de Guadalupe: Historias, estampas y leyendas*, 143.

26. By definition, cofradías are "associations of devotees organized institutionally by the church, specifically by the bishop to promote Christian life, devotional acts, charity and social work. In its most practical definition, many cofradías developed and adapted according to the necessities of the community." Alicia Bazarte Martínez and Clara García Ayluardo, *Los costos de la salvación: Las cofradías y la ciudad de México* (Mexico City: Instituto Politécnico Nacional/ Archivo General de la Nación, 2001), 29–30. At the same time, *cofradías* were markers of socioethnic and socioeconomic differences created by colonial and Christian expansion. See Alicia Bazarte Martínez, *Las cofradías de españoles en la ciudad de México (1526–1869)* (Mexico City: Universidad Autónoma de México, 1989); Ana Rita Valero de García Lascurain, "Los primeros cofrades de Guadalupe: Algunas reflexiones en torno a su intensa devoción," *Boletín Guadalupano* 34 (2003): 17–19; and John K. Chance and William B. Taylor, "Cofradías and Cargos: An Historical Perspective on the Mesoamerican Civil-Religious Hierarchy," *American Ethnologist* 12, no. 1 (1985): 1–26.

27. Sentíes Rodriguez, *La villa de Guadalupe: Crónica centenaria*, 12.

28. One of the most important early colonial projects that exploited indigenous labor was the construction of causeways that connected different industrial and commercial locations within Mexico City. In 1604 the viceroy Marqués de Montesclaros ordered the renovation of the causeway of Guadalupe—a second entryway that joined Santiago Tlatelolco with Tepeyac. Using two thousand laborers to layer kilometers of earth and reeds, fray Juan de Torquemada oversaw the completion of the project in a mere five months. In 1675 Basilica officials renamed this Calzada de Tepeyac the Calzada de los Misterios, after the construction of fifteen Stations of the Cross alongside the road. Religious-minded city planners hoped these markers would encourage peregrinas/os to

pray the rosary on their way to Tepeyac. The Calzada de los Misterios exemplifies how devotees built and legitimized religious/civil projects.

29. Sentíes Rodriguez, *La villa de Guadalupe: Historias, estampas, y leyendas*, 19. See also Lafayé, *Quetzalcóatl and Guadalupe*, 67.

30. For a broader sense of race- and class-based social stratification in New Spain see, Ilona Katzew, *Casta Painting: Images of Race in Eighteenth-Century Mexico* (New Haven, CT: Yale University Press, 2005); Herman L. Bennett, *Africans in Colonial Mexico: Absolutism, Christianity, and Afro-Creole Consciousness, 1570–1640* (Bloomington: Indiana University Press, 2003); and Laura Lewis, *Hall of Mirrors: Power, Witchcraft, and Caste in Colonial Mexico* (Durham, NC: Duke University Press, 2003).

31. Manuel Alvarez, one of the most respected architects in New Spain, oversaw the construction of the aqueduct, which cost 124,796 *medio reales*. For a discussion of Mexico's colonial economic structure, see J.F. Schwaller, *Origins of Church Wealth in Mexico: Ecclesiastical Revenues and Church Finances, 1523–1600* (Albuquerque: University of New Mexico Press, 1985), 19–29.

32. O'Gorman, *Destierro de sombra*, 17.

33. Sentíes Rodriguez, *La villa de Guadalupe: Historias, estampas, y leyendas*, 27.

34. Ibid., 25.

35. See Miranda, *Dos cultos fundantes;* Horacio Sentíes Rodriguez, "Evolución urbana del Santuario de Nuestra Señora de Guadalupe," in Aguilera and Montero García, *Tepeyac estudios históricos*, 195–226; Watson Marrón, *Los templos del Tepeyac;* Pedro Ramírez Vázquez, "Basílica de Guadalupe, Santuario de los Mexicanos," in Aguilera and Montero García, *Tepeyac estudios históricos*, 227–38; and Martinez de la Serna, *Los santuarios de la Virgen de Guadalupe*.

36. David A. Brading, *Mexican Phoenix: Our Lady of Guadalupe: Image and Tradition across Five Centuries* (Cambridge: Cambridge University Press, 2001), 6. See also O'Gorman, *Destierro de sombra*, 284.

37. Castillo, *Guadalupe: Goddess of the Americas*.

38. Sentíes Rodriguez, *La villa de Guadalupe: Crónica centenaria*, 49.

39. Sentíes Rodriguez, *La villa de Guadalupe: Historias, estampas, y leyendas*, 27.

40. María Dolores Morales, "Espacio, propiedad y organos de poder en la ciudad de México en el siglo XIX," in *Ciudad de México: Instituciones, actores sociales, y conflicto politico, 1774–1931*, ed. Carlos Illades and Ariel Rodriguez (Zamora: Colegio de Michoacán, 1996), 158; see also William Roseberry, *Anthropologies and Histories: Essays in Culture, History, and Political Economy* (New Brunswick, NJ: Rutgers University Press, 1994), 95–97.

41. The exact figure is 0.21 percent of the city's proprietors and 0.18 percent of the city's property value. Morales, "Espacio, propiedad, y organos de poder en la ciudad de México en el siglo XIX," 161–64.

42. Basilica officials renovated the sanctuary between 1929 and 1938 at an estimated cost of 2.3 million pesos. See Brading, *Mexican Phoenix*, 317. It is also worth noting that the Basilica's civil status changed when the city of Guadalupe Hidalgo became integrated into Mexico City's district system in 1931,

thereby acquiring official affiliation as the delegación Gustavo A. Madero. See Sentíes Rodríguez, *La villa de Guadalupe: Historias, estampas y leyendas,* 12.

43. Sentíes Rodriguez, *La villa de Guadalupe: Crónica centenaria,* 73; Luis Everaert Dubernard, "El tratado de Guadalupe Hidalgo: Algunas consideraciones sobre las diversas circunstancias que predicieron su firma," in Aguilera and Montero García, *Tepeyac estudios históricos,* 187.

44. Pompa y Pompa, *El gran acontecimiento guadalupano,* 118.

45. Regarding church property, see *El Universal: Relaciones entre la iglesia y el estado,* vol. 1, "El Enfrentamiento (1916–1929)," and vol. 2, "La Tolerancia (1930–1977)": "Sólo seis templos en el Distrito Federal" (14 de octubre 1924), 85; "Los templos, convertidos en escuelas" (6 de octubre 1925), 106–7; "Un veradero escándalo produjo ayer en la villa de Guadalupe la clausura de los colegios católicos" (18 de febrero de 1926), 111–14; "Las reformas penales y la intolerancia religiosa" (5 de julio 1926), 129–30; "Comenzó la entrega de los templos" (1 de agosto 1926), 136. In volume 2, see "Estudio de expedientes de nacionalización de bienes" (8 de agosto 1936), 25–26.

46. These associations established headquarters throughout the republic, but they organized their efforts most successfully in central Mexico—Michoacán, Querétaro, Guanajuato, México, and Hidalgo. Although officially documented as a three-year conflict, the Cristiada prompted counter-uprisings that challenged the security and authority of the Catholic Church throughout the period. A bomb set off in the Basílica Antigua on November 14, 1921, for example, was one of the most public responses to the tension. This attack was an unsuccessful attempt to destroy the Virgin's image. Although it exploded dangerously close to ayate, it only twisted a crucifix, which is now on display in the modern Basílica as evidence of the anti-Guadalupan fanatic's failed act. During this same period the state suffered great losses, the greatest perhaps being General Alvaro Obregón's assassination on July 18, 1928, by the religious fundamentalist León Torral. These violent acts, which are only a few among many, offer evidence of the historical and ideological discontinuities between church and state in Mexico. For overviews of the Cristero conflict, see David C. Bailey, *Viva Cristo Rey! The Cristero Rebellion and the Church-State Conflict in Mexico* (Austin: University of Texas Press, 1974); Jean Meyer, *La cristiada* (Mexico City: Siglo XXI, 1973) and *The Cristero Rebellion: The Mexican People between Church and State, 1926–1929* (New York: Cambridge University Press, 1976); Roberto Blancarte, *Historia de la iglesia católica en México* (Mexico City: Fondo de Cultura Económica, 1992) and "Modernidad, secularización y religión; La iglesia católica. El estado y la sociedad mexicana en el umbral del Siglo XXI," in *México a fines del siglo,* vol. 2, ed. José Woldenberg and José Joaquin Blanco (Mexico City: Fondo de Cultura Económica, 1993); Marta Elena Negrete, *Relaciones entre la iglesia y el estado de México, 1930–1940* (Mexico City: Colegio de Mexico, 1988); Alicia Olivera Sedano, *Aspectos del conflicto religioso de 1926 a 1929: Sus antecedentes y consecuencias* (Mexico City: Instituto Nacional de Antropologia e Historia, 1966). For more information on violence against the Catholic Church, see *El Universal: Relaciones entre la iglesia y el estado,* vol. 1, "El Enfrentamiento (1916–1929)," and vol. 2, "La Tolerancia (1930–1977)": "Dos bombas de dinamita en un templo" (17 de diciembre 1924), 86; "Se incia

en México una intensa cruzada por el catolicismo" (28 de enero 1925), 87–88; "Hubo desórdenes en Tabasco por la cuestión religiosa" (9 de noviembre 1925), 107; "El asesinato del señor general Alvaro Obregón" (18 de julio 1928), 169–75; "Murió el jefe de la rebelión en Jalisco" (4 de junio de 1929), 185. In volume 2, see "Hizo explosión una bomba en el templo de la Profesa" (1 de septiembre 1931), 7–8.

47. Roberto Blancarte, "Aspectos internacionales del conflicto religioso mexicano en la década de los treinta," in *Cultura e identidad nacional* (Mexico City: Fondo de Cultura Económica, 1994), 233.

48. For international and intercultural studies of pilgrimage and tourism, see Ellen Badone and Sharon R. Roseman, eds., *Intersecting Journeys: The Anthropology of Pilgrimage and Tourism* (Urbana: University of Illinois Press, 2004); K.A. Shinde, "Religious Tourism at Sacred Sites in India," in *Religious Tourism and Pilgrimage Festivals Management: An International Perspective*, ed. Razaq Raj and Nigel D. Morpeth (Cambridge, MA: CAB International, 2007), 184–97; and Maria I.R.B. De Pinho and Isabel M.R.T. de Pinho, "Case Study 8: Fátima—the Religious Tourism Altar," in Raj and Morpeth, *Religious Tourism and Pilgrimage Festivals Management*, 211–21.

49. Daniel Morales, "Gracias, Señor Presidente," *Voz Guadalupana* 12 (1945–46): 31.

50. Three state officials—Judge Manuel Rivera Vázquez, police chief Miguel Z. Martínez, and chief of the secret service José Gómez Anaya—publicly approved this change because "tradition should be conserved [Rivera Vázquez]," "the historic name is preferable [Martínez]," "and it justifies the tradition of the community which persists in our souls [Gómez Anaya]." See *El Universal: Relaciones entre la iglesia y el estado*, vol. 2, "La Tolerancia (1930–1977): "'Guadalupe,' nombre que une a todo el pais" (7 de septiembre 1943), 34; and "La villa de Guadalupe finalmente recupera su nombre" (27 de octubre 1943), 35.

51. Edmundo Félix Belmonte, "El presidente Kennedy en la Basílica de Guadalupe," *Voz Guadalupana* 28 (1962–63): 3.

52. Elisabeth Bumiller and Marc Lacey, "McCain Winds up Latin Trip in Mexico," *New York Times,* July 4, 2008, U.S./Politics.

53. "El señor presidente inauguró las obras y visitó la Basílica," *Voz Guadalupana* 18 (1952–53): 10–11.

54. "Atrio y plaza de la Basílica del Tepeyac," *Voz Guadalupana* 19 (1953–54): 6–7.

55. Adrian García Cortes, "La plaza de las Americas," *Voz Guadalupana* 16 (1960a): 13–4.

56. "Importancia de la obras en la Villa," *Voz Guadalupana* 16 (1960–61): 6.

57. García Cortes, "La plaza de las Americas," 12.

58. "Moderno mercado para la Villa," *Voz Guadalupana* 21 (1955–56): 21.

59. One criticism of the project is that the architects should have sought out alternative areas to expand the space, such as the actual hill of Tepeyac, so that people would not have to relocate. See Ruiz Sandoval, "Obras arquitectónicas embellecen el Tepeyac," *Voz Guadalupana* 23 (1957); and "Importancia de la obras en la Villa," *Voz Guadalupana* 16 (1960): 6–7, for an extended discussion of the institutional elements of the twentieth-century renovation.

60. Adrian García Córtes, "La plaza de las Américas," *Voz Guadalupana* 16 (1960b).

61. "Atrio y plaza de la Basílica del Tepeyac," 6–7.

62. Sentíes Rodriguez, *La villa de Guadalupe: Crónica centenaria,* 79.

63. Ramírez Vázquez, "Basílica de Guadalupe, Santuario de los Mexicanos," 229.

64. Pope Pio X proclaimed the Basílica Antigua a "Basílica menor" on May 24, 1904. This title signifies that the shrine surpasses standards set by Canon Law 1234, which stipulates that "the space safeguards the remains or relic of a saint, a sacred image, or is important historically and culturally." The title "Basílica menor" is different from the title "santuario." According to Canon Law 1230, the latter is given to a church or sacred space that is "special" for a particular reason and attracts numerous persons of faith. See Guillermo Schulenburg Prado, *Memorias del "último Abad de Guadalupe"* (Mexico City: Porrua, 2003), 345–50.

65. Ramírez Vázquez, "Basílica de Guadalupe, Santuario de los Mexicanos," 236.

66. Ibid., 230.

67. Ibid., 228.

68. Schulenburg Prado, *Memorias del "último Abad de Guadalupe."*

69. Schulenberg Prado later resigned/was dismissed from his post because of a comment he made in the winter edition of IXTUS magazine (Year 3, no. 15) in which he suggested that Juan Diego never existed. His comments set off a whirlwind of negative media attention and investigations into intrachurch corruption and embezzlement. For explanation and analysis, see Schulenburg Prado, *Memorias del "último Abad de Guadalupe,"* 285; and César Aguilar, "Un misterio las finanzas de la Basílica," *Vértigo* 4, no. 195 (2004): 35.

70. See the following articles in *El Universal: Relaciones entre la iglesia y el estado:* Fidel Sanmaniego and Enrique Aranda Pedroza, "Modernizar relaciones con la iglesia, propone CSG," vol. 3. (2 de diciembre, 1988), 1; Fidel Sanmaniego, "Recibió Salinas en Los Pinos a 130 prelados católicos," vol. 3. (11 de diciembre, 1991), 129; Eleazar Franco, "Schulenberg: ha sido decisivo el papel de la iglesia en la defensa de la paz social," vol. 3. (10 de diciembre, 1990), 56; and Gumersindo Magaña Negrete, "El nuevo régimen legal de la iglesias," vol. 3. (23 de julio, 1992), 195.

71. Maria del Carmen Macías, "Un nuevo amanacer en Tepeyac de Norteamerica," *Católico* (October 2001): 10.

72. For a discussion of shrine origin stories and the impact of a Marian year, see Mary Lee Nolan, "Christian Pilgrimage Shrines in Western Europe and India: A Preliminary Comparison," in *Trends in the Geography of Pilgrimages,* ed. R.L. Singh and Rana P.B. Singh (Kamachha, Varanasi: National Geographical Society of India, 1987), 18–26; and Gisbert Rinschede, "Pilgrimage Studies at Different Levels," in Stoddard and Morinis, *Sacred Places, Sacred Spaces,* 95–116.

73. The sacred edifices that make up la Villa have served as the model for replicas across North America and beyond, even in the service of other Virgins. For a related case study, see Vásquez and Friedmann Marquardt, *Globalizing the Sacred,* 79.

74. Del Carmen Macías, "Un nuevo amanacer," 10.

75. Marcela Vallecillo Gómez and María Concepción Castillo de Jiménez, "Santa María de Guadalupe une América en el amor y la fe para un mundo de Esperanza," *Boletín Guadalupano* 66 (2006): 18–19.

76. Robert A. Orsi, "Everyday Miracles: The Study of Lived Religion," in *Lived Religion in America: Toward a History of Practice,* ed. David D. Hall (Princeton, NJ: Princeton University Press, 1997), 3–21.

77. Harvey, *The Condition of Postmodernity.*

78. For a full version of the song, see Appendix.

79. Fieldwork in the Chicago area and central Mexico has shown that devotees proudly sing these lyrics at Tepeyac, on foot to Tepeyac, and at the Second Tepeyac, among other locations. See Elaine Peña, "Making Space Sacred: Devotional Capital, Political Economy, and the Transnational Expansion of the Cult of la Virgen de Guadalupe" (Ph.D. diss., Northwestern University, 2006).

80. Taylor, *The Archive and the Repertoire,* 28–9.

81. Ibid., 46–47.

82. De Certeau, *The Practice of Everyday Life,* 117.

83. For a study of the value of sacred relics (bodies or portions of bodies, particles of clothing or objects associated with saints), see Patrick Geary, "Sacred Commodities: the Circulation of Medieval Relics," in *The Social Life of Things,* ed. Arjun Appadurai (Cambridge: Cambridge University Press, 1988), 169–91.

84. See McDannell, *Material Christianity,* 144–45; and Robert Orsi, "The Cult of the Saints and the Reimagination of the Space and Time of Sickness in Twentieth-Century American Catholicism," *Literature and Medicine* 8 (1989): 63–77.

85. In late September 2003 thousands rallied across the nation to support the Immigrant Workers Freedom Ride. Inspired by the Freedom Riders of the civil rights movement and sponsored by AFL-CIO, Coalition of Black Trade Unionists, Hotel Employees and Restaurant Employees International Union (HEREIU), National Asian Pacific American Legal Consortium, and United Farmworkers of America (UFW), among others, immigrants and activists collaborated to "educate the public and elected officials about three key requirements of a new immigration policy." They encouraged Congress to initiate an immigration policy that would make "legalization and a road to citizenship for all immigrant workers in the country, the right to re-unite families, and protection of worker rights on the job without regard to legal status" a reality for millions of undocumented workers in the United States. Participants journeyed fifteen days (September 20–October 4) across the nation from West Coast cities—Seattle, San Francisco, and Los Angeles—toward two key East Coast destinations—Washington D.C., where participants met with members of Congress on October 1 and 2, and New York City. In addition to towns and small cities along the route, coordinators held recruitment rallies in Las Vegas, Minneapolis, Houston, Miami, and Chicago.

86. According to a study conducted by the Inter-American Development Bank (IADB), there are approximately 2.5 million adult Central Americans (the report refers solely to Guatemalans, Hondurans, and Salvadorans) residing in

the United States, 78 percent of whom sent remittances to their families in 2007. Between 2006 and 2007 the amount of remittances in U.S. dollars increased approximately 8 percent, to $9.95 billion. The majority of migrants work in construction and landscaping, followed by domestic work and the service sector. For more details, see www.iadb.org/news/docs/remitmex.pdf.

87. The Sanctuary Movement, which began in 1980, created safe political spaces and offered legal and humanitarian assistance to Central American refugees displaced by war, violence, and poverty in their home countries; many of those scenarios were promulgated by U.S. interests. The movement inspired churches—across faith-based and cultural boundaries—to openly defy government mandates advising deportation. Chicago played a key role in this movement. For more information about the Sanctuary Movement, see Ignatius Bau, *This Ground Is Holy: Church Sanctuary and Central American Refugees* (Mahwah, NJ: Paulist Press, 1985); Susan Coutin, *The Culture of Protest* (Boulder, CO: Westview Press, 1993); and Renny Golden and Michael McConnell, *Sanctuary: The New Underground Railroad* (Maryknoll, NY: Orbis Books, 1986).

88. This impassioned speech resonates with the case and cause of Elvira Arellano, an unauthorized Mexican migrant who sought sanctuary for over a year in a church in Chicago's Humboldt Park neighborhood to avoid deportation and separation from her son, who is a U.S. citizen. Often likened to Rosa Parks, Arellano has become an international symbol and speaker for comprehensive U.S. immigration reform. Unfortunately, Arellano, who left Chicago to give a speech at an immigration rally in Los Angeles, California, in August 2007, faced deportation.

89. *Pastoral Response to Immigration Reform* (Chicago: Maryville Academy Publishing Center, 1997).

90. Gardner, *Global Migrants, Local Lives;* Tweed, *Our Lady of the Exile;* McCarthy Brown, *Mama Lola;* Korom, *Hosay Trinidad;* and Elizabeth McAllister, *Rara! Vodou, Power, and Performance in Haiti and Its Diaspora* (Berkeley: University of California Press, 2002).

91. Matovina and Poyo, *Presente!* 56.

92. Ibid., 95.

93. Utilizing pan-Latinoism for mobilization purposes is strategic. Yet as many pro pan-Latino theorists have suggested, when U.S. government agencies, naive intellectuals, mass media, and marketing agencies invoke the mythologies of pan-Latinoism, the results can be detrimental. The implicit homogenizing power of this term makes stigmatizing, categorizing, and disciplining across the board easy for self-interested parties. After all, each "Latino" group has a long and specific political, economic, and cultural history of interrelating with other "Latinos." Further, the politics of citizenship challenges any attempts to generalize along ethnic lines. I agree with de Genova and Ramos-Zayas when they suggest that "the basis for such commonalities must be located in an analysis of the shared historicity of peoples throughout Latin America in relation to the colonial and imperialist projects of the U.S. nation-state, in concert with the concomitant historical as well as contemporary racializations of both Latin America, as a whole, and Latinos in the U.S. in relation to a sociopolitical order of white supremacy." Without that connection, categorizations, in

my opinion, harm more than help. See De Genova and Ramos-Zayas, *Latino Crossings,* 20.

2. "¡QUÉ RISA ME DA!"

1. I transcribed this chant to emphasize the women's tone and inflection. This method, known as ethnopoetic transcription, attempts to convey what the written word has omitted. For a conceptual analysis, see Roland Barthes, *The Grain of the Voice: Interviews, 1962–1980,* trans. Linda Coverdale (New York: Hill and Wang, 1985); Michel de Certeau, *The Capture of Speech and Other Political Writings,* trans. Tom Conley (Minneapolis: Minnesota University Press, 1997). For practical approaches, see Anna Deveare Smith, *Fires in the Mirror: Crown Heights, Brooklyn, and Other Identities* (New York: Anchor Books/Doubleday, 1993) and *Twilight: Los Angeles, 1992 on the Road: A Search for American Character* (New York: Anchor Books, 1994); and Della Pollock, *Telling Bodies Performing Birth: Everyday Narratives of Childbirth* (New York: Columbia University Press, 1999).

2. Schulenburg Prado, *Memorias del "ultimo abad de Guadalupe,"* 350.

3. Yvonne Yabro-Bejarano explains, "La Virgen represents the redemption of her gender through self-abnegation and resignation. She is Mother, yet miraculously intact. The equation of female sexuality with enslavement is translated through la Virgen into the cultural values of love/devotion, reinforcing women's subordinate position of servitude and obedience with a rigidly heterosexual hierarchy." Yabro-Bejarano, "The Female Subject in Chicano Theatre," 135. See also Cisneros, "Guadalupe the Sex Goddess," 43–46. For a broader critique of traditional notions of femininity, see J.S. Mill, *The Subjection of Women* (New York: Appleton, 1869); and Simone de Beauvoir, *The Second Sex* (New York: Knopf, 1952).

4. Victor Turner and Edith Turner suggest, "In studies of human culture and behavior the tension between motivation and scientific objectivity can sometimes prove fruitful. When the deeper levels of the self . . . are reflexively engaged, the knowledge brought back from the encounter between self as subject and self as object may be just as valid as knowledge acquired by 'neutral' observation of others." Victor Turner and Edith Turner, *Image and Pilgrimage in Christian Culture: Anthropological Perspectives* (New York: Columbia University Press, 1978), xv. The Turners implicitly challenge researchers to break the participant observation divide, to recognize that the interpreter of the ritual is also an integral part of the process. For recent examples, see Paula Elizabeth Holmes-Rodman, "'They Told What Happened on the Road': Narrative and the Construction of Experiential Knowledge on the Pilgrimage to Chimayo, New Mexico," in Badone and Roseman, *Intersecting Journeys,* 24–51; and Phillip L. Wagner, "Pilgrimage: Culture and Geography," in Stoddard and Morinis, *Sacred Places, Sacred Spaces,* 299–323.

5. A number of scholars suggest that the act is guided not solely by canonical law but also by institutional requisites, individual practitioners' needs, and the communities' sociopolitical and economic conditions. Shadow and Rodriguez emphasize, "It is necessary to locate the pilgrimage text in relation to the social

group that produces it, situate it inside class and power structures, and conceptualize the act as an ideological phenomenon that has arisen and has been reproduced as part of a historical process that is linked to dynamic class struggles." Robert Shadow and María Rodriguez V., "Símbolos que amarran, símbolos que dividen: hegemonía e impugnación en una peregrinación campesina a Chalma," *Mesoamérica* 19 (June 1990): 36. See also Robert Shadow and María Rodriguez Shadow, "La peregrinación en América Latina: Enfoques y perspectivas," in *Las peregrinaciones religiosas: Una aproximación* (Mexico City: Universidad Autonoma Metropolitana, 1994); Walter R. Adams, "Political and Economic Correlates of Pilgrimage Behavior," *Anales de Antropología* 20 (1983): 147–72; Beatriz Barba de Piña Chan, ed., "Introducción," in *Caminos terrestres al cielo: Contribución al estudio del fenómeno romero*, 10, ed. Beatriz Barba de Piña Chan, Serie Antropología Social (Mexico City: Instituto Nacional de Antropología e Historia, 1998); Fernando Cámara Barbachano and Teófilo Reyes, "Los santuarios y la peregrinaciones. Una expresión de relaciones sociales en una sociedad compleja: El caso de México," *Boletín Bibliográfico de Antropología Americana* 35, no. 2 (1972): 29–45; Ross N. Crumrine and Alan Morinis, eds., *Pilgrimage in Latin America* (New York: Greenwood Press, 1991); Alan Morinis, ed., *Sacred Journeys: The Anthropology of Pilgrimage* (Westport, CT: Greenwood Press, 1992); D. Gross, "Ritual and Conformity: A Religious Pilgrimage to Northern Brazil," *Ethnology* 10 (1971): 129–48; John Eade and Michael J. Sallnow, eds., *Contesting the Sacred: The Anthropology of Christian Pilgrimage* (London: Routledge, 1991); Paolo Giuriatti and Elio Masferrer Kan, *No temas . . . yo soy tu madre: Un estudio socioantropológico de los peregrinos a la Basílica de la Virgen de Guadalupe* (Mexico City: Plaza y Valdes, 1998); Ricardo F. Macip, "Creación de espacios y paisaje sagrado en una peregrinación campesina a Chalma," in Barba de Piña Chan, *Caminos terrestres al cielo*, 73–91; Genoveva Orvaños Busto, "Peregrinación femenina de la diócesis de Querétaro al Tepeyac," *Investigación: Revista Informativa de los Centros de Investigación de la Universidad Autonoma de Querétaro Secretaria Academica* 5, no. 18 (1986): 5–14.

6. De Certeau, *The Practice of Everyday Life,* 97.

7. The all-male pilgrimage dates to 1886. See Valentin F. Frías, "Las peregrinaciones al Tepeyac," in *Léyendas y tradiciones Queretanas,* vol. 3, 170–75 (Mexico City: Plaza y Valdes, 1989).

8. According to the Instituto Nacional de Estadística y Geografia (INEGI), 1,598,139 residents live in Querétaro Arteaga. Like any region, however, Querétaro is constantly giving and taking residents. In 2005, 25,894 Queretanos left the state for another state in the republic, but 69,140 new inhabitants settled in Querétaro. From 1997 to 2002 Querétaro sent 38,391 residents to the United States, 23,485 of whom did not return. In 2000 a study measuring the intensity of state-based migration to the United States conducted by the Consejo Nacional de Población (CONAPO), suggested approximately 5 percent of the state's households receive remittances from family members living abroad. For more statistics, see CONAPO, "Indice de intensidad migratoria México-Estados Unidos por entidad federativa" and "Migración a Estados Unidos por entidad federativa, según migrantes de

retorno y migrantes a Estados Unidos durante el quinquenio, 1997–2002," www.conapo.gob.mx.

9. After a long and tumultuous fight for agrarian reform, the region moved from an agriculture-based economy to an industrial model in the 1940s. World War II pressures and political support from local and state officials guided this shift. According to Martha Morales Garza, Querétaro's governor from 1943 to 1949, Agapito Pozo Balbás, offered legal support for industrial developers with the "law for the protection of industry," which exempted industrial plants from taxes over a ten-year period. By the 1970s and 1980s this sector employed over 75 percent of the state's population, though agriculture and gaming industries remain throughout the state, especially in indigenous regions such as Amealco, a nucleus of Querétaro's Otomí-speaking population. The Mexican republic's series of economic crises in the 1980s and 1990s, however, capped Querétaro's industrial production at 40 percent of its potential (Rámirez Velázquez 1995: 222). This figure has changed with the regenerative effects of the North American Free Trade Agreement (NAFTA). See Martha Gloria Morales Garza, *Grupos, partidos y cultura política en Querétaro* (Querétaro: Universidad Autonoma de Querétaro, 1993), 53–55; and Blanca Rebecca Ramírez Velázquez, *La región en su diferencia: Los valles centrales de Querétaro 1940–1990* (Puebla: Red Nacional de Investigación Urbana, 1995), 222. For an overview of the state's economic development, see Donna J. Keren, *Trabajo y transformación económica de Querétaro* (Mexico City: Instituto Nacional de Antropología e Historia, 1997).

10. According to INEGI data, Mexico is predominantly Catholic, at 88 percent, but Protestantism is on the rise. Roderic Ai Camp writes, "From 1992 to 1994, the Secretariat of Government registered 2,010 religious associations in response to newly introduced constitutional reforms. Of those, only 21 percent were Catholic, and 77 percent were evangelical Protestant. The evangelicals could be subdivided as follows: independent groups, 48 percent; Baptists, 29 percent; Pentecostals, 21 percent; and traditional Protestants (such as Methodists), 2 percent." See Roderic Ai Camp, *Politics in Mexico: The Democratic Transformation*, 4th ed. (Oxford: Oxford University Press, 2002), 88. For a wider lens, see James W. Dow and Alan R. Sandstrom, eds. *Holy Saints and Fiery Preachers: The Anthropology of Protestantism in Mexico and Central America* (New York: Praeger, 2001); and André Corten and Ruth Marshall-Fratani, eds., *From Babel to Pentecost: Transnational Pentecostalism in Africa and Latin America* (Bloomington: Indiana University Press, 2001).

11. Turner and Turner, *Image and Pilgrimage in Christian Culture*, 28.

12. Barba de Piña Chan, *Caminos terrestres al cielo*, 9; and Ana Rita Valero de García Lascurain, "Peregrinación al Tepeyac: Una observación analítica de las romerías guadalupanas," in Barba de Piña Chan, *Caminos terrestres al cielo*, 64.

13. Alicia M. Barabas argues, "La discusión sobre la persistencia de la cosmovisión y ritualidad de origen mesoamericano en las culturas indígenas actuales ha sido retomada por casi todos los mesoamericanistas y estudiosos de las religiones indígenas, sin llegar a un acuerdo definitivo. No obstante, parece que superadas las etnografías de la continuidad que postulaban "supervivencias" del pasado prehispánico, buscando las concordancias entre los rasgos culturales

de la etnias actuales y de las culturas arqueológicas, como apuntara J. Galinier, las obras actuales por lo común explícitas acerca de la existencia de fracturas, transformaciones y cambios, pero tambíen de procesos de reinterpretación de dos vías que se operan en las matrices antiguas de lo sagrado. Los antropólogos nos referimos a estos complejos procesos de creación cultural como sincretismos, apropiación selectiva, resignificación, reinterpretación simbólica o reconfiguración, entre otros términos." See Alicia M. Barabas, "Introducción: Una mirada etnográfica sobre los territorios simbólicos indígenas," in *Diálogos con el territorio: Procesiones, santuarios, y peregrinacions,* vol. 4 (Mexico City: Instituto Nacional de Antropología e Historia, 2004), 18, 28.

14. Turner and Turner, *Image and Pilgrimage in Christian Culture,* 25; my emphasis.

15. Taylor, *The Archive and the Repertoire,* xviii.

16. Victor Turner built the concept of social drama—a cycle of happenings that involves four stages: breach, crisis, redressive action, and reintegration—from Arnold van Gennep's structuralist analysis of ritual, which includes the categories separation, margin or limen, and aggregation. Separation occurs when the individual leaves his home and the comforts and rituals of everyday life. The second phase, margin or limen, is a space of innovation and creativity that develops as a result of the extraordinary circumstances. The third stage, aggregation, is comparable to reintegration or the return to daily life and social roles. For Turner, the "breach" occurs when the devotee leaves her home space, its comforts, and everyday rituals, as well as the laws, hierarchy, and status roles associated with that environment. The "crisis" is the journey itself. This stage is a time of reflection in which the individual battles what she left behind (problems, guilt, hopes, dreams, etc.) and contemplates what she will encounter. Turner refers to this part of the process as liminal space—a threshold individuals cross, breaking free from mundane regulations and constraints to cultivate new political, artistic, or social viewpoints. The third phase—"redressive action"—is taken when the devotee arrives at her destination. The combination of suffering and meditation experienced along the pilgrimage paired with the euphoria of completing the task creates compensation for a wrong or a loss. "Reintegration" happens when she immerses herself once again in everyday life. This last stage of the experience displays her altered viewpoints and perspectives as an individual and as a social subject. See Arnold van Gennep, *The Rites of Passage* (Chicago: University of Chicago Press, 1960); Victor Turner, *The Ritual Process: Structure and Anti-Structure* (Chicago: Aldine, 1969) and *Dramas, Fields, and Metaphors: Symbolic Action in Human Society* (Ithaca, NY: Cornell University Press, 1974); Shadow and Rodriguez V., "Símbolos que amarran, símbolos que dividen"; Macip, "Creación de espacios"; and Pnina Werbner and Helene Basu, eds., *Embodying Charisma: Modernity, Locality and the Performance of Emotion in Sufi Cults* (London: Routledge, 2002).

17. Victor Turner, *The Anthropology of Performance* (New York: Performing Arts Journal, 1986), 157.

18. Simon Coleman and John Eade, "Introduction: Reframing Pilgrimage," in *Reframing Pilgrimage: Cultures in Motion,* ed. Simon Coleman and John Eade (London: Routledge, 2004), 3.

19. Shadow and Rodriguez V., "Símbolos que amarran, símbolos que dividen," 59.

20. Ellen Badone and Sharon R. Roseman, "Approaches to the Anthropology of Pilgrimage and Tourism," in *Intersecting Journeys: The Anthropology of Pilgrimage and Tourism* (Urbana: University of Illinois Press, 2004), 3–5. See also Alan E. Morinis, "Introduction: The Territory of the Anthropology of Pilgrimage," in Morinis, *Sacred Journeys*, 1–27; and John Eade and Michael J. Sallnow, Introduction to Eade and Sallnow, *Contesting the Sacred*, 1–29.

21. In using the verb *sacralize* as opposed to the substantive, Coleman and Eade emphasize the "often partial, performative, contested character of appropriating something or someone as 'holy.'" Coleman and Eade, "Introduction: Reframing Pilgrimage," 18.

22. Roach, *Cities of the Dead*, 26.

23. De Certeau, *The Practice of Everyday Life*, 97–98. Here de Certeau is referring to J.R. Searle's notion of a "speech act" and J.L. Austin's notion of a "performative"—"the issuing of the utterance is the performing of an action." See J.R. Searle, Speech Acts: An Essay in the Philosophy of Language (London: Cambridge University Press, 1969), 16; and J.L. Austin, *How to Do Things with Words*, 2nd ed. (Cambridge, MA: Harvard University Press, 1975), 6.

24. James Fernandez, "Emergence and Convergence in Some African Sacred Places," in *The Anthropology of Space and Place: Locating Culture*, ed. Setha M. Low and Denise Lawrence-Zúñiga (Malden, MA: Blackwell, 2003), 190.

25. Richard Schechner proposes, "The habits, ritual, and routines of life are restored behaviors. Restored behavior is living behavior treated as a film director treats a strip of film. These strips of behavior can be rearranged and reconstructed; they are independent of causal systems (personal, social, political, technological, etc.) that brought them into existence. They have a life of their own. . . . Restored behavior is the key process of every kind of performing, in everyday life, in healing, in ritual, in play, and in the arts." See Richard Schechner, *Performance Studies: An Introduction*, 1st ed. (New York: Routledge, 2002), 28. For his initial conceptualization of the term, see his *Between Theater and Anthropology* (Philadelphia: University of Pennsylvania Press, 1985), 35.

26. América E. Arredondo Huerta, *Semblanza histórica de la peregrinación femenina: Querétaro-Tepeyac 1936–1995* (Querétaro: Universidad Autonoma de Querétaro, 1996), 31.

27. Ibid., 34.

28. Ibid., 34–35.

29. Ibid., 35.

30. Mary Douglas, *Purity and Danger* (London: Routledge, 1966), 4.

31. This rite also occurs during the all-male pilgrimage. A noteworthy difference is that the boys dress as Juan Diego.

32. Prayer booklet, "Sin siembra no hay cosecha, sin palabra no hay Eucaristía," Directiva Seglar de la 47a Peregrinación Femenina a pie de Querétaro al Tepeyac, Querétaro, 2005, 4–5.

33. Ibid., 5.

34. According to INEGI, 70 percent of Querétaro's residents are based in urban areas, 30 percent in rural areas. See www.inegi.org.mx.

35. Orvaños Busto, "Peregrinación femenina," 5; my emphasis.

36. "47ª Peregrinación Femenina a pie de Querétaro al Tepeyac, Santiago de Querétaro, Querétaro, 2005, 34.

37. There are several studies of the business-related dimensions of pilgrimage. See, e.g., Vitor Ambrósio and Margarida Pereira, "Case Study 2: Christian/ Catholic Pilgrimage-Studies and Analyses," in *Religious Tourism and Pilgrimage Festivals Management: An International Perspective,* ed. Razaq Raj and Nigel D. Morpeth (Cambridge, MA: CAB International, 2007), 140–52. For an international perspective of how business affects sacred space, see Singh and Singh, *Trends in the Geography of Pilgrimages.*

38. Orvaños Busto, "Peregrinación femenina," 12.

39. For more on religious ritual and socioeconomic benefits, see Mary O'Connor, "The Virgin of Guadalupe and the Economics of Symbolic Behavior," *Journal for the Scientific Study of Religion* 28, no. 2 (1989): 105–19; and John M. Giggie and Diane Winston, eds., *Faith in the Market: Religion and the Rise of Urban Commercial Culture* (New Brunswick, NJ : Rutgers University Press, 2002).

40. Censo Económicos, "Querétaro Arteaga: Resultados generales," 2004. www.inegi.gob.mx.

41. According to CONAPO (2005), the national median income was 79,551 pesos (roughly US$7,955). www.conapo.gob.mx.

42. Mary Weismantel, *Cholas and Pishtacos: Tales of Race and Sex in Andean South America* (Chicago: University of Chicago Press, 2001), 187–88.

43. Pilgrimage coverage insert, *Diario de Querétaro,* July 14 and 15, 2006.

44. Quoted in Anna McCarthy, *Ambient Television: Visual Culture and Public Space* (Durham, NC: Duke University Press, 2001), 16. For Feurer's full discussion, see Jane Feurer, "The Concept of Live Television: Ontology as Ideology," in *Regarding Television: Critical Approaches—An Anthology,* ed. E. Ann Kaplan (Frederick, MD: AFI/University Publications of America, 1983), 12–22. For terrific essays that engage television and other forms of media, see Purnima Mankekar, *Screening Culture, Viewing Politics: An Ethnography of Television, Womanhood, and Nation in Postcolonial India* (Durham, NC: Duke University Press, 1999); and Faye D. Ginsburg, Lila Abu-Lughod, and Brian Larkin, eds., *Media Worlds: Anthropology on a New Terrain*(Berkeley: University of California Press, 2002).

45. Song booklet, "Peregrinación Femenina a pie de Querétaro al Tepeyac," Directiva Seglar de la 47a Peregrinación Femenina a pie de Querétaro al Tepeyac, Querétaro, 2005, 45.

46. Personal correspondence, William B. Taylor, December 2006.

47. According to CONAPO, Querétaro is 95 percent Catholic. www.conapo .gob.mx.

48. Adams, "Political and Economic Correlates of Pilgrimage Behavior," 149.

3. FEELING HISTORY

1. Like many dotting preindependence Spanish territories in Latin America, government buildings, markets, and a Catholic church surround the central

plaza, which functions as a "psychological focus" of certain towns. See Setha Low, *On the Plaza: The Politics of Public Space and Culture* (Austin: University of Texas Press, 2000), 51–52.

2. Saba Mahmood, *The Politics of Piety: The Islamic Revival and the Feminist Subject* (Princeton: Princeton University Press, 2005), 37.

3. Ibid.

4. Ibid., 15.

5. Phillip L. Wagner suggests, "If we look on pilgrimage as an epitome of devout life, the laborious procession up to Guadalupe can be seen to exemplify the virtuous regime of humility and simplicity, unswerving faith, and patient effort held essential to salvation. It certifies the devotees as worthy of the spiritual benefits (and practical assistance) that they expect the entry into the holy places to confer, and may even atone for derelictions in the past." See Wagner, "Pilgrimage: Culture and Geography," 305. Wagner articulates an interpretation often superimposed on the ritual of pilgrimage. This case study does corroborate his perspective. The evidence, however, delves deeper into the moments of interaction and exchange that make suffering absolute not only to spectators but also to fellow devotees.

6. De Certeau, *The Practice of Everyday Life,* 129.

7. INEGI, "Perspectiva estadística. Serie por entidad federativa, Michoacán de Ocampo," 2006. www.inegi.gob.mx.

8. CONAPO, "Migración a Estados Unidos por entidad federativa, según migrantes de retorno y migrantes a Estados Unidos durante el quinquenio, 1997–2002," 2002. www.conapo.gob.mx.

9. INEGI, "Ingresos-remesas familiares en la entidad Michoacán de Ocampo," Balanza de pago: Ingresos por remesas familiares, 2003, www.inegi.gob .mx.

10. INEGI, "Consulta de: Población total con estimación Por: Entidad municipio y loc/Según: Sexo," 2005. www.inegi.gob.mx.

11. Paul Connerton, *How Societies Remember* (Cambridge: Cambridge University Press, 1989), 5.

12. Elaine Scarry, *The Body in Pain: The Making and Unmaking of the World* (New York: Oxford University Press, 1985), 162.

13. See, e.g., Carolyn Rouse, "Shopping with Sister Zubayda: African American Sunni Muslim Rituals of Consumption and Belonging," in *Women and Religion in the African Diaspora: Knowledge, Power, and Performance,* ed. R. Marie Griffith and Barbara Dianne Savage (Baltimore, MD: Johns Hopkins University Press, 2006), , 245–65; Gardner, *Global Migrants, Local Lives;* Mahmood, *Politics of Piety;* Sherry B. Ortner, *High Religion: A Cultural and Political History of Sherpa Buddhism* (Princeton, NJ: Princeton University Press, 1989); and C.J. Fuller, *The Renewal of the Priesthood: Modernity and Traditionalism in a South Indian Temple* (Princeton, NJ: Princeton University Press, 1989).

14. Barba de Piña Chan, "Introducción."

15. The regenerative effects of pilgrimage transcend religious and cultural affiliations. As Nancy L. Frey writes in her study of the aftermath of the Camino de Santiago, "For some, the journey continues as a spiritual path of prayer, a budding interest in religion, a springboard to other pilgrimages and journeys,

and even a conversation. For others, the journey continues as a path of personal growth or leads to other humanitarian interests or a new career. Many feel a strong sense of gratitude to the Camino." See Nancy L. Frey, "Stories of the Return: Pilgrimage and Its Aftermaths," in *Intersecting Journeys: The Anthropology of Pilgrimage and Tourism,* ed. Nancy Badone and Sharon R. Roseman (Urbana: University of Illinois Press, 2004), 102.

16. For an analysis of the New York–bound pilgrimage in Manhattan, see Gálvez, "'She Made Us Human.'"

17. For the full version of the song, see Appendix.

18. See Gail Mummert, ed., *Fronteras fragmentadas* (Morelia: Colegio de Michoacán/Centro de Investigaciones y Desarrollo del Estado de Michoacán, 1999); Roberto Lovato, "A Migrant Summit," *Nation* (July 13, 2007); David A. Badillo, "Religion and Transnational Migration in Chicago: The Case of the Potosinos," *Journal of the Illinois State Historical Society* (Winter 2001–2), 420–40; Gerardo Necoechea Gracia, "Customs and Resistance: Mexican Immigrants in Chicago, 1910–1930," in *Border Crossings: Mexican and Mexican-American Workers,* ed. John Mason Hart (New York: Rowman and Littlefield, 1998), 185–208; Roger Rouse, "Migración al suroeste de Michoacán durante el Porfiriato: El caso de Aguililla," in *Movimientos de población en el occidente de México,* ed. Thomas Calvo and Gustavo López (Mexico City and Zamora: CEMCA and Colegio de Michoacán, 1988).

4. DEVOTION IN THE CITY

1. Vásquez and Friedmann Marquardt, *Globalizing the Sacred,* 72. For a full-length discussion, see also Karen McCarthy Brown, "Staying Grounded in a High-Rise Building: Ecological Dissonance and Riual Accommodation in Haitian Vodou," in Orsi, *Gods of the City,* 79–102.

2. Eliade proposes that an axis mundi "represents an ideal point which belongs not to profane geometrical space, but to sacred space; a point in which communication with Heaven or Hell may be realized. [A place] where the planes intersect, the point at which the sensuous world can be transcended." See Mircea Eliade, *Images and Symbols: Studies in Religious Symbolism,* trans. Phillip Mairet (Princeton, NJ: Princeton University Press, 1991), 75.

3. The fear or apprehension these ethnonational performances engender tie into larger xenophobic sentiments about illegal immigration to the United States. In Chicago one way this anti-immigration anxiety manifests itself is through political campaigns. Jim Oberweis, a two-time Republican nominee for the Illinois State Senate, for example, targeted Mexican immigration as a problem that he would fix. One of his televised campaign commercials panned across Soldier Field (home of the Chicago Bears) filling up with an estimated 10,000 people while a voice-over compared this figure to the daily influx of Mexicans to the Chicago area. Anti-Mexican sentiments like Oberweis's are not new. We can trace police harassment, segregation, rights limitations, and the verbal and physical mistreatment of Mexicans and other migrants as "temporary" or second-class foreigners back to the Great Depression. The government deported tens of thousands of Mexican laborers and then brought them back during the Bracero Program. In

1971 Illinois state senators and congressional representatives put out an alarmist report,the "Illegal Mexican Alien Problem." The prevalence of these images and texts has created a culture of fear among Chicago-area residents that directly affects public interpretations of ethnoreligious devotion in Rogers Park. For more information, see De Genova and Ramos-Zayas, *Latino Crossings,* 37–38.

4. Orsi, *Gods of the City,* 41.

5. Roach, *Cities of the Dead,* 76.

6. Orsi, *Gods of the City,* 47.

7. Carl Sandburg, *Chicago Poems* (New York: Henry Holt and Co., 1916), 3–4.

8. Gregory D. Squires, Larry Bennett, Kathleen McCourt, and Phillip Nyden, *Chicago: Race, Class, and the Response to Urban Decline* (Philadelphia: Temple University Press, 1987), 26.

9. Established in the 1830s by an Irishman, Phillip Rogers, who had purchased land "ceded" by the Potawatomi Indians, the eponymous township provided newly arriving immigrants from Ireland, England, Sweden, Germany, and Luxembourg with 1,600 acres of farmland. The area remained sparsely populated for much of the nineteenth century. The construction of the Chicago and Milwaukee Railroad in 1859, however, increased economic and social activity. In the 1870s Patrick L. Touhy and other area developers—Greenleaf, Lunt, Morse, Farwell, and Pratt—established the Rogers Park Land Association. For more on Rogers Park in the nineteenth century, see Neal Samors, Mary Jo Doyle, Martin Lewin, and Michael Williams, *Chicago's Far North Side: An Illustrated History of Rogers Park and West Ridge* (Chicago: Rogers Park/West Ridge Society, 1997), 151; Neal Samors, Michael Williams, and Mary Jo Doyle, *Neighborhoods within Neighborhoods: Twentieth-Century Life on Chicago's Far North Side* (Chicago: Rogers Park/West Ridge Society, 2002); James R. Grossman, Ann Durkin Keating, and Janice L. Reiff., eds., "Rogers Park," in *The Encyclopedia of Chicago* (Chicago: University of Chicago Press, 2004), 714–15; and David K. Fremon, *Chicago Politics Ward by Ward* (Bloomington: Indiana University Press, 1988), 326.

10. The U.S. policies of contracting laborers, deporting them, and even interning them, in response to the fluctuating political and economic climate, continues to be a lucrative enterprise for American employers. This mobile labor source is essentially cheap, fearful, and expendable. They work for subminimum wages, do not require benefits, and will not contest harsh labor conditions for fear of deportation or incarceration. One incentive to persevere through dismal working conditions and endure political prejudice is establishing informal economic circuits, or networking "from below," through which to send remittances. Achille Mbembe's study of mobilization of spaces and resources in Africa as well as Alejandro Portes's work on North American immigration examine how this type of mobilization develops "from below." Unlike multinational and transnational corporations that have financial and political muscle, informal development is contingent on social capital, especially kin and friendship networks that migrants develop in the workplace, the community, and other social spaces. Yet processes "from above" and "from below" are not

mutually exclusive. See Alejandro Portes, "Global Villagers: The Rise of Trans-national Communities," *American Prospect* 25 (March–April 1996): 74–77. See also Achille Mbembe, "At the Edge of the World: Boundaries, Territoriality, and Sovereignty in Africa," in Appadurai, *Globalization,* 259–84; Smith and Guarnizo, *Transnationalism from Below;* Saskia Sassen, *Globalization and Its Discontents* (New York: New Press, 1998); Sassen, "Spatialities and Temporalities of the Global"; Roger Rouse, "Making Sense of Settlement: Class Transfor-mation, Cultural Struggle, and Transnationalism among Mexican Migrants in the United States," in *Towards a Transnational Perspective on Migration: Race, Class, Ethnicity, and Nationalism,* ed. Nina Glick-Schiller, Linda Basch, and Christina Szanton-Blanc (New York: New York Academy of Sciences, 1992), 25–52; Nina Glick-Schiller and Georges Fouron, "'I Am Not a Problem with-out a Solution': Poverty and Transnational Migration," in *The New Poverty Studies: The Ethnography of Power, Politics, and Impoverished People in the United States,* ed. Judith Goode and Jeff Maskovsky (New York: New York University Press, 2001), 321–63; and Josiah Heyman, "State Effects on Labor Exploitation," *Critique of Anthropology* 18, no. 2 (1998): 157–80.

11. The Immigration Act of 1965, drafted in an era of heightened racial ten-sion, first initiated the practice of applying quotas less selectively by focusing on hemispheric migration rather than on individual countries. Many immigration analysts and scholars of religion choose to focus on immigrant community for-mation after 1965 because of the changes brought about by this legislation. Al-though there is evidence that substantial shifts in population growth, ethnic makeup, and religious diversity occurred after 1965, it is by no means a starting point. Twenty years later the Reagan administration formulated "the answer" to illegality in the form of an amnesty to approximately three million undocu-mented laborers who could prove that they were working in the country prior to 1982. This Immigration and Reform Act of 1986 also increased penalties to employers who knowingly hired undocumented personnel. These superficial in-terventions proved a temporary solution, as, for example, they actually strength-ened chain-migration networks among migrants. In the 1990s the temperamen-tal political backlash against immigrant laborers resurfaced. In November 1994, under Governor Pete Wilson, California voters passed Proposition 187, denying public benefits to illegal aliens across the state. Following California's lead, the federal government, in conjunction with state legislators, initiated the Illegal Im-migration Reform and Immigrant Responsibility Act of 1996, which imposed nationwide barriers (i.e., proof of documentation) to social services and medical care, thus denying undocumented individuals basic human rights. National law-makers, constrained by the illusion of bipartisan politics, continue to struggle with comprehensive immigration reform.

12. Betancur, Córdova, and de los Angeles Torres, "Economic Restructur-ing"; see also Saskia Sassen, *The Mobility of Labor and Capital: A Study in International Investment and Labor Flow* (Cambridge: Cambridge University Press, 1988).

13. Pierrette Hondagneu-Sotelo, *Gendered Transitions: Mexican Experi-ences of Immigration* (Berkeley: University of California Press, 1994), 5.

14. Alejandro Portes and Robert A. Bach, *Latin Journey: Cuban and Mexican Immigrants in the United States* (Berkeley: University of California Press, 1985), 7–8.

15. Douglas S. Massey, "The Settlement Process among Mexican Migrants to the United States," *American Sociological Review* 51 (1986): 683. See also Douglas S. Massey, Jorge Durand, and Nolan J. Malone, *Beyond Smoke and Mirrors: Mexican Immigration in an Era of Economic Integration* (New York: Russell Sage Foundation, 2002); Frank D. Bean, *At the Crossroads: Mexican Migration and U.S. Policy* (Lanham, MD: Rowman and Littlefield, 1997); Frank D. Bean and Stephanie Bell-Rose, eds., *Immigration and Opportunity: Race, Ethnicity, and Employment in the United States* (New York: Russell Sage Foundation, 1999); Alejandro Portes and Rubén G. Rumbaut, *Immigrant America: A Portrait* (Berkeley: University of California Press, 1996); and Marcelo M. Suárez-Orozco, *Crossings: Mexican Immigration in Interdisciplinary Perspectives* (Cambridge, MA: Harvard University, David Rockefeller Center for Latin American Studies, 1998).

16. The majority of this community moved westward toward the South Lawndale neighborhood, now Little Village. Theoretically, this process should not have benefited institutions or city projects because 1954 legislation limited urban renewal to residential spaces. Daley's machine politics, "favoritism based on political criteria in personnel decisions, contracting, and administration of laws," however, redirected funds to the expansion and/or renovation of universities, hospitals, and "industrially depressed areas." See Squires et al., *Chicago*, 63, 104.

17. Squires and his colleagues address the function and motives of four institutional actors who manipulate neighborhood space—banks and savings and loan institutions, municipal zoning regulations, government agencies, and real estate companies. These players determine who receives and does not receive mortgage money, housing plans in particular metropolitan areas, where racial groups will be "steered," and the enforcement or relaxation of federal guidelines See Squires et al., *Chicago*, 93–94.

18. Samors et al., *Chicago's Far North Side*, 120, 123–24.

19. Citing a speech by Anthony Downs to the Chicago Real Estate Board in 1964, Dwight Conquergood, in his study of tenement housing in Albany Park, examines the links among property politics, multiculturalism, and how structural factors direct lower-income communities toward "gray areas." Drawing from de Certeau, Conquergood argues that these nonwhites, often perceived as "immigrants," "floaters," or "transients"—communities unattached to a "proper place"—"embody the instability of 'transitional' neighborhoods they pass through and upset. No one wants to recognize that their nomadic practices are economically constrained." See Conquergood, "Life in Big Red," 99, 138–39.

20. Fremon, *Chicago Politics Ward by Ward*, 326–30.

21. See Samors, Williams, and Doyle, *Neighborhoods within Neighborhoods*, 26. For an idealized interpretation of religious practice in Rogers Park, see Lowell Livezey, "Communities and Enclaves: Where Jews, Christians, Hindus, and Muslims Share the Neighborhoods" in *Public Religion and Urban*

Transformation: Faith in the City, ed. Lowell Livezey (New York: New York University Press, 2001), 133–62.

22. Manuel A. Vásquez, "Historicizing and Materializing the Study of Religion," in *Immigrant Faiths: Transforming Religious Life in America* (New York: AltaMira, 2005), 220.

23. For more on religious pluralism in America, see Diana L. Eck, *On Common Ground: World Religions in America* (New York: Columbia University Press, 1997); Orsi, *Gods of the City;* R. Stephen Warner and Judith G. Wittner, eds., *Gatherings in Diaspora: Religious Communities and the New Immigration* (Philadelphia: Temple University Press, 1998); Barbara McGraw and Jo Renee Formicola, eds., *Taking Religious Pluralism Seriously: Spiritual Politics on America's Sacred Ground* (Waco, TX: Baylor University Press, 2005); and Stephen Prothero, ed., *A Nation of Religions: The Politics of Pluralism in Multireligious America* (Chapel Hill: University of North Carolina Press, 2006).

24. Personal correspondence, June 12, 2006.

25. Samors et al., *Chicago's Far North Side,* 126.

26. Fremon, *Chicago Politics Ward by Ward,* 327.

27. According to the 2000 U.S. census, Rogers Park residents were 70.21 percent white, 9.91 percent black, 10.96 percent Hispanic, 8.92 percent Asian and other.

28. Samors, Williams, and Doyle, *Neighborhoods within Neighborhoods,* 140–41.

29. Squires et al., *Chicago,* 112; Fremon, *Chicago Politics Ward by Ward,* 330.

30. Samors, Williams, and Doyle, *Neighborhoods within Neighborhoods,* 69.

31. Victor Turner, *Dramas, Fields, and Metaphors: Symbolic Action in Human Society* IIthaca, NY: Cornell University Press, 1974), 46.

32. Julia Lieblich, "Believers See Apparition of Virgin: Image on Tree in Rogers Park Comforts Many," *Chicago Tribune,* July 11, 2001, 7.

33. Ibid.

34. Historians, sociologists, and literary figures have written extensively about the symbolic and literal qualities of altars. The museum honoring the Virgin of Guadalupe located at Tepeyac/La Villa in Mexico City, for example, has a permanent exhibition dedicated to these devotional acts. For an excellent overview of Catholic altars and migration issues on the U.S-Mexico border, see Jorge Durand and Douglas Massey, *Miracles on the Border: Retablos of Mexican Migrants to the United* States (Tucson: University of Arizona Press, 1995).

35. Although it focuses explicitly on the notion of an informal sector, studies of informal economic activity owe much to the following article: Keith Hart, "Informal Income Opportunities and Urban Employment in Ghana," *Journal of Modern African Studies* 11, no. 1 (1973): 61–89. For a recent overview of scholarship, see Keith Hart, "Bureaucratic Form and the Informal Economy," in *Linking the Formal and Informal Economy: Concepts and Policies,* ed. B. Guha-Khasnobis, R. Kanbur, and E. Ostrom (Oxford: Oxford University Press, 2006), 21–35.

36. Betancur et al., "Economic Restructuring," 110.

37. He seemed like a reasonable man until he told me that he used to work as a homicide detective in the "really bad parts" of the city, where between two and five people would die a night. "Gangbangers," he said knowingly. He also reported that he witnessed a "cleansing" with all of the violence. After this charming conversation, he proceeded to invite me out for a drink. I ran away from him.

38. Matechine dance is rooted in popular conceptions of Mexico's indigenous culture. Men and women of all ages perform this dance, which consists of repetitive choreographed movements and sometimes features a good versus evil narrative, to enhance communion with la Virgen de Guadalupe. The substance and practice of this dance is different from region to region across the Americas. For a site-specific look at matechine dancing, see Sklar, *Dancing with the Virgin.*

39. Incarnations of Mary have appeared numerous times across the United States and especially in the Chicago area. For example, in summer 1999 there was a sighting in the suburb of Joliet. In summer 2001 la Virgen de Guadalupe appeared in Rogers Park. More recently, in 2005, an image of Mary appeared under an expressway in Chicago. This apparition received national and international attention from CBS, MSNBS, the *Chicago Tribune,* and other news sources.

40. I use "constituents" here, as opposed to "residents," in order to look more deeply at the circuits of power and privilege running through the development of sacred space in that urban landscape. The constituents, or voters, in the neighborhood have open communication with the Chicago Police Department because they are legally able to voice their opinion. Undocumented Guadalupan devotees do not have this luxury.

41. Wesley G. Skogan, Lynn Steiner, Jill DuBois, J. Erik Gudell, and Aimee Fagan, "Community Policing and 'The New Immigrants,'" *NIJ Research Report*-NCJ 189908 (Washington, DC: U.S. Department of Justice, 2002), 1.

42. Wesley G. Skogan, Lynn Steiner, Jill DuBois, J. Erik Gudell, and Aimee Fagan, "Taking Stock: Community Policing in Chicago," *NIJ Research Report*-NCJ 189909 (Washington, DC: U.S. Department of Justice, 2002), 1–4.

43. Ibid., 8.

44. See Micaela di Leonardo, *Exotics at Home: Anthropologies, Others and American Modernity* (Chicago: University of Chicago Press, 1998), 32; and Dwight Conquergood, "The Power of Symbols," *One City* (Summer 1996): 11–13.

45. Lefebvre, *The Production of Space,* 33–34.

CONCLUSION

1. De Certeau, *The Practice of Everyday Life,* 35.

2. Adapting Marcel Mauss's work on the phenomenon of gift exchange alerts us to how devotional labor or presentations of spirituality can shape intracommunity power circuits and status positions. He astutely proposes, "Presentations which are in theory voluntary, disinterested and spontaneous, are in fact obligatory and interested." See Marcel Mauss, *The Gift: Forms and Func-*

tions of Exchange in Archaic Societies, trans. Ian Cunnison (Glencoe, IL: Free Press, 1954), 77; and Bourdieu, *Outline of a Theory of Practice,* 171–77.

3. Lefebvre, *The Production of Space,* 33–39.

4. Roach, *Cities of the Dead,* 39.

5. Their anthropological claims and comparisons of religion positioned science, not religion or magic, as humanity's triumph—the impetus for civilization's evolution from superstition to progress via empirical fact. Though critiqued for their methodological shortcomings, their analyses remain elemental to any contemporary understanding of religion.

6. See Daniel L. Pals, "Reductionism and Belief: An Appraisal of Recent Attacks on the Doctrine of Irreducible Religion," *Journal of Religion* 66 (1986): 18; see also Ivan Strenski, "Reduction without Tears," in *Religion and Reductionism* (New York: Brill, 1994), 95–107; Robert Segal, "In Defense of Reductionism," in *Religion and the Social Sciences: Essays on the Confrontation* (Atlanta: Scholars Press, 1989), , 5–36; and Charlotte Allen, "Is Nothing Sacred? Casting out the Gods from Religious Studies," *Lingua Franca* (November): 30–40.

7. See Rudolf Otto, *The Idea of the Holy,* trans. John W. Harvey (London: Oxford University Press, 1923), 4.

8. Anti-irreductionist critics use Otto's treatise and Eliade's condemnation of "the audacious and irrelevant interpretations of religious realities made by psychologists, sociologists, or devotees of various reductionist ideologies" to argue that they too are complicit in a reductionist enterprise. Ivan Strenski further cites Eliade's approach as "reductionist (by replacement)": " Eliade rejects all explanations of religion which do not reflect their 'spiritual nature' (whatever that means). . . . Eliade tries to replace all other definitions and theories of religion by his well-known interpretation of data in terms of their reflection of transcendental archetypes." Strenski, "Reduction without Tears," 95, 102.

9. Guadalupan committee members in Des Plaines, for example, chose to hang various flags from different nations at the Second Tepeyac, thereby metaphorically expanding the boundaries of sacred space.

10. Manuel A. Vásquez, "Historicizing and Materializing the Study of Religion," in *Immigrant Faiths: Transforming Religious Life in America,* ed. Karen I. Leonard, Alex Stepick, Manuel A. Vásquez, and Jennifer Holdaway (New York: AltaMira Press, 2005), 222.

11. Thomas Tweed productively suggests, "Theories are simultaneously proposals for a journey, representations of a journey, and the journey itself." See Thomas Tweed, *Crossing and Dwelling: A Theory of Religion* (Cambridge, MA: Harvard University Press, 2006), 9.

12. Lefebvre, *The Production of Space,* 33–34.

13. Ibid., 33–39.

14. Ibid., 44.

15. David Harvey's call to grapple with how "spatial constructs are created and used as fixed markers of human memory and of social values in a world of rapid flux and change," played a key role in bringing these types of interventions to the foreground of this analysis. See David Harvey, "Between Space and Time: Reflections on the Geographical Imagination," *Annals of the Association of American Geographers* 80, no. 3 (1990): 429.

16. Catherine Bell, "Performance," in *Critical Terms for Religious Studies*, ed. Mark C. Taylor (Chicago: University of Chicago Press, 1998), 208.

17. Ibid.

18. As Margaret Thompson Drewal suggests in her critical evaluation of research in Africa, "Performance participants can self-reflexively monitor their behavior in the process of doing. Therefore, more than simply observing that performance is emergent, it is crucial to examine the rhetoric of performers situated in time and place. For performance as a mode of activity is often tactical and improvisational." Thompson Drewal's intervention advocates for a relationship based on reciprocity, one that is focused on the performer's agency, how these communities continually theorize their traditions, the temporal and spatial components of their performances, and on the researcher's role as coactor and interpreter. See Margaret Thompson Drewal, "The State of Research on Performance in Africa," *African Studies Review* 34, no. 3 (1991): 2–3.

19. Conquergood, "Performance Studies." For implementation of these ideas, see Conquergood, "Health Theatre in a Hmong Refugee Camp" and "Life in Big Red."

Bibliography

Adams, Walter R. "Political and Economic Correlates of Pilgrimage Behavior." *Anales de Antropología* 20 (1983): 142–72.

Aguilar, César. "Un misterio las linanzas de la Basílica." *Vértigo* 4, no. 195 (2004): 35.

Aguilera, Carmen, and Arturo Montero García, eds. *Tepeyac estudios históricos*. Mexico City: Universidad del Tepeyac, 2000.

Ai Camp, Roderic. *Politics in Mexico: The Democratic Transformation*. 4th ed. Oxford: Oxford University Press, 2002.

Alarcón, Norma. "Chicana's Feminist Literature: A Re-Vision through Malintzin/or Malintzin: Putting Flesh Back on the Object." In *This Bridge Called My Back: Writings by Radical Women of Color*, edited by Cherríe Moraga and Gloria Anzaldúa, 182–90. New York: Kitchen Table/Women of Color Press, 1983.

Alvarez, Robert. *Mangos, Chiles, and Truckers: The Business of Transnationalism*. Minneapolis: University of Minnesota Press, 2005.

Ambrósio, Vitor, and Margarida Pereira. "Case Study 2: Christian/Catholic Pilgrimage-Studies and Analyses." In *Religious Tourism and Pilgrimage Festivals Management: An International Perspective*, edited by R. Raj and N.D. Morpeth, 140–52. Cambridge, MA: CAB International, 2007.

Anderson, Benedict. *Imagined Communities*. London: Verso Press, 1983.

Anon. *Las peregrinaciones religiosas en la humanidad, en el cristianismo y en México*. Mexico City: Tip. Berrueco Hmos San Felipe Neri, 1887.

Anzaldúa, Gloria. *Borderlands/La Frontera: The New Mestiza*. San Francisco: Aunt Lute Books, 1987.

Año Nuevo Kerr, Louise. "The Chicano Experience in Chicago, 1920–1970." Ph.D. diss., University of Illinois at Chicago, 1976.

Appadurai, Arjun, ed. *The Social Life of Things.* Cambridge: Cambridge University Press, 1988.

Araiza Velázquez, Elvira. "La Virgen de Guadalupe de México: Para América." *Boletín Guadalupano* 2, no. 34 (2003): 8–10.

Arias Jirasek, Rita, and Carlos Tortolero. *Images of America: Mexican Chicago.* Chicago: Arcadia, 2001.

Arredondo, Gabriela F. *Mexican Chicago: Race, Identity, and Nation, 1916–39.* Urbana: University of Illinois Press, 2008.

Arredondo Huerta, América E. *Semblanza histórica de la peregrinación femenina: Querétaro-Tepeyac, 1936–1995.* Querétaro: Universidad Autonoma de Querétaro, 1996.

Austin, J.L. *How to Do Things with Words.* 2nd ed. Cambridge, MA: Harvard University Press, 1975.

Avalos, Hector, ed. *Introduction to the U.S. Latina and Latino Religious Experience.* Boston: Brill, 2004.

Bachin, Robin F. *Building on the South Side: Urban Space and Civic Culture in Chicago, 1890–1919.* Chicago: University of Chicago Press, 2004.

Badillo, David A. *Latinos and the New Immigrant Church.* Baltimore, MD: Johns Hopkins University Press, 2006.

———. "Religion and Transnational Migration in Chicago: The Case of the Potosin." *Journal of the Illinois State Historical Society* (Dec.–Jan. 2001): 420–40.

Badone, Ellen, and Sharon R. Roseman. *Intersecting Journeys: The Anthropology of Pilgrimage and Tourism.* Urbana: University of Illinois Press, 2004.

Bailey, David C. *Viva Cristo Rey! The Cristero Rebellion and the Church-State Conflict in Mexico.* Austin: University of Texas Press, 1974.

Baker-Cristales, Beth. *Salvadoran Migration to Southern California: Redefining el Hermano Lejano.* Gainesville: University Press of Florida, 2004.

Barabas, Alicia M. "Introducción: Una mirada etnográfica sobre los territorios simbólicos indígenas." In *Diálogos con el territorio: Procesiones, santuarios y peregrinaciones.* Vol. 4. Mexico City: Instituto Nacional de Antropología e Historia, 2004.

Barba de Piña Chan, Beatriz, ed. "Introducción." In *Caminos terrestres al cielo: Contribución alestudio del fenómeno romero* 10. Serie Antropología Social. Mexico City: Instituto Nacional de Antropología e Historia, 1998.

Barthes, Roland. *The Grain of the Voice: Interviews, 1962–1980.* Translated by Linda Coverdale. New York: Hill and Wang, 1985.

Basch, Linda, Nina Glick-Schiller, and Cristina Blanc-Szanton. *Nations Unbound: Transnational Projects, Postcolonial Predicaments, and Deterritorialized Nation-States.* Langhorne, PA: Gordon and Breach, 1994.

Bau, Ignatius. *This Ground Is Holy: Church Sanctuary and Central American Refugees.* Mahwah, NJ: Paulist Press, 1985.

Bazarte Martínez, Alicia. *Las cofradías de españoles en la ciudad de México (1526–1869).* Mexico City: Universidad Autonoma de México, 1989.

Bazarte Martínez, Alicia, and Clara García Ayluardo. *Los costos de la salvación: Las cofradías y la Ciudad de México.* Mexico City: Instituto Politécnico Nacional/Archivo General de la Nación, 2001.

Bean, Frank D. *At the Crossroads: Mexican Migration and U.S. Policy.* Lanham, MD: Rowman and Littlefield, 1997.

———. *Immigration and Opportunity: Race, Ethnicity, and Employment in the United States.* Edited by Stephanie Bell-Rose. New York: Russell Sage Foundation, 1999.

Bean, Frank D., and B. Lindsay Lowell. "Unauthorized Migration." In *The New Americans: A Guide to Immigration since 1965,* edited by Mary C. Waters and Reed Ueda, 70–82. Cambridge, MA: Harvard University Press, 2007.

Beauvoir, Simone de. *The Second Sex.* New York: Knopf, 1952.

Becker, Marjorie. *Setting the Virgin on Fire: Lázaro Cárdenas, Michoacán Peasants, and the Redemption of the Mexican Revolution.* Berkeley: University of California Press, 1995.

Bell, Catherine. *Ritual Theory, Ritual Practice.* Oxford: Oxford University Press, 1992.

Belmonte, Edmundo Félix. "El presidente Kennedy en la Basílica de Guadalupe." *La Voz Guadalupana* 28 (1962–63): 3.

Bennett, Herman L. *Africans in Colonial Mexico: Absolutism, Christianity, and Afro-Creole Consciousness, 1570–1640.* Bloomington: Indiana University Press, 2003.

Berger, John. *About Looking.* New York: Vintage, 1980.

Bernstein, Nina. "Wait for U.S. Residency Soars over 18-Month Span." *New York Times,* April 6, 2004, New York Region ed.

Betancur, John, Teresa Córdova, and María De los Angeles Torres. "Economic Restructuring and the Process of Incorporation of Latinos in the Chicago Economy." In *Latinos in a Changing U.S. Economy: Comparative Perspectives on Growing Inequality,* edited by Rebecca Morales and Frank Bonilla, 109–32. Newbury Park, CA: Sage, 1993.

Blancarte, Roberto, "Aspectos internacionales del conflicto religioso mexicano en la década de los treinta." In *Cultura e identidad nacional,* edited by Roberto Blancarte, 233–60. Mexico City: Fondo de Cultura Económica, 1994.

———. *Historia de la iglesia católica en México.* Mexico City: Fondo de Cultura Económica, 1992.

———. "Modernidad, secularización y religión; La iglesia Católica. El estado y la sociedad mexicana en el umbral del Siglo XXI." In *México a fines del siglo,* vol. 2, edited by José Woldenberg and José Joaquin Blanco. Mexico City: Fondo de Cultura Económica, 1993.

Boehm, Deborah A. "Our Lady of Resistance: The Virgin of Guadalupe and Contested Constructions of Community in Santa Fe, New Mexico." *Journal of the Southwest* 44 (Spring 2002): 95–104.

Bourdieu, Pierre. *Distinction: A Social Critique of the Judgment of Taste.* Translated by Richard Nice. Cambridge: Cambridge University Press, 1984.

———. *The Logic of Practice.* Translated by Richard Nice. Stanford: Stanford University Press, 1980.

———. *Outline of a Theory of Practice.* Translated by Richard Nice. Cambridge: Cambridge University Press, 1977.

Brading, David A. *Mexican Phoenix. Our Lady of Guadalupe: Image and Tradition across Five Centuries.* Cambridge: Cambridge University Press, 2001.

Broadway, Bill. "Carrying a Torch for Hope: Bearers of Flame from Our lady of Guadalupe Relay Message to Immigrants in U.S." *Washington Post,* November 30, 2002, B9.

Bumiller, Elisabeth, and Marc Lacey. "McCain Winds up Latin Trip in Mexico." *New York Times,* July 4, 2008, U.S./Politics.

Burns, Kathryn. *Colonial Habits: Convents and the Spiritual Economy of Cuzco, Peru.* Durham, NC: Duke University Press, 1999.

Cámara Barbachano, Fernando, and Teófilo Reyes. "Los santuarios y la peregrinaciones: Una expresión de relaciones sociales en una sociedad compleja: El caso de México." *Boletín Bibliográfico de Antropología Americana* 35, no. 2 (1972): 29–45.

Carlson, Marvin. *Performance: A Critical Introduction.* London: Routledge, 1996.

Carrasco, Dávid. *City of Sacrifice: Violence from the Aztec Empire to the Modern Americas.* Boston: Beacon, 1999.

Carrasco, Dávid, and Scott Sessions. *Daily Life of the Aztecs: People of the Sun and Earth.* New York: Greenwood Press, 1998.

Carrilo y Pérez, Ignacio. *1797. Pensil americano florido en el origen del invierno, la imagen de María Santisima de Guadalupe aparecida en la corte de la septentrional América México, en donde escribía esta historia.* Mexico City: Librería Religiosa, 1895.

Castillo, Ana, ed. *Guadalupe: Goddess of the Americas/La Diosa de Las Américas; Writings on la Virgen de Guadalupe.* New York: Riverhead, 1996.

Censo Económicos. Querétaro Arteaga: Resultados Generales, 2004. www.inegi .gob.mx.

Certeau, Michel de. *The Capture of Speech and Other Political Writings.* Translated by Tom Conley. Minneapolis: University of Minnesota Press, 1997.

———. *The Practice of Everyday Life.* Berkeley: University of California Press, 1984.

Chance, John K., and William B. Taylor. "Cofradías and Cargos: A Historical Perspective on the Mesoamerican Civil-Religious Hierarchy." *American Ethnologist* 12, no. 1 (1985): 1–26.

"Chicago's Cardinal George Forced to Issue Another Press Release to Correct False Reporting by Chicago Sun-Times." Catholic Citizens of Illinois. www .CatholicCitizens.org (accessed 2003).

Cisneros, Sandra. "Guadalupe the Sex Goddess: Unearthing the Racy Past of Mexico's Most Famous Virgin." *Ms.* (July-August) 1996: 45.

Clifford, James. *The Predicament of Culture: Twentieth-Century Ethnography, Literature, and Art.* Cambridge, MA: Harvard University Press, 1988.

Coleman, Simon, and John Eade. "Introduction: Reframing Pilgrimage." In *Reframing Pilgrimage: Cultures in Motion,* edited by Simon Coleman and John Eade, 1–26. London: Routledge, 2004.

Collins, Jane. *Threads: Gender, Labor and Power in the Global Apparel Industry.* Chicago: University of Chicago Press, 2003.

Combs-Schilling, M.E. *Sacred Performances: Islam, Sexuality, and Sacrifice.* New York: Columbia University Press, 1989.

Conquergood, Dwight. "Health Theatre in a Hmong Refugee Camp." *TDR: The Drama Review* 32 (1988): 174–208.

———. "Life in Big Red: Struggles and Accommodations in a Chicago Polyethnic Tenement." In *Structuring Diversity,* edited by Louise Lamphere, 95–144. Chicago: University of Chicago Press, 1994.

———. "Performance Studies: Interventions and Radical Research." *TDR: The Drama Review* 46 (2002): 145–56.

———. "Performing as a Moral Act: Ethical Dimensions of the Ethnography of Performance." *Literature in Performance* 5, no. 2 (1985): 1–13.

———. "The Power of Symbols." *One City* (Summer 1996): 11–13.

———. "Rethinking Ethnography: Towards a Critical Cultural Politics." In *The Sage Handbook of Perfomance Studies,* edited by D.S. Madison and J. Hamera, 351–65. Thousand Oaks, CA: Sage, 2006.

Connerton, Paul. *How Societies Remember.* Cambridge: Cambridge University Press, 1989.

Consejo Nacional de Población (CONAPO). "Indice de intensidad migratoria México-Estados Unidos por entidad federativa." www.conapo.gob.mx.

———. "Migración a Estados Unidos por entidad federativa, según migrantes de retorno y migrantes a Estados Unidos durante el quinquenio, 1997–2002." www.conapo.gob.mx.

Corten, André. *From Babel to Pentecost: Transnational Pentecostalism in Africa and Latin America.* Edited by Ruth Marshall-Fratani. Bloomington: Indiana University Press, 2001.

Coutin, Susan. *The Culture of Protest.* Boulder, CO: Westview Press, 1993.

Cross, John C. "Co-Optation, Competition, and Resistance: State and Street Vendors in Mexico City." *Latin American Perspectives* 25, no. 2 (1998): 41–61.

———. *Informal Politics: Street Vendors and the State in Mexico City.* Stanford: Stanford University Press, 1998.

Crumrine, Ross N. *Pilgrimage in Latin America.* Edited by Alan Morinis. New York: Greenwood Press, 1991.

Cruz García, Mauricio. *Historia regional de Querétaro: Perfil socioeconomica.* Mexico City: Limusa Noriega, 2000.

Dagodag, Tim W. "Source Regions and Composition of Illegal Mexican Immigration to California." *International Migration Review* 9, no. 4 (1975): 499–511.

Davalos, Karen Mary. "The Real Way of Praying: The Via Crucis, Mexicano Sacred Space, and the Architecture of Domination." In *Horizons of the Sacred: Mexican Traditions in the U.S. Catholicism,* edited by Timothy Matovina and Gary Riebe-Estrella, 41–68. Ithaca, NY: Cornell University Press, 1993.

Davalos, Mary Karen. "Ethnic Identity among Mexican and Mexican American Women in Chicago, 1920–1991." Ph.D. diss., Yale University, 1993.

Davis, Kenneth G., Eduardo C. Fernández, and Verónica Méndez. *United States Hispanic Catholics: Trends and Works, 1990–2000.* Scranton, PA: University of Scranton Press, 2002.

De Genova, Nicholas, and Ana Ramos-Zayas. *Latino Crossings: Mexicans, Puerto Ricans, and the Politics of Race and Citizenship.* New York: Routledge, 2003.

De Genova, Nicholas. "Migrant 'Illegality' and Deportability in Everyday Life." *Annual Review of Anthropology* 31 (2002): 419–47.

De la Maza, Francisco. *El guadalupanismo mexicano.* Mexico City: Fondo de Cultura Económica, 1981.

De la Mota, Ignacio. *Diccionario guadalupano.* Mexico City: Panorama Editorial, 1997.

De la Torre Villar, Ernesto, and Ramiro Navarro de Anda, eds. *Testimonios históricos guadalupanos.* Mexico City: Fondo de Cultura Económica, 1982.

Del Carmen Macías, Maria. "Un nuevo amanacer en Tepeyac de Norteamerica." *Católico* (October 2001): 10.

Delgadillo, Theresa. "Forms of Chicana Feminist Resistance: Hybrid Spirituality in Ana Castillo's 'So Far From God.'" In *Modern Fiction Studies* 44: 888–916.

Deveare Smith, Anna. *Fires in the Mirror: Crown Heights, Brooklyn, and Other Identities.* New York: Anchor Books/Doubleday, 1993.

———. *Twilight: Los Angeles, 1992, on the Road: A Search for American Character.* New York: Anchor Books, 1994.

Diaz del Castillo, Bernal. *The Discovery and Conquest of Mexico, 1517–1521.* Translated by A.P. Maudslay. New York: Harper, 1928.

Di Leonardo, Micaela. *Exotics at Home: Anthropologies, Others, and American Modernity.* Chicago: University of Chicago Press, 1998.

———. *The Gender/Sexuality Reader: Culture, History, and Political Economy.* Edited by Roger Lancaster. New York: Routledge, 1997.

Dolan, Jay P. *In Search of an American Catholicism: A History of Religion and Culture in Tension.* Oxford: Oxford University Press, 2002.

———. *The American Catholic Experience: A History from Colonial Times to the Present.* Garden City, NY: Doubleday, 1985.

Dolan, Jay P., and Allan Figueroa Deck, S.J. *Hispanic Catholic Culture in the U.S.: Issues and Concerns.* Notre Dame, IN: Notre Dame University Press, 1994.

Dolan, Jay P., and Gilberto M. Hinojosa. *Mexican Americans and the Catholic Church, 1900–1965.* Notre Dame, IN: University of Notre Dame Press, 1994.

Douglas, Mary. *Purity and Danger.* London: Routledge, 1966.

Dow, James W., and Alan R. Sandstrom, eds. *Holy Saints and Fiery Preachers: The Anthropology of Protestantism in Mexico and Central America.* New York: Praeger, 2001.

Drewal, Margaret. "The State of Research on Performance in Africa." *African Studies Review* 34, no. 3 (1991): 1–64.

———. *Yoruba Ritual: Performance, Play, Agency.* Bloomington: Indiana University Press, 1994.

Dubin, Steven C. *Arresting Images: Impolitic Art and Uncivil Actions.* New York: Routledge, 1992.

Dunnington, Jacqueline Orsini . *Guadalupe: Our Lady of New Mexico.* Santa Fe: Museum of New Mexico Press, 1999.

Dunnington, Jacqueline Orsini, and Charles Mann. *Viva Guadalupe! The Virgin in New Mexican Popular Art.* Santa Fe: Museum of New Mexico Press, 1997.

Duntley, Madeline. "Heritage, Ritual, and Translation: Seattle's Japanese Presbyterian Church." In *Gods of the City,* edited by Robert A. Orsi, 289–309. Bloomington: Indiana University Press, 1999.

Durand, Jorge, and Douglas S. Massey. *Miracles on the Border: Retablos of Mexican Migrants to the United States.* Tucson: University of Arizona Press, 1995.

Durkheim, Emile. *The Elementary Forms of Religious Life.* New York: Free Press, [1912] 1995.

Eade, John, and Michael J. Sallnow, eds. *Contesting the Sacred: The Anthropology of Christian Pilgrimage.* London: Routledge, 1991.

Eck, Diana L. *On Common Ground: World Religions in America.* New York: Columbia University Press, 1997.

Eliade, Mircea. *Images and Symbols: Studies in Religious Symbolism.* Translated by Phillip Mairet. Princeton, NJ: Princeton University Press, 1991.

Elizondo, Virgil P. *Guadalupe: Mother of the New Creation.* Maryknoll, NY: Orbis Books, 1997.

———. *La Morenita: Evangelizer of the Americas.* San Antonio, TX: Mexican American Cultural Center, 1980.

England, Sarah. *Afro Central Americans in New York City: Garifuna Tales of Transnational Movements in Racialized Space.* Gainesville: University Press of Florida, 2006.

Espinosa, Gaston, Virgilio Elizondo, and Jesse Miranda. *Latino Religions and Civic Activism in the United States.* Oxford: Oxford University Press, 2005.

Everaert Dubernard, Luis. "El tratado de Guadalupe Hidalgo: Algunas consideraciones sobre las diversas circunstancias que predicieron su firma." In *Tepeyac estudios históricos,* edited by Carmen Aguilera and Ismael Arturo Montero García. Mexico City: Universidad del Tepeyac, 2000).

Fabian, Johannes. *Power and Performance: Ethnographic Explorations through Proverbial Wisdom and Theater in Shaba, Zaire.* Madison: University of Wisconsin Press, 1990.

———. *Time and the Other: How Anthropology Makes Its Object.* New York: Columbia University Press, 1983.

Fernandez, James F. "Emergence and Convergence in Some African Sacred Places." In *The Anthropology of Space and Place: Locating Culture,* edited by Setha M. Low and Denise Lawrence-Zúñiga, 187–203. Malden, MA: Blackwell, 2003.

Feuer, Jane. "The Concept of Live Television: Ontology as Ideology?" In *Regarding Television: Critical Approaches?An Anthology,* edited by E. Ann Kaplan, 12–22. Frederick, MD: AFI/University Publications of America, 1983.

Flowers for Guadalupe/Flores para Guadalupe. VHS. Produced by Judith Gleason with the Collaboration of the Colectivo Feminists de Xalapa and Elisa Mereghetti. New York: Filmmakers Library, 1995.

Foucault, Michel. *The Archeology of Knowledge.* Translated by A.M. Sheridan Smith. London: Tavistock, 1972.

———. *Discipline and Punish: The Birth of the Prison.* Translated by Alan Sheridan. New York: Vintage Press, 1977.

———. "Of Other Spaces." *Diacritics* 16, no. 1 (1986): 22–27.

Franco, Eleazar. "Schulenberg: Ha sido decisivo el papel de la iglesia en la defensa de la paz social?" *El Universal: Relaciones entre la Iglesia y el Estado* 3 (Dec. 10, 1990): 56.

François, Pierre Louis. *Haitians in New York City: Transnationalism and Hometown Associations.* Gainesville: University Press of Florida, 2006.

Frías, Valentin F. "Las peregrinaciones al Tepeyac." In *Léyendas y tradiciones Queretanas,* vol. 3: 170–75. Mexico City: Plaza y Valdez, 1989.

Fremon, David K. *Chicago Politics Ward by Ward.* Bloomington: Indiana University Press, 1988.

Frey, Nancy L. "Stories of the Return: Pilgrimage and Its Aftermaths." In *Intersecting Journeys: The Anthropology of Pilgrimage and Tourism,* edited by Nancy Badone and Sharon R. Roseman, 89–109. Urbana: University of Illinois Press, 2004.

Fuller, C. J. *The Renewal of the Priesthood: Modernity and Traditionalism in a South Indian Temple.* Princeton, NJ: Princeton Univeristy Press, 1989.

Gálvez, Alyshia, ed. "'She Made Us Human': The Relationship between the Virgin of Guadalupe, Popular Religiosity, and Activism among Members of Mexican Devotional Organizations in New York City." In *Performing Religion in the Americas: Media, Politics, and Devotional Practices of the 21st Century,* 141–57. New York: Seagull Books, 2007.

Gamio, Manuel. *Mexican Immigration to the U.S.* Chicago: University of Chicago Press, 1930.

García, Sebastián. *Guadalupe en Extremadura en America.* Madrid: Gráficas Don Bosco, Arganda del Rey, 1991.

———, ed. *Guadalupe: Siete siglos de fe y de cultura.* Madrid: Ediciones Guadalupe, 1993.

García Canclini, Nestór. *Las culturas populares en el capitalismo.* Mexico City: Nueva Imagen, 1982.

García Cortez, Adrian. "La plaza de las Americas." *Voz Guadalupana* 16 (1960): 13–14.

Gardner, Katy. *Global Migrants, Local Lives: Travel and Transformation in Rural Bangladesh.* Oxford: Clarendon Press, 1995.

Gaspar de Alba, Alicia, and Tomas Ybarra Frausto. *Velvet Barrios: Popular Culture and Chicana/o Sexualities.* New York: Palgrave Macmillan, 2003.

Geary, Patrick. "Sacred Commodities: The Circulation of Medieval Relics." In *The Social Life of Things,* edited by Arjun Appadurai, 169–91. Cambridge: Cambridge University Press, 1988.

Geertz, Clifford. *The Interpretation of Cultures.* New York: Basic Books, 1973.

———. *Islam Observed: Religious Development in Morocco and Indonesia.* Chicago: University of Chicago Press, 1968.

Giggie, John M., and Diane Winston, eds. *Faith in the Market: Religion and the Rise of Urban Commercial Culture.* New Brunswick, NJ: Rutgers University Press, 2002.

Ginsburg, Faye D. *Media Worlds: Anthropology on a New Terrain.* Edited by Lila Abu-Lughod and Brian Larkin. Berkeley: University of California Press, 2002.

Giuriatti, Paolo, and Elio Masferrer Kan. *No temas . . . Yo soy tu madre: Un estudio socioantropológico de los peregrinos a la Basílica de la Virgen de Guadalupe.* Mexico City: Plaza y Valdes, 1998.

Glick-Schiller, Nina, and Georges Fouron. "'I Am Not a Problem without a Solution': Poverty and Transnational Migration." In *The New Poverty Studies: The Ethnography of Power, Politics, and Impoverished People in the United States,* edited by Judith Goode and Jeff Maskovsky, 321–63. New York: New York University Press, 2001.

Goffman, Erving. *The Presentation of Self in Everyday Life.* Garden City, NY: Doubleday, 1959.

Golden, Renny, and Michael McConnell. *Sanctuary: The New Underground Railroad.* Maryknoll, NY: Orbis Books, 1986.

Gómez, Marcela Vallecillo, and María Concepción Castillo de Jiménez. "Santa María de Guadalupe une América en el amor y la fe para un mundo de Esperanza." *Boletín Guadalupano* 66 (2006): 17–20.

Gómez-Peña, Guillermo. *Dangerous Border Crossers: The Artist Talks Back.* London: Routledge, 2000.

———. *Ethnotechno: Writings on Performance, Activism, and Pedagogy.* Edited by Elaine A. Peña. London: Routledge, 2005.

Gramsci, Antonio, and David Forgacs. *The Antonio Gramsci Reader: Selected Writings.* New York: New York University Press, 2000.

———. *Selections from Cultural Writings.* Edited by David Forgacs and Geoffrey Nowell Smith, translated by William Boelhower. Cambridge, MA: Harvard University Press, 1985.

———. *Selections from the Prison Notebooks of Antonio Gramsci.* Edited by Quintin Hoare and Geoffrey Nowell Smith, translated by Quintin Hoare and Geoffrey Nowell Smith. Cambridge, MA: Harvard University Press, 1971.

Griffith, R. Marie, and Barbara Dianne Savage. *Women and Religion in the African Diaspora: Knowledge, Power, and Performance.* Baltimore, MD: Johns Hopkins University Press, 2006.

Gross, D. "Ritual and Conformity: A Religious Pilgrimage to Northern Brazil." *Ethnology* 10 (1971): 129–48.

Grossman, James R., and Ann Durkin Keating. "Rogers Park." In *The Encyclopedia of Chicago,* edited by Janice L. Reiff, 714–15. Chicago: University of Chicago Press, 2004.

Guglielmo, Thomas A. *White on Arrival: Italians, Race, Color, and Power in Chicago.* Oxford: Oxford University Press, 2003.

Hall, David D., ed. *Lived Religion in America: Toward a History of Practice.* Princeton, NJ: Princeton University Press, 1997.

Hamilton, Nora, and Norma Stoltz Chinchilla. "Central American Migration: A Framework for Analysis." In *Challenging Fronteras: Structuring Latina and Latino Lives in the U.S.,* edited by Mary Romero, Pierrette Hondagneu-Sotelo, and Vilma Ortiz, 81–100. New York: Routledge, 1997.

Hannerz, Ulf. *Transnational Connections*. London: Routledge, 1996.

Hart, Keith. "Bureaucratic Form and the Informal Economy." In *Linking the Formal and Informal Economy: Concepts and Policies,* edited by B. Guha-Khasnobis, R. Kanbur, and E. Ostrom, 21–35. Oxford: Oxford University Press, 2006.

———. "Informal Income Opportunities and Urban Employment in Ghana." *Journal of Modern African Studies* 11, no. 1 (1973): 61–89.

Harvey, David. "Between Space and Time: Reflections on the Geographical Imagination." *Annals of the Association of American Geographers* 80, no. 3 (1990): 418–34.

———. *The Condition of Postmodernity*. Cambridge, MA: Blackwell, 1990.

———. *Justice, Nature and the Geography of Difference*. Oxford: Blackwell, 1996.

———. *Spaces of Hope*. Edinburgh: Edinburgh University Press, 2000.

———. *The Urbanization of Capital: Studies in the History and Theory of Capitalist Urbanization*. Baltimore, MD: Johns Hopkins University Press, 1985.

Hayden, Dolores. *Building Suburbia: Green Fields and Urban Growth, 1820–2000*. New York: Pantheon Books, 2003.

———. *The Power of Place* Cambridge, MA: MIT Press, 1995.

Herbert, Bob. "Op-ed: Stifling an Opportunity." *New York Times,* March 16, 2009, A27.

Heyman, Josiah. "State Effects on Labor Exploitation." *Critique of Anthropology* 18, no. 2 (1998): 157–80.

Higgins, John, ed. *The Raymond Williams Reader*. Malden, MA: Blackwell, 2001.

Hinojosa, Francisco. *Mexican Chicago*. Mexico City: CONACULTA, 1999.

Holmes-Rodman, Paula Elizabeth. "'They Told What Happened on the Road': Narrative and the Construction of Experiential Knowledge on the Pilgrimage to Chimayo, New Mexico." In *Intersecting Journeys: The Anthropology of Pilgrimage and Tourism,* edited by Ellen Badone and Sharon R. Roseman, 24–51. Urbana: University of Illinois Press, 2004.

Hondagneu-Sotelo, Pierrette. *Gendered Transitions: Mexican Experiences of Immigration*. Berkeley: University of California Press, 1994.

Hondagneu-Sotelo, Pierrette, Genelle Gaudinez, Hector Lara, and Billie C. Ortiz. "There's a Spirit That Transcends the Border: Faith, Ritual, and Postnational Protest at the U.S.-Mexico Border." *Sociological Perspectives* 47, no. 2 (2004): 137.

Huhndorf, Shari M. *Mapping the Americas: The Transnational Politics of Contemporary Native Culture*. Ithaca, NY: Cornell University Press, 2009.

Hurston, Zora Neale. *Dust Tracks on a Road*. Urbana: University of Illinois Press, [1942] 1984.

INEGI. "Consulta de población total con estimación por entidad municipio y loc/según: Sexo." www.inegi.gob.mx.

———. "Ingresos-remesas familiares en la entidad Michoacán de Ocampo, balanza de pago: Ingresos por remesas familiares." 2008. www.inegi.gob.mx.

———. "Perspectiva estadística. Serie por entidad federativa, Michoacán de Ocampo." www.inegi.gob.mx.

Jackson, Kenneth T. *Crabgrass Frontier: The Suburbanization of the United States.* New York: Oxford University Press, 1985.

Jackson, Shannon. *Lines of Activity: Performance, Historiography, Hull House Domesticity.* Ann Arbor: University of Michigan Press, 2001.

Jefferson, Cowie P. *Capital Moves: RCA's Seventy-Year Quest for Cheap Labor.* Ithaca, NY: Cornell University Press, 1999.

Johnson, Benjamin, and Andrew R. Graybill, eds. *Bridging National Borders in North America: Transnational and Comparative Histories.* Durham, NC: Duke University Press, 2010.

Johnson, Geoffrey. "A Common Altar: Chicago's Immigrant Catholics." *Chicago* (September 2005): 79.

Johnson, Patrick E. *Appropriating Blackness: Performance and the Politics of Authenticity.* Durham, NC: Duke University Press, 2003.

———. *Sweet Tea: Black Gay Men of the South.* Chapel Hill: University of North Carolina Press, 2008.

Jones, Anita Edgar. "Conditions Surrounding Mexicans in Chicago: A Dissertation." Master's thesis, University of Chicago, 1928.

Joyce, Rosemary A. *Gender and Power in Prehispanic Mesoamerica.* Austin: University of Texas Press, 2000.

Katzew, Ilona. *Casta Painting: Images of Race in Eighteenth-Century Mexico.* New Haven, CT: Yale University Press, 2005.

Keren, Donna J. *Trabajo y transformación económica de Querétaro.* Mexico City: Instituto Nacional de Antropología e Historia, 1997.

Korom, Frank J. *Hosay Trinidad: Muharram Performances in an Indo-Caribbean Diaspora.* Philadelphia: University of Pennsylvania Press, 2003.

Lafayé, Jacques. *Quetzalcóatl and Guadalupe: The Formation of National Consciousness, 1531–1813.* Translated by Benjamin Keene. Chicago: University of Chicago Press, 1976.

Lavie, Smadar, and Ted Swedenburg. *Displacement, Diaspora, and Geographies of Identity.* Durham, NC: Duke University Press, 1996.

Lefebvre, Henri. *The Production of Space.* Translated by Donald Nicholson-Smith. Oxford: Basil Blackwell, 1991.

León, Luis D. *La Llorona's Children: Religion, Life, and Death in the U.S.-Mexican Borderlands.* Berkeley: University of California Press, 2004.

León-Portilla, Miguel. *Aztec Thought and Culture: A Study of the Ancient Nahuatl Mind.* Translated by Jack Emory Davis. Norman: University of Oklahoma Press, 1963.

———. *Bernardino de Sahagún: First Anthropologist.* Norman: University of Oklahoma Press, 2002.

———. *Tonantzin Guadalupe: Pensamiento náhuatl y mensaje cristiano en el Nican Mopohua.* Mexico City: Colegio Nacional y Fondo de Cultura Económica, 2000.

León-Portilla, Miguel, Jorge Klor de Alva, and Lysander Kemp. *The Broken Spears: The Aztec Account of the Conquest of Mexico.* Boston: Beacon, 2006.

Levitt, Peggy. *God Needs No Passport: Immigrants and the Changing American Religious Landscape*. New York: New Press, 2009.

———. *The Transnational Villagers*. Berkeley: University of California Press, 2001.

Levitt, Peggy, and Sanjeev Khagram, eds. *The Transnational Studies Reader: Intersections and Innovations*. New York: Routledge, 2007.

Lewis, Laura. *Hall of Mirrors: Power, Witchcraft, and Caste in Colonial Mexico*. Durham, NC: Duke University Press, 2003.

Lieblich, Julia. "Believers See Apparition of Virgin: Image on Tree in Rogers Park Comforts Many." *Chicago Tribune*, July 11, 2001, Trib West.

"Life in Des Plaines." www.desplaines.org (accessed Dec. 13, 2003).

Livezey, Lowell. "Communities and Enclaves: Where Jews, Christians, Hindus, and Muslims Share the Neighborhoods." In *Public Religion and Urban Transformation: Faith in the City*, edited by Lowell Livezey, 133–62. New York: New York University Press, 2001.

Logan, John R., and Harvey L. Molotch. *Urban Fortunes: The Political Economy of Place*. Berkeley: University of California Press, 1987.

Lovato, Roberto. "A Migrant Summit." *Nation*, July 13, 2007.

Low, Setha. *On the Plaza: The Politics of Public Space and Culture*. Austin: University of Texas Press, 2000.

Low, Setha M., and Denise Lawrence-Zúñiga, eds. *The Anthropology of Space and Place: Locating Culture*. Malden, MA: Blackwell, 2003.

Macip, Ricardo F. "Creación de espacios y paisaje sagrado en una peregrinación campesina a Chalma." In *Caminos terrestres al cielo: Contribución al estudio del fenómeno romero*, 73–91. Serie Antropología Social. Mexico City: Instituto Nacional de Antropología e Historia, 1998.

Madison, D. Soyini. "Co-Performative Witnessing." *Cultural Studies* 21, no. 6 (2007): 826–31.

Magaña Negrete, Gumersindo. "El nuevo régimen legal de la iglesias." *El Universal: Relaciones entre la Iglesia y el Estado* 3 (July 23, 1992): 195.

Mahmood, Saba. *The Politics of Piety: The Islamic Revival and the Feminist Subject*. Princeton, NJ: Princeton University Press, 2005.

Mankekar, Purnima. *Screening Culture, Viewing Politics: An Ethnography of Television, Womanhood, and Nation in Postcolonial India*. Durham, NC: Duke University Press, 1999.

Marcus, George E. *Ethnography through Thick and Thin*. Princeton, NJ: Princeton University Press, 1998.

Martinez de la Serna, Esteban. *Los santuarios de la Virgen de Guadalupe*. Mexico City: Editora Escalante, 2003.

Marx, Karl. *Capital: A Critique of Political Economy*. Chicago: Charles H. Kerr, 1919.

Marx, Karl, and Friedrich Engels. *Karl Marx and Friedrich Engels on Religion*. New York: Schocken Books, 1964.

Massey, Douglas S. "The Settlement Process among Mexican Migrants to the United States." *American Sociological Review* 51 (1986): 670–84.

Massey, Douglas S., Jorge Durand, and Nolan J. Malone. *Beyond Smoke and Mirrors: Mexican Immigration in an Era of Economic Integration.* New York: Russell Sage Foundation, 2002.

Matovina, Timothy. *Guadalupe, and Her Faithful: Latino Catholics in San Antonio from Colonial Origins to the Present.* Baltimore, MD: Johns Hopkins University Press, 2005.

Matovina, Timothy, and Gerald E. Poyo, eds. *¡Presente! U.S. Latino Catholics from Colonial Origins to the Present.* Maryknoll, NY: Orbis Books, 2000.

Maurer, Karl. "Hundreds Rally to Protest Maryville Closing." Catholic Citizens of Illinois. www.CatholicCitizens.org (accessed 2003).

Mauss, Marcel. *The Gift: Forms and Functions of Exchange in Archaic Societies.* Translated by Ian Cunnison. Glencoe, IL: Free Press, 1954.

Mbembe, Achille. "At the Edge of the World: Boundaries, Territoriality, and Sovereignty in Africa." In *Globalization,* edited by Arjun Appadurai, 259–84. Durham, NC: Duke University Press, 2001.

McAllister, Elizabeth. *Rara! Vodou, Power, and Performance in Haiti and Its Diaspora.* Berkeley: University of California Press, 2002.

McCarthy, Anna. *Ambient Television: Visual Culture and Public Space.* Durham, NC: Duke University Press, 2001.

McCarthy Brown, Karen. *Mama Lola: A Vodou Priestess in Brooklyn.* Berkeley: University of California Press, 1999.

———. "Staying Grounded in a High-Rise Building: Ecological Dissonance and Riual Accommodation in Haitian Vodou." In *Gods of the City,* edited by Robert A. Orsi, 79–102. Bloomington: Indiana University Press, 1999.

McCloud, Aminah Beverly. *Transnational Muslims in American Society.* Gainesville: University Press of Florida, 2006.

McDannell, Colleen. *Material Christianity.* New Haven, CT: Yale University Press, 1995.

McGraw, Barbara. *Taking Religious Pluralism Seriously: Spiritual Politics on America's Sacred Ground.* Edited by Jo Renee Formicola. Waco, TX: Baylor University Press, 2005.

Meyer, Jean. *The Cristero Rebellion: The Mexican People between Church and State, 1926–1929.* New York: Cambridge University Press, 1976.

———. *La cristiada.* Mexico City: Siglo XXI, 1973. Mill, J.S. *The Subjection of Women.* New York: Appleton, 1869.

Mintz, Sidney. "The Localization of Anthropological Practice: From Area Studies to Transnationalism." *Critique of Anthropology* 18, no. 2 (1998): 117–33.

Miranda, Francisco. *Dos cultos fundantes: Los remedios y Guadalupe, 1521–1649; Historia documental.* Zamora: Colegio de Michoacán, 1998.

Morales, Daniel. "Gracias, Señor Presidente." *Voz Guadalupana* 12 (1945–46): 31.

Morales, María Dolores. "Espacio, propiedad y organos de poder en la Ciudad de México en el siglo XIX." In *Ciudad de México: Instituciones, actores sociales y conflicto político, 1774–1931,* edited by Carlos Illades and Ariel Rodriguez, 155–90. Zamora: Colegio de Michoacán, 1996.

Morales Garza, Martha Gloria. *Grupos, partidos y cultura política en Queré-taro.* Querétaro: Universidad Autonoma de Querétaro, 1993.

Morinis, Alan E. "Introduction: The Territory of the Anthropology of Pilgrim-age." In *Sacred Journeys: The Anthropology of Pilgrimage,* edited by Alan E. Morinis, 1–29. Westport, CT: Greenwood Press, 1992.

———, ed. *Sacred Journeys: The Anthropology of Pilgrimage.* Westport, CT: Greenwood Press, 1992.

Mummert, Gail, ed. *Fronteras fragmentadas.* Morelia: Colegio de Michoacán/Centro de Investigaciones y Desarrollo del Estado de Michoacán, 1999.

Muro Castillo, Matilde. *Guadalupe: La llamada de la luz.* Guadalupe: Junta de Extremadura, 2007.

Nakano Glenn, Evelyn. *Unequal Freedom: How Race and Gender Shaped American Citizenship and Labor.* Cambridge, MA: Harvard University Press, 2002.

Nebel, Richard. "The Cult of Santa Maria Tonantzin, Virgin of Guadalupe in Mexico." In *Sacred Space: Shrine, City, Land,* edited by Benjamin K. Zedar and R.J. Zwi Werblowsky, 250–58. New York: New York University Press, 1998.

———. *Santa María Tonantzin Virgen de Guadalupe: Continuidad y transfor-mación religiosa en México.* Mexico City: Fondo de Cultura Económica, 1996.

Necoechea Gracia, Gerardo. "Customs and Resistance: Mexican Immigrants in Chicago, 1910–1930." In *Border Crossings: Mexican and Mexican-American Workers,* ed. John Mason Hart, 185–208. New York: Rowman and Littlefield, 1998.

Negrete, Marta Elena. *Relaciones entre la Iglesia y el estado de México, 1930–1940.* Mexico City: Colegio de Mexico, 1988.

Noguez, Xavier. *Documentos guadalupanos: Un estudio sobre las fuentes de información tempranas en torno a las Mariofanías en el Tepeyac.* Mexico City: Fondo de Cultural Económica, 1995.

Nolan, Mary Lee. "Christian Pilgrimage Shrines in Western Europe and India: A Preliminary Comparison." In *Trends in the Geography of Pilgrimages,* edited by R.L. Singh and Rana P.B. Singh, 18–26. Kamachha, Varanasi: National Geographical Society of India, 1987.

O'Conner, Mary. "The Virgin of Guadalupe and the Economics of Symbolic Behavior." *Journal for the Scientific Study of Religion* 28, no. 2 (1989): 105–19.

O'Donnell, Maureen. "Franciscan Nun to Run Maryville." www.Catholic citizens.org (accessed February 2005).

O'Gorman, Edmundo. *Destierro de sombra: Luz en el origen de la imagen y culto de Nuestra Señora de Guadalupe del Tepeyac.* Mexico City: Universidad Nacional Autonoma de México, 1991.

Olivera Sedano, Alicia. *Aspectos del conflicto religioso de 1926 a 1929: Sus antecedentes y consecuencias.* Mexico City: Instituto Nacional de Antropología e Historia, 1966.

Ong, Aihwa. *Flexible Citizenship: The Cultural Logics of Transnationality.* Durham, NC: Duke University Press, 1999.

Orsi, Robert. "The Cult of the Saints and the Reimagination of the Space and Time of Sickness in Twentieth-Century American Catholicism." *Literature and Medicine* 8 (1989): 63–77.

———. "Everyday Miracles: The Study of Lived Religion." In *Lived Religion in America: Toward a History of Practice,* edited by David D. Hall, 3–21. Princeton, NJ: Princeton University Press, 1997.

———, ed. *Gods of the City: Religion and the American Urban Landscape.* Bloomington: Indiana University Press, 1999.

Ortner, Sherry B. *High Religion: A Cultural and Political History of Sherpa Buddhism.* Princeton, NJ: Princeton University Press, 1989.

Orvaños Busto, Genoveva. "Peregrinación femenina de la diócesis de Querétaro al Tepeyac." *Investigación: Revista Informativa de los Centros de Investigación de la Universidad Autonoma de Querétaro Secretaria Academica* 5, no. 18 (1986): 5–14.

Otto, Rudolph, and John W. Harvey. *The Idea of the Holy.* London: Oxford University Press, 1923.

Padilla, Felix M. *Latino Ethnic Consciousness: The Case of Mexican Americans and Puerto Ricans in Chicago.* Notre Dame, IN: Notre Dame University Press, 1985.

Pals, Daniel L. "Reductionism and Belief: An Appraisal of Recent Attacks on the Doctrine of Irreducible Religion." *Journal of Religion* 66 (1986): 18–36.

———. *Seven Theories of Religion.* Oxford: Oxford University Press, 1996.

Paral, Rob, Michael Norkewicz, Madura Wijewardena, and Christina Diaz Peterson. *Mexican Immigration in the Midwest: Meanings and Implications.* Chicago: Chicago Council on Global Affairs, 2009.

Park, Robert E. *Human Communities: The City and Human Ecology.* Glencoe, IL: Free Press, 1952.

Parot, John Joseph. *Polish Catholics in Chicago, 1850–1920: A Religious History.* DeKalb: Northern Illinois University Press, 1981.

Paz, Octavio. *The Labyrinth of Solitude and Other Writings.* Translated by Lysander Kemp. New York: Grove Press, 1985.

Peña, Elaine A. "Beyond México: Guadalupan Sacred Space Production and Mobilization in a Chicago Suburb." *American Quarterly* 60, no. 3 (2008): 721–47.

———. "Making Space Sacred: Devotional Capital, Political Economy, and the Transnational Expansion of the Cult of la Virgen de Guadalupe." Ph.D. diss., Northwestern University, 2006.

Peterson, Anna L., and Manuel A. Vásquez. *Latin American Religions: Histories and Documents in Context.* New York: New York University Press, 2008.

Pollock, Della. *Telling Bodies Performing Birth: Everyday Narratives of Childbirth.* New York: Columbia University Press, 1999.

Pompa y Pompa, Antonio. *El gran acontecimiento guadalupano.* Mexico City: Editorial Jus, 1967.

Poole, Stafford. *Our Lady of Guadalupe: The Origins and Sources of a National Symbol.* Tucson: University of Arizona Press, 1995.

Portes, Alejandro. "Global Villagers: The Rise of Transnational Communities." *American Prospect* 25 (Mar.–Apr. 1996): 74–77.

Portes, Alejandro, and Robert A. Bach. *Latin Journey: Cuban and Mexican Immigrants in the United States*. Berkeley: University of California Press, 1985.

Portes, Alejandro, and Rubén G. Rumbaut. *Immigrant America: A Portrait*. Berkeley: University of California Press, 1996.

Prothero, Stephen, ed. *A Nation of Religions: the Politics of Pluralism in Multireligious America*. Chapel Hill: University of North Carolina Press, 2006.

Quintero, Josefina. "Los recursos provendrán de 'donaciones del pueblo: La Plaza Mariana costará unos $500 millones: Responsable del proyecto." *La Jornada*, Nov. 2, 2002. www.jornada.unam.mx.

Ramírez Vázquez, Pedro. "Basílica de Guadalupe, Santuario de los Mexicanos." In *Tepeyac Estudios Historicos,* edited by Carmen Aguilera and Ismael Arturo Montero García, 237–38. Mexico City: Universidad del Tepeyac, 2000.

Ramiíez Velázquez, Blanca Rebecca. *La región en su diferencia: Los valles centrales de Querétaro 1940–1990*. Puebla: Red Nacional de Investigación Urbana, 1995.

Randolph Adams, Walter. "Political and Economic Correlates of Pilgrimage Behavior." *Anales de Antropologia* 20 (1983): 147–72.

Reed-Danahay, Deborah E. *Auto/Ethnography: Rewriting the Self and the Social*. Oxford: Berg, 1997.

Reich, Peter L. *Mexico's Hidden Revolution: The Catholic Church in Law and Politics since 1929*. Notre Dame, IN: Notre Dame University Press, 1995.

Reisler, Mark. *By the Sweat of Their Brow: Mexican Immigrant Labor in the United States*. Wesport, CT: Greenwood Press, 1976.

———. "The Mexican Immigrant in the Chicago Area during the 1920s." *Journal of the Illinois State Historical Society* 66, no. 2 (Summer 1973): 144–58.

Ricard, Robert. *The Spiritual Conquest of Mexico: An Essay on the Apostles and the Evangelizing Methods of the Mendicant Order in New Spain: 1523–1572*. Berkeley: University of California Press, 1966.

Ricardo, David. *Economic Essays*. Edited by E.C.K. Gonner. London: G. Bell and Sons, 1923.

Rinschede, Gisbert. "Pilgrimage Studies at Different Levels." In *Sacred Places, Sacred Spaces: The Geography of Pilgrimages,* edited by Robert H. Stoddard and Alan Morinis, 95–116. Baton Rouge, LA: Geoscience Publications.

Roach, Joseph. *Cities of the Dead: Circum-Atlantic Performance*. New York: Columbia University Press, 1996.

Rodriguez, Jeanette. *Our Lady of Guadalupe: Faith and Empowerment among Mexican-American Women*. Austin: University of Texas Press, 1994.

Rosaldo, Renato. *Culture and Truth: The Remaking of Social Analysis*. Boston: Beacon, 1993.

Rosales, Francisco A. "Regional Origins of Mexicano Immigrants to Chicago during the 1920s." *Aztlán: International Journal of Chicano Studies Research* 7 (Summer 1976): 187–201.

Roseberry, William. *Anthropologies and Histories: Essays in Culture, History, and Political Economy*. New Brunswick, NJ: Rutgers University Press, 1994.

Rouse, Carolyn. "Shopping with Sister Zubayda: African American Sunni Muslim Rituals of Consumption and Belonging." In *Women and Religion in the*

African Diaspora: Knowledge, Power, and Performance, edited by R. Marie Griffith and Barbara Dianne Savage, 245–65. Baltimore, MD: Johns Hopkins University Press, 2006.

Rouse, Roger. "Making Sense of Settlement: Class Transformation, Cultural Struggle and Transnationalism among Mexican Migrants in the United States." In *Towards a Transnational Perspective on Migration: Race, Class, Ethnicity and Nationalism,* edited by Nina Glick-Schiller, Linda Basch, and Christina Szanton-Blanc, 25–52. New York: New York Academy of Sciences, 1992.

———. "Migración al suroeste de Michoacán durante el Porfiriato: El caso de Aguililla." In *Movimientos de población en el occidente de México,* edited by Thomas Calvo and Gustavo López, 231–52. Mexico City and Zamora: CEMCA and Colegio de Michoacán, 1988.

Saldívar-Hull, Sonia. *Feminism on the Border: Chicana Gender Politics and Literature.* Berkeley: University of California Press, 2000.

Salzinger, Leslie. *Genders in Production: Making Workers in Mexico's Global Factories.* Berkeley: University of California Press, 2003.

Samors, Neal, Mary Jo Doyle, Martin Lewin, and Michael Williams. *Chicago's Far north Side: An Illustrated History of Rogers Park and West Ridge.* Chicago: Rogers Park/West Ridge Society, 1997.

Samors, Neal, Michael Williams, and Mary Jo Doyle. *Neighborhoods within Neighborhoods: Twentieth-Century Life on Chicago's Far North Side.* Chicago: Rogers Park/West Ridge Society, 2002.

Sanchez, Miguel. "Imagen de la Virgen María, madre de Dios de Guadalupe, milagrosamente aparecida en la ciudad de México." 1648. MS., Brown University, Providence, RI, Nican Mopohua.

Sandburg, Carl. *Chicago Poems.* New York: Henry Holt and Co., 1916.

Sandoval, Ruiz. "Obras arquitectónicas embellecen el Tepeyac." *Voz Guadalupana* 23 (1957).

Sanmaniego, Fidel. "Recibió salinas en Los Pinos a 130 prelados católicos." *El Universal: Relaciones entre la Iglesia y el Estado* 3 (December 11, 1991): 129.

Sanmaniego, Fidel, and Enrique Aranda Pedroza. "Modernizar relaciones con la iglesia, propone CSG." *El Universal: Relaciones entre la Iglesia y el Estado* 3 (December 2, 1988): 1.

Sassen, Saskia. *Globalization and Its Discontents.* New York: New Press, 1998.

———. *The Mobility of Labor and Capital: A Study in International Investment and Labor Flow.* Cambridge: Cambridge University Press, 1988.

———. "Spatialities and Temporalities of the Global: Elements for Theorization." In *Globalization,* edited by Arjun Appadurai, 260–78. Durham, NC: Duke University Press, 2001.

Scarry, Elaine. *The Body in Pain: The Making and Unmaking of the World.* New York: Oxford University Press, 1985.

Schechner, Richard. *Between Theater and Anthropology.* Philadelphia: University of Pennsylvania Press, 1985.

———. *Performance Studies: An Introduction.* 1st ed. New York: Routledge, 2002.

Schulenburg Prado, Guillermo. *Memorias del "último Abad de Guadalupe."* Mexico City: Porrua, 2003.

Schwaller, J.F. *Origins of Church Wealth in Mexico: Ecclesiastical Revenues and Church Finances, 1523–1600.* Albuquerque: University of New Mexico Press, 1985.

Scott, James C. *Domination and the Arts of Resistance.* New Haven, CT: Yale University Press, 1990.

———. *Weapons of the Weak: Everyday Forms of Peasant Resistance.* New Haven, CT: Yale University Press, 2003.

Searle, J.R. *Speech Acts: An Essay in the Philosophy of Language.* London: Cambridge University Press, 1969.

Segal, Robert. "In Defense of Reductionism." In *Religion and the Social Sciences: Essays on the Confrontation,* 5–36. Atlanta: Scholars Press.

Sentíes Rodriguez, Horacio. "Evolución urbana del Santuario de Nuestra Señora de Guadalupe." In *Tepeyac Estudios Historicos,* edited by Carmen Aguilera and Ismael Arturo Montero García, 195–226. Mexico City: Universidad del Tepeyac, 2000.

———. *La villa de Guadalupe: Crónica centenaria.* Mexico City: Gobierno del Distrito Federal/ Delegación Gustavo A. Madero, 1999.

———. *La villa de Guadalupe: Historias, estampas y leyendas.* Mexico City: Portico de la Ciudad de México, 1991.

Shadow, Robert, and Maria Rodriguez Shadow. "La peregrinación en América Latina: Enfoques y perspectivas." In *Las peregrinaciones religiosas: Una aproximación,* edited by Carlos Garma Navarro and Robert Shadow. Mexico City: Universidad Autonoma Metropolitana, 1994.

Shadow, Robert, and Maria Rodriguez V. "Símbolos que amarran, símbolos que dividen: Hegemonía e impugnación en una peregrinación campesina a Chalma." *Mesoamérica* 19 (1990): 33–72.

Shaw, Stephen J. *The Catholic Parish as a Way-Station of Ethnicity and Americanization: Chicago's Germans and Italians, 1903–1939.* New York: Carlson, 1991.

Shinde, K.A. "Case Study 6: Visiting Sacred Sites in India: Religious Tourism or Pilgrimage." In *Religious Tourism and Pilgrimage Festivals Management: An International Perspective,* edited by R. Raj and N.D. Morpeth, 184–97. Cambridge, MA: CAB International, 2007.

Sin siembra no hay cosecha, sin palabra no hay eucasristía. Querétaro: Directiva Seglar de la 47a Peregrinación Femenina a Pie de Querétaro al Tepeyac, 2005.

Singh, Rana P.B. "Sacred Space and Pilgrimage in Hindu Society: The Case of Varanasi." In *Sacred Places, Sacred Spaces: The Geography of Pilgrimages,* edited by Robert H. Stoddard and Alan Morinis, 191–208. Baton Rouge, LA: Geoscience Publications, 1997.

Singh, R.L., and Rana P.B. Singh. *Trends in the Geography of Pilgrimages: Homage to David E. Sopher.* Varanasi: National Geographic Society of India, 1987.

Sklar, Deidre. *Dancing with the Virgin: Body and Faith in the Fiesta of Tortugas, New Mexico.* Berkeley: University of California Press, 2001.

Skogan, Wesley G., Lynn Steiner, Jill DuBois, J. Erik Gudell, and Aimee Fagan. *Community Policing and the New Immigrants.* NIJ Research Report–NCJ. Report no. 189908. Washington, DC: U.S. Department of Justice, 2002.

———. *Taking Stock: Community Policing in Chicago.* NIJ Research Report–NCJ. Report no. 189909. Washington, DC: U.S. Department of Justice, 2002.

Smith, Jonathon Z. "Constructing a Small Place." In *Sacred Space: Shrine, City, Land,* edited by R.J. Zwi Werblowsky and Benjamin K. Zedar, 18–31. New York: New York University Press, 1998.

Smith, Michael Peter, and Luis Esuardo Guarnizo. *Transnationalism from Below.* New Brunswick, NJ: Transaction, 1998.

Smith, Robert Courtney. *Mexican New York: Transnational Lives of New Imigrants.* Berkeley: University of California Press, 2006.

Soja, Edward W. *Postmetropolis: Critical Studies of Cities and Regions.* Malden, MA: Blackwell, 2000.

Squires, Gregory D., Larry Bennett, Kathleen McCourt, and Phillip Nyden. *Chicago: Race, Class, and the Response to Urban Decline.* Philadelphia: Temple University Press, 1987.

Stark, Robert. "Religious Ritual and Class Formation: The Story of Pilsen St. Vitus Parish, and the 1977 Via Crucis." Ph.D. diss., University of Chicago Divinity School, 1981.

Stephen, Lynn. *Transborder Lives: Indigenous Oaxacans in Mexico, California, and Oregon.* Durham, NC: Duke University Press, 2007.

Stevens-Arroyo, Antonio M. *Prophets Denied Honor: An Anthology of the Hispanic Church in the United States.* Maryknoll, NY: Orbis, 1980.

Stevens-Arroyo, Antonio, and Ana M. Díaz-Stevens. *An Enduring Flame: Studies on Latino Popular Religiosity.* New York: Bildner Center for Western Hemisphere Studies, 1994.

Stewart, Kathleen. *A Space on the Side of the Road: Cultural Poetics in an 'Other' America.* Princeton, NJ: Princeton University Press, 1996.

Strenski, Ivan. "Reduction without Tears." In *Religion and Reductionism,* 95–107. New York: Brill, 1994.

Suárez-Orozco, Marcelo M. *Crossings: Mexican Immigration in Interdisciplinary Perspectives.* Cambridge, MA: Harvard University, David Rockefeller Center for Latin American Studies, 1998.

Taylor, Diana. *The Archive and the Repertoire: Performing Cultural Memory in the Americas.* Durham, NC: Duke University Press, 2003.

Taylor, Paul S. *Mexican Labor in the United States: Chicago and the Calumet Region.* Berkeley: University of California Press, 1932.

Taylor, William B. "Mexico's Virgin of Guadalupe in the Seventeenth Century: Hagiography and Beyond." In *Colonial Saints: Discovering the Holy in the Americas,* edited by Allan Greer and Jodi Bilinkoff, 277–98. New York: Routledge, 2003.

———. "The Virgin of Guadalupe in New Spain: An Inquiry into the Social History of Marian Devotion." *American Ethnologist* 1 (1987): 9–24.

Trueba Arámburu, Evangelina. *La procesión del silencio en Querétaro: Un caso especifico.* Thesis, Escuela Nacional de Antropología e Historia, 1998.

Tuan, Yi-Fu. *Space and Place: The Perspective of Experience*. Minneapolis: University of Minnesota Press, 2001.

Turnbull, Colin. "Postscript: Anthropology as Pilgrimage, Anthropologist as Pilgrim." In *Sacred Journeys: The Anthropology of Pilgrimage*, edited by Alan Morinis, 257–74. Wesport, CT: Greenwood Press, 1992.

Turner, Victor. *The Anthropology of Performance*. New York: Performing Arts Journal, 1986.

———. *Dramas, Fields, and Metaphors: Symbolic Action in Human Society*. Ithaca, NY: Cornell University Press, 1974.

———. *The Ritual Process: Structure and Anti-Structure*. Chicago: Aldine, 1969.

Turner, Victor, and Edith Turner. *Image and Pilgrimage in Christian Culture: Anthropological Perspectives*. New York: Columbia University Press, 1978.

Tweed, Thomas. *Our Lady of the Exile: Diasporic Religion at a Cuban Catholic Shrine in Miami*. Oxford: Oxford University Press, 1997.

"Unidos por la fe: Canonización de Juan Diego Cuauhtlatoatzin ¡Nuestra Señora de Guadalupe ha cumplido lo que ha prometido!" *Católico* 17 (2002): cover.

Valdés, Dionicio N. *Barrios Norteños: St. Paul and Midwestern Mexican Communities in the Twentieth Century*. Austin: University of Texas Press, 2000.

Valero de García Lascurain, Ana Rita. "Peregrinación al Tepeyac: Una observación analítica de las romerías guadalupanas." In *Caminos terrestres al cielo: Contribución al estudio del fenómeno romero* 10, edited by Beatriz Barba de Piña Chan, Serie Antropología Social. Mexico City: Instituto Nacional de Antropología e Historia, 1998.

———. "Los primeros cofrades de Guadalupe: Algunas reflexiones en torno a su intensa devoción." *Boletín Guadalupano* 34 (2003): 17–19.

Van Gennep, Arnold. *The Rites of Passage*. Chicago: University of Chicago Press, 1960.

Vásquez, Manuel A. "Historicizing and Materializing the Study of Religion." In *Immigrant Faiths: Transforming Religious Life in America*, edited by Karen I. Leonard, Alex Stepick, Manuel A. Vásquez, and Jennifer Holdaway, 220. New York: AltaMira, 2005.

Vásquez, Manuel A., and Marie F. Marquardt. *Globalizing the Sacred: Religion across the Americas*. Piscataway, NJ: Rutgers University Press, 2003.

Vergara, Camilo José. "Queen of L.A." *Print* 53 (May–June 1999): 86–89.

Wacquant, Loïc. *Body and Soul: Notebooks of an Apprentice Boxer*. New York: Oxford University Press, 2003.

Wagner, Phillip L. "Pilgrimage: Culture and Geography." In *Sacred Places, Sacred Spaces: The Geography of Pilgrimages*, edited by Robert H. Stoddard and Alan Morinis, 299–323. Baton Rouge, LA: Geoscience Publications, 1997.

Warner, R. Stephen. *Gatherings in Diaspora: Religious Communities and the New Immigration*. Edited by Judith G. Wittner. Philadelphia: Temple University Press, 1998.

Watson Marrón, Gustavo. *Los templos del Tepeyac*. Mexico City: Arzobispado de México, 2001.

Weismantel, Mary. *Cholas and Pishtacos: Tales of Race and Sex in Andean South America.* Chicago: University of Chicago Press, 2001.

Werbner, Pnina, and Helene Basu, eds. *Embodying Charisma: Modernity, Locality and the Performance of Emotion in Sufi Cults.* London: Routledge, 2002.

Williams, Raymond. *The Country and the City.* New York: Oxford University Press, 1973.

———. *Culture and Society, 1780–1950.* London: Chatto and Windus, 1958.

———. *Keywords: A Vocabulary of Culture and Society.* New York: Oxford University Press, 1976.

Wolf, Eric R. *Europe and the People without History.* Berkeley: University of California Press, 1982.

———. "The Virgin of Guadalupe: A Mexican National Symbol." *Journal of American Folklore* 71 (1959): 34.

Wolfinger, Raymond E. "Why Political Machines Have Not Withered Away and Other Revisionist Thoughts." *Journal of Politics* 34 (1972): 374–75.

Yabro-Bejarano, Yvonne. "The Female Subject in Chicano Theatre: Sexuality, 'Race,' and Class." In *Performing Feminisms: Feminist Critical Theory and Theatre,* edited by Sue-Ellen Case, 131–49. Baltimore, MD: Johns Hopkins University Press, 1990.

Zurita, Martha. "Latino Population in Illinois and Metropolitan Chicago: Young and Growing Fast!" *Latino Research at Notre Dame* 1 (2003): 1.

Index

TEXT
10/13 Sabon

DISPLAY
Sabon

COMPOSITOR
Westchester Book Group

INDEXER
Do Mi Stauber

PRINTER AND BINDER
IBT Global